"Jesus, a single man who lived in close community with women as well as men, affirmed that 'in the beginning, God made them male and female.' In the future, history itself will give way to eternity in the form of a new heaven, a new earth, and a bride (the church) beautifully dressed for her husband (Jesus). Whether we are married, divorced, widowed, or single, our deepest understanding of personhood, truth, beauty, goodness, theology, and God will depend on the degree to which we let ourselves be influenced by these realities. Elyse and Eric have done a masterful job to help us along that path."

—**Scott Sauls**, senior pastor of Christ Presbyterian Church; author of *Jesus Outside the Lines* and *Beautiful People Don't Just Happen*

"What does it mean to be created in God's image? How does this influence our relationships as spouses, parents, children, church leaders, friends, coworkers, neighbors, and more? Elyse and Eric answer these questions by exploring how Jesus's life, death, and resurrection relate to issues about who we are as men and women. This book overflows with theological understanding, deep comfort, and wise insights."

—**Justin S. Holcomb and Lindsey A. Holcomb**, authors of *God Made All of Me*, *God Made Me in His Image*, *Is It My Fault?*, and *Rid of My Disgrace*

"If you only ever read one book about God's intention for female and male relationships, read this one. In *Jesus and Gender*, Elyse and Eric masterfully move the conversation forward by going back to the often overlooked 'key aspect of our faith, as it relates to gender, ... the incarnation.' It is impossible to overstate the significance of this book in terms of bringing freedom to both men and women, naming and dismantling dangerous and damaging beliefs, impacting future generations, and helping to prepare and mobilize the church for her mission and witness."

—**Christine Caine**, founder of A21 and Propel Women

"Powerful. Enlightening. Inspiring. And hopeful. Those are words that describe how I felt reading *Jesus and Gender* by Elyse and Eric. This is a 'right now' moment book. They teach us by exploring the depths of Scripture to be Christic instead of complementarian or egalitarian. This book is a gift to all siblings in Christ."

—**Derwin L. Gray,** cofounder and lead pastor of Transformation Church; author of *How To Heal Our Racial Divide*

"I'm deeply thankful for *Jesus and Gender* because in it Elyse and Eric steadfastly refuse to allow anything or anyone but Jesus dictate what it means to be a Christian man or woman. What better standard could I want as a husband, a father of daughters, and as a pastor? I love how these pages reflect the dignity and wholeness Jesus gave to women and men alike, and how Elyse and Eric don't shy away from difficult or painful areas of life (just like Jesus). This is a refreshing read, especially for someone who is burned out on gender roles debates and is looking for a meaningful way to uphold and celebrate God's image in all our brothers and sisters."

—**Barnabas Piper**, pastor and author

"In *Jesus and Gender*, Elyse and Eric help us understand what Scripture really says about how women and men ought to relate to one another—not as temptations to be avoided, subjects to be ruled, or objects to be used, but as sisters and brothers, allies and friends. I was challenged and convicted as I considered how we've added to the word of God by creating stricter rules around those relationships than God ever did. I was encouraged and emboldened to recognize the freedom women and men have in Christ to love each other deeply as family and to support one another as we stand shoulder to shoulder on mission together. *Jesus and Gender* is a welcome addition to the conversation formerly known as 'biblical manhood and womanhood,' and I can easily imagine this book becoming a go-to reference for a new generation of Christic women and men."

—**Lucy Crabtree**, disability advocate

"*Jesus and Gender* is a marvelous, maddening book that will challenge your assumptions and help you love Jesus more. Through deep yet accessible analysis, Fitzpatrick and Schumacher confront narrowly gendered interpretations of Scripture that distort the beauty of our brotherhood and sisterhood in Christ. Their refreshing perspective offers new language to embrace what men and women have in common while honoring the distinctives that make us unique."

—**Joanna Meyer**, Denver Institute for Faith and Work; founder of the Women and Vocation Initiative

"There's a lot to love about *Jesus and Gender*—first, because authors Elyse Fitzpatrick and Eric Schumacher restore Jesus to his rightful place of prominence in the discussion of what it means to be male or female. That alone revolutionizes this discussion and opens up an expansive horizon for how Jesus transforms human relationships in ways that enable all of us to flourish. Second, because both authors are lifelong learners—willing to ask uncomfortable questions, to challenge long-held, previously proclaimed beliefs about male/female relationships, and to make whatever changes Scripture requires. And third, because they practice what they preach. They model the kind of male/female partnership to which Jesus calls us all. Two distinct voices blend into one strong message that, if heeded, will bless and distinguish the body of Christ as a place of uncommon oneness."

—**Carolyn Custis James**, author of *Half the Church: Recapturing God's Global Vision for Women* and *Malestrom: Manhood Swept into the Currents of a Changing World*

Jesus & Gender

Living as Sisters & Brothers in Christ

Jesus & Gender

Living as Sisters & Brothers in Christ

ELYSE M. FITZPATRICK

ERIC SCHUMACHER

KIRKDALE PRESS

KIRKDALE PRESS

Jesus & Gender: Living as Sisters and Brothers in Christ

Copyright 2022 Elyse Fitzpatrick and Eric Schumacher

Kirkdale Press, an imprint of Lexham Press, 1313 Commercial St., Bellingham, WA 98225
KirkdalePress.com

Print ISBN 9781683595878
Digital ISBN 9781683595885
Library of Congress Control Number 2021947078

Lexham Editorial: Deborah Keiser, Abigail Stocker, Elizabeth Vince, Kelsey Matthews, Mandi Newell
Cover Design: Brittany Schrock, Christine Christophersen
Typesetting: ProjectLuz.com

To my brother, Richard. A day will come when all will be healed, and we'll laugh and play again like we did when we were young.

Elyse Fitzpatrick

To my sons—Josiah, Micah, Elijah, and Judson. May you be conformed into the image of our Big Brother, the humble King Jesus.

Eric Schumacher

Contents

Foreword

Perhaps there are few more life-giving, hope-infusing passages than 1 Peter 5:10–11: "And after you have suffered a little while, the God of all grace, who has called you to his eternal glory in Christ, will himself restore, confirm, strengthen, and establish you. To him be the dominion forever and ever. Amen" (ESV). What an incredible way to talk about our salvation; what an amazing way to define and explain the Christian life. By grace, we have been invited into an eternal glory, *in Christ*. The glory we have been invited into is from Christ, through Christ, and to Christ. It is a comprehensively *christological* glory. We have been welcomed by rescuing, forgiving, empowering, and transforming grace into a life that is Christ-centered in every way. We are to look at everything through the lens of his presence, promises, power, and grace, and when we do, everything—yes, everything—changes.

For this to happen, we need to be restored.

Did you notice that word in Peter's wonderful summary of our salvation? I think *restoration* is an under-discussed, under-appreciated aspect of our Lord's saving work. Consider the process of restoring an old, run-down house. You know right away from the size of the tools outside whether a home is being restored or condemned. If you see a crane with a wrecking ball in the front yard, you know the house isn't being restored; it has been condemned. So, the fact that we are being restored tells us that we are no longer under a sentence of condemnation.

But there is more. When a house is run down, two approaches can be taken. The easiest, quickest approach is to remodel the home.

The goal of remodeling is to make the house livable. So, you throw paneling over cracked walls. You do quick fixes to the electricity and plumbing. Your goal is to make the house look nicer, function a little bit better, and be a bit more livable.

God didn't send his Son to remodel you—that is, to make you a little bit more likable and livable. No, he came to completely restore you. When you commit to restoring a house, your goal is to return it to its original beauty, functionality, and purpose.

So, you have to tear down walls to expose and replace faulty wiring and plumbing. You may even have to jack up the house and restore the foundation or tear off the roof because the supporting structures have rotted. Restoration is a process of deconstruction followed by reconstruction. Restoration is seldom an event but most often a long, arduous process. You will only ever give yourself to the long, laborious process of restoration because you deeply love the thing you're working on. The word "restore" in 1 Peter 5:10 tells how deeply and fully our Lord loves us.

Joining our Lord in his restorative zeal, we should always be deconstructing and reconstructing our faith so that in every area of our life, we are living in a way that has been rebuilt by what it means to be *in Christ*. When it comes to our commitment to God's deconstructing and reconstructing grace, there must not be anything off-limits, nothing untouchable, and no closed closets. When it comes to what we think, what we believe, and how we live, we need to stand before our Savior with our knees bent and our hearts open, living in a constant state of humility, willingness, honesty, submission, confession, and celebration, ready for him to tear down another wall, expose another thing that is still broken, and move us yet another step closer toward what he died for us to be.

I know for me, none of this is natural. So, I need grace to be at all excited about and willing to participate in the process of restorative grace. But I also know that there is no better, more joyful life than when you have surrendered your heart and life to the hammers and saws of restorative grace, eyes fixed on Jesus, heart ready for what he will deconstruct and reconstruct next.

This restoration I have been writing about here is why I love *Jesus and Gender*.

This wonderful, thoroughly biblical, gospel-saturated book is an invitation to a journey to allow what it means to be *in Christ*, to deconstruct and reconstruct how you think, desire, decide, speak, and act in one inescapable area of your life as a child of God—that is, gender. How does our new identity as those who now are *in Christ* change the way we live together as brothers and sisters in the house of God? And how do we get from where we are to where God, in Christ, calls us and welcomes us to be?

There is evidence in us and all around us that when it comes to our lives together as brothers and sisters in the body of Christ, there remains a huge and pressing need for God's restorative deconstructing and reconstructing work.

I found the book you are about to read to be deeply convicting and encouraging at the same time. I experienced the pain of having some of my walls torn down and experienced the joy of restorative mercy. So, I invite you to humbly open your heart and read with willingness and joy. Your Savior is in the house and still doing his deconstructing, reconstructing work.

May this wonderful book be for you a tool of restorative grace in his infinitely capable hands.

—Paul David Tripp
October 8, 2021

Acknowledgments

I'm thankful for the many women and men who have walked with me over the last 50 years as I've sought to walk with Christ. I'm thankful for pastors and teachers who have taught me to love and value the Lord and his word. They are legion.

In the process of this book, I'm particularly thankful for the ongoing ministry of each of the elders of my church, Grace Bible, in Escondido. I'm thankful for their care for women and their humility—and particularly for Tom Maxham (and his wife, Patty) and his desire to lovingly shepherd me and to protect and care for the women in our church.

I'm thankful for the work of Deb Keiser and the team at Kirkdale/Lexham Press. True professionals. I'm also thankful for my dear friend, Scott Lindsey, Logos Ninja and coffee-connoisseur. You've blessed me, my brother.

I'm thankful for my co-author and dear brother, Eric Schumacher. I'm so glad that you were willing to step into this arena with me. You've taught me so much. I'm thankful also for the wonderful men and women who took time from their very busy ministries to share in these pages about the Lord's call on their life and their work for him. I'm so encouraged by the way they follow the Lord and by the way they've persevered to bring life to the world.

I'm thankful for my children and their spouses and children and for the many conversations around this topic I've had with them...and how they're patient when I keep asking them questions and saying,

"Yeah, but what about...?" It's a joy to call you my children and my brothers and sisters.

And I'm mostly thankful for dear Phil, who through the years and the books wrestled with and written, and the struggles to really think, has stood by my side, my biggest cheerleader, dear brother, and best friend. None of this happens without you, dear friend.

—Elyse

I'm beyond grateful to my wife, Jenny, who encourages me to write, celebrates these projects, and never complains about them (even when the writing takes me away for too long).

Thanks to my sons and daughter, who know that Daddy writes but don't care to read his books. Even if you never read them, I pray they contribute to a better world for you and yours.

I'm blessed by the saints at Grand Avenue Baptist Church in Ames and the staff who pray me through projects.

I can't adequately express my gratitude for my co-writer, co-host, co-belligerent, co-worker, and co-heir, Elyse Fitzpatrick—a strong ally and buttress in the Lord's service.

Much appreciation to our editor, Deb Keiser, and the incredible team at Kirkdale for believing in this project and seeing it through.

A huge "THANK YOU" to all the Worthy podcast guests and listeners. Your conversations and stories motivate me to keep thinking and writing on this topic.

Finally, to my big brother, Jesus: I don't deserve you, but you love me anyway. Thank you, friend.

—Eric

Introduction

Be warned: there is no end to the making of many books,
and much study wearies the body. When all has been
heard, the conclusion of the matter is this: fear God and
keep his commands, because this is for all humanity. For
God will bring every act to judgment, including every
hidden thing, whether good or evil.
—Ecclesiastes 12:12–14

Like you, we've read arguments from every side about relationships and roles and rules between men and women and, honestly, we we're beginning to think that poor dead horse just needs a proper burial. Which of course begs the question: Why on earth have we written another book on the subject?

In the chapters that follow we'll answer that question more fully, but for now let us say this: *Jesus and Gender* was written because a very key aspect—in fact the most important one—has been largely overlooked.

ELYSE'S STORY

Before we explain more about where we're going, we want to introduce ourselves and share why it matters to us. I am a woman who was saved in 1971 at the age of twenty-one. Yes, that makes me seventy years old as I write this introduction. That also means that I've been a Christian for fifty years. I was not raised in a Christian home and really didn't have any sort of family role models; my father was out of our home early on and my mother worked a full-time job. Hardly the model of a conservative Christian household. Immediately after my conversion, I enrolled in a little Bible college where I earned a Bachelor of Theology degree and met and married my husband, Phil. The churches I attended during those early years didn't really talk much about women's or men's roles. In fact, women could be ordained, and I was encouraged by my leaders and by my husband to pursue whatever God had gifted me to do. Eventually I pursued biblical counseling education and started my writing career.

It wasn't until the mid-1990s that I began to hear about gender roles and to experience restrictions placed on me in the church. But don't assume that I pushed back against them. No. In fact, I embraced them wholeheartedly. The more I learned, the more I bought into what I would come to understand as a "complementarian" perspective. It was during those years that I wrote *Helper By Design: God's Perfect Plan for Women in Marriage* (Moody, 2003). At the time I wrote that book, of course I really did believe everything I said. And since I've written over twenty books, I'll admit that there are parts of some of them that, let's just say, I've reexamined. Of course, there are bedrock truths I remain committed to—yet there are others I would nuance and still more I turn from today.

One particularly meaningful season was when I came to understand the centrality of the gospel. Sure, in the past I knew it and believed it, but I didn't really see how fundamental the good news of Jesus' life, death, and resurrection was to every area of life. It was then that I wrote *Because He Loves Me: How Christ Transforms Our Daily Life* (Crossway, 2008), which became central in my thinking. Everything I've written since then has been my attempt to apply the truths of the gospel consistently to specific areas of living.[1] Then, in 2013 I wrote *Found in Him: The Joy of the Incarnation and Our Union with Christ*, a deeper look at one facet of the gospel message: the incarnation. My study of God the Son becoming Man has continued as a prevailing paradigm since that time.

However, it was during the writing of *Good News for Weary Women: Escaping the Bondage of To-Do Lists, Steps, and Bad Advice* (Tyndale, 2014) that I grew to understand how damaging a lot of what had been written about women, their roles, and the implications of those teachings have been to so many. I ran a social media experiment and heard from hundreds of women; over 20,000 women read the post within twenty-four hours. Many responded over the days and weeks that followed. I polled women in a large church and heard the same stories repeatedly about how they had felt ignored, pressured, disrespected, judged, and objectified by their church's leaders and eventually by their husbands who had bought into the teaching. There wasn't a place in any woman's life where she was free from the burdens placed on her simply because she is a woman. These Christian-woman "shoulds" were proof of her godliness and shouted at her from every corner—her home, her church, the Christian culture, and even from her own mind.

By this point in my life, I knew enough about the gospel and what happens to believers when they don't hear it—when they're given only law disconnected from Jesus' perfect keeping of it—that the responses I heard from these women were unfortunately commonplace. Only the gospel has the power to transform lives and lift burdens. The problem with this teaching on gender roles: It is devoid of the good news. Of course women were struggling! Burdens too heavy to bear were being placed on their backs.

I knew I would have to respond. This book is the culmination of these two facets in my ongoing understanding: the centrality of the gospel, especially the incarnation, and my concern that much of the teaching on gender in the church is devoid of the gospel and is therefore soul-crushing and conflict-producing.

ERIC'S STORY

Growing up in small-town Iowa in a traditional home that faithfully attended a conservative Lutheran church shaped my views on women and men. I say that first because none of us approach the Scriptures as blank slates. The idea that we are born "blank slates" or become such at conversion is mistaken—the Bible knows nothing about it. Our cultural environment, family of origin, school, peers, church, marriage, work, and hobbies all impact how we understand what it means to be men and women. We're primed to affirm some beliefs and be offended by others. Such an admission is no cause for suspicion of interpretation. The first step to accurate reading is awareness of what impacts us.

My father and mother were my first guides. Dad went to work and grilled the hamburgers. Mom did the laundry and cooked in the kitchen. Dad sang in the choir, taught me to hunt, and cried at funerals. Mom beat me in footraces, taught me to cross-stitch, and worked the soil, growing garden vegetables by the sweat of her brow. They both disciplined me, cheered for me, and talked about our faith. They were both tough. They were both tender. They were both parents. Dad was a male, so he was my father. Mom was a female, so she was my mother.

Our church didn't use words like "manhood" and "womanhood." It knew nothing of "complementarianism" and "egalitarianism." Our pastor and elders were always men. Our denomination ordained both men and women as deacons. Men and women taught me in Sunday school. Men and women worked side by side to put on the annual chicken supper. A woman taught my catechism classes while men quizzed me on Scripture memory verses. Women and men read the Old Testament and Epistle readings in the service. The pastor read the Gospel reading and gave the sermon. Men and women were friends with one another, though they often gathered by gender for some activities.

It wasn't until my college years that I was told there were "roles" for men and women. It was then that I received a copy of *Recovering Biblical Manhood and Womanhood*. Shortly after this, I got engaged. Wanting to be the best husband that I could be, I purchased the set of John Piper's 1989 sermon series, "Biblical Manhood and Womanhood." I absorbed these over the summer, along with material from the Council on Biblical Manhood and Womanhood (CBMW).

I must confess that I did not approach these resources with an open mind. I had recently read Piper's *Desiring God* and *Let the Nations Be Glad*, and I had listened to dozens of his sermons. He had a profound impact on opening my eyes to God's beauty and glory, as well as taking the Bible seriously. So, turning to his other sources, I assumed that whatever they said was the truth. Period.

Later, I attended The Southern Baptist Theological Seminary in Louisville, where I received an MDiv in Biblical and Theological Studies. To be honest, I can't recall ever hearing anything about "biblical manhood and womanhood" in the classroom. There was, however, a particular culture. I only had one female professor during my time on campus (one of my favorites and one of the best). While women were spoken of respectfully in public, it seemed anyone who wasn't complementarian was suspect.

Early in my time there, the student body received a letter from President Mohler on the subject of female students. It stated in no uncertain terms that the seminary was happy to have female students at every level of study. Those who made female students feel unwelcome would be subject to discipline. It shocked me that there were issues in the seminary body at a level warranting such a communication.

My first few years of pastoral ministry brought conflict regarding how men and women should serve in the church. Seminary had said little to these things, so I dove into materials from CBMW looking for clarification.

I attended conferences and read books that reinforced what I believed. I preached sermons on these matters and even hosted a CBMW conference at a church I pastored. It was at that conference that my conscience began to grow uncomfortable. At one point, to illustrate what it looks like to raise "masculine boys," the speaker shared a vignette about his son asking if he could eat an earthworm. He encouraged him enthusiastically. A member raised her hand and asked what he would do if his daughter asked the same question. The speaker said he'd probably encourage her too. What then, I wondered, was "masculine" about eating an earthworm if girls could do it too?

That incident brought a plethora of questions. I heard celebrity pastors encourage pastors to maintain a "masculine feel" in the worship service. Next they discouraged pastors from from allowing women to lead or participate in certain activities because it "might appear" to be endorsing female eldership. But where does the New Testament even hint at this emphasis? If it's there, I haven't found it after two decades of looking. Maybe it's next to the verse detailing how Jesus proved his manhood by eating a worm.

Beyond this, I began to see how biblical passages on specific topics—like marriage and eldership—became general principles for how all men and women should relate in the church and the world. These principles were extrapolated into implications that shaped everything from who initiated family prayer and Bible reading to how one should deliver the mail or offer driving directions. The consciences of church members were bound by teaching beyond what the Scripture clearly said. While extrabiblical extrapolations may look good on paper, they had terrible consequences in marriages, child-raising, and church relationships.

Then, I realized that Jesus wasn't a perfect model for the "biblical manhood" offered to me. Undoubtedly the virtues of "biblical manhood" can be illustrated with the life of Jesus. But, just as quickly, the virtues of "biblical womanhood" can be as well. And, beyond a few scattered verses, why did the New Testament have almost *nothing* to say about male discipleship versus female discipleship? Putting on Christ and bearing the fruit of the Spirit didn't come with male and female icons.

Perhaps that's why so many of the illustrations for "biblical manhood" looked to athletes, MMA fighters, soldiers, and outdoorsmen. We had to give a nod to Jesus in the discussion, of course. But, in the end, manhood looked much more like Bear Grylls and Teddy Roosevelt.

And perhaps that's why women were asking me (in private—they didn't dare say these things out loud) whether Jesus was the model they should follow in life. If he was the perfect male, how could he be *their* example? But, if he wasn't their example, did he understand them, could he sympathize with them? If he didn't enter into both male and female humanity, how could his life, death, and resurrection atone for all our sins? This view of manhood has implications for the gospel.

All this drove me back to the text of the Bible. I wanted to read it and see what was *and was not* there. Where I came with assumptions or conclusions, I wanted to ask if it was really there. I hear too many fellow Christians become little more than people parroting Pastor Celebrity. I want to be controlled by the text and not by gatekeepers. As with *Worthy: Celebrating the Value of Women*, this book is a continuation of that journey. Come, join us in reading the Bible and asking God to show us what he's said and free us from what he hasn't said.

OUR SHARED PERSPECTIVE

Over the last thirty years, primarily in response to the rise of feminism, dozens of Christian books have been written about the nature and roles of men and women. In response to those books, others have been written asserting a different perspective. Both have tried to develop descriptions of what it looks like to define and live out gender "biblically." Many have sought to faithfully consider the biblical record, while others have been far too enamored with American cultural norms.

The more conservative side of these models, called *complementarianism,* has focused on gender equality with role distinctions, with the overall emphasis that the Bible consistently teaches male authority and female subordination, especially in the home and the church. This perspective has so gained in popularity in the evangelical world that it is now functionally treated as a first-tier doctrine by many. And some assume that if one is not complementarian, then they couldn't possibly have a high view of the Bible. In fact, they may not even be a Christian at all.

The opposing side of this debate, *egalitarianism,* also seeks to define gender "biblically." Like complementarians, egalitarians believe that men and women are equally created in the image of God; however,

they don't believe the Bible consistently teaches de facto male authority and female subordination. They believe that a proper reading of
the biblical record, particularly the New Testament, demonstrates
that the patriarchal structures common in the ancient Near East are
annulled by a better understanding of the Bible and particularly the
gospel. Like their complementarian counterparts, many egalitarians
mistrust both the scholarship and motives of their opposites. Some
believe that a complementarian view is evidence of misogyny and a
thirst for power. And like their opposites, they have gone to Scripture
to demonstrate the truth of their perspective.

Although we would say that we're very thankful for all that we've
learned from these scholars, we're going to offer something different. This book is not going to be like either category of those books.
That's because the gospel, and in particular the incarnation, should
transform how we think about what it means to be male and female.

Much of the focus on the Genesis narrative needs to be understood
in light of the incarnation, life, death, and resurrection of Jesus Christ.
This gracious reality is most important: God made himself little; he
became human. We have to question whether any Christian understanding of gender that fails to take into account the implication of
the incarnation is actually Christian at all.

The condescension of the Second Person of the Trinity must be
the guiding principle of any rubric we develop as we seek to answer
the questions: *As a woman, who am I? As a man, who am I? What does
it mean to be one who is created in the image of God but also recreated
in the image of the incarnate Christ?*

In the pages to come, we'll show more about how the life, death,
resurrection, and ascension must inform every discussion we have as
men and women and answer many questions about gender identity.
We hope this book will be a fresh, gospel-driven, wise, and—yes—fresh
look at who Jesus is and what he's accomplished for both women
and men.

So, this is our ask: First, pray. Pray that the Lord will help us all to
put aside any preconceived ideas not based solely in the gospel. And,

second, ask for the heart of one who can receive the word of the gospel with eagerness and examine the Scriptures daily to see if what we're saying is true or not (see Acts 17:11). And then, ask the Spirit for help to embrace what is true. All we ask is the gift of a fair and charitable reading. Our goal is to bring glory and praise to the one who humbled himself, took on the form of a servant, and became obedient unto death so that he might bring life to women and men, boys and girls.

And, finally, together let's question whether all that's been said about gender has brought us to the one most important truth: Jesus Christ came to transform women and men into sisters and brothers who know they are loved, forgiven, and made one.

1

Sisters, Brothers, and the Gospel

"[The Father] gave [the Son] authority over all flesh, so that he may give eternal life." —John 17:2 EHV

L et's stop now to consider why it would be important to view ourselves and how we relate to one another through a distinctly gospel-focused lens. How many times have you heard squabbling little children scream, "You're not the boss of me!" as they marched off in anger. Sometimes when I've heard that from little ones, I've chuckled and thought, *Oh, I get that.* And although I probably wouldn't ever put it in exactly that way, I'm sure I've said it thousands of times, at least in my own heart. For instance, when I see a blinking sign that tells me I'm exceeding the speed limit, my heart's response is all too often, *You're not the boss of me.*

Which brings us to the importance of defining what it means to be male and female through an incarnationally informed lens. How do you react to the *You're not the boss of me* impulse in your own heart? The most common response to resistance against authority is to give more rules and consequences. *Maybe if we made the rules and consequences clearer, more reasonable, or more firm or applicable, people would respond better.* But is that what we learn in the New Testament?

Is that a gospel-shaped perspective? We don't think so.

The Bible teaches that only One can quench the desire to define ourselves, and our lives, the way we think is best, and he is the humble King who used his own power to serve others (not himself) and then died. It is only as we learn that his way really is the only way to true freedom and peace that we will find our thirst for independence and authority quieted by his love.

We're building a different perspective on men and women because so much of what has been written about the topic, especially in modern American evangelicalism, isn't all that different from the norms of the ancient world when the power of the state, and the men who ran it, was the only acceptable norm. Patriarchy informed every relationship, from the lowliest foot-washing slave to the legion commander. Women and men, children and slaves were all expected to live within strict social roles, and no one dared challenge them without risking the ire of those in authority, which is why Jesus and his message of self-sacrifice shocked and repelled them so much. His humility was not only foolish but also repulsive to them. And it was frightening: It threatened the very structures they relied on for prosperity and civil society. Jesus shattered all their rules of *who's the boss* when he stooped down and became the King who washed feet.

> The Bible teaches that only One can quench the desire to define ourselves, and our lives, the way we think is best, and he is the humble King who used his own power to serve others.

But it isn't only Jesus who shattered those paradigms. Paul's statements about sexual equality between husbands and wives in 1 Corinthians 7 would have been inconceivable to his readers, who viewed wives as little more than chattel or broodmares, while also affirming the right of husbands to consort with female or male household slaves (of any age), or prostitutes. Paul's shocking assertion that husbands and wives were equal, especially in this most intimate area of relationship, and that husbands were to lay down their lives for their

wives and love them as Christ loved the church was utterly anathema
to the Corinthians and the Ephesians, as it would have been to any
ancient society.

We find it troubling that even though many Christians accept the
gospel accounts of Jesus's life and the letters of Paul as truth, they
frequently disregard them when framing discussions about relationships between women and men. Rather than living in amazement
at Jesus' humility and serving, some revert back to old patriarchal
models of the ancient Near East, striving to somehow blend Christ's
message of humility and service with Rome's message of power and
rule. On the contrary, the New Testament is meant to stand, at least
in part, as a rebuke against the structures of that day, structures that
prized and guarded power over the weak, the use of authority for self-
aggrandizement and ambition, and the denigration and disregard of
those considered less valuable.

This book is important because we will reshape our paradigms
about relationships between men and women, parents, children,
church leaders, and parishioners from the perspective of the gospel.
We aren't saying that others who have written about gender and particularly gender roles before us don't love and believe the gospel. We
assume that they do and that they are our brothers and sisters in the
faith. What we do question, however, is whether their perspectives
on this topic have been as deeply informed by and tied to the gospel
and the incarnation as they should have been.

Again, why would it be important to develop a distinctly gospel-
centered perspective on what it means to be men and women? And how
would that perspective speak to our *You're not the boss of me* dilemma?

Not surprisingly, the apostle Paul has something to say to us about
it. In Romans 7 he confessed his struggle with God's law: although he
knew it was "holy and just and good" (7:12), he also sensed a sinful
predisposition to react against it. For instance, when he heard the
command, "Do not covet," it didn't stop him from coveting. In fact, it
produced in him "coveting of every kind" (7:8). Even though he knew
that God had the right to command him and even though he knew

all God's commands were righteous, he confessed that he was resistant to being told what to do. He understood that all his underlying *You're not the boss of me* resistance could never be overcome by rules. That's why, at the end of Romans 7, after confessing his powerlessness to respond rightly to the law, he cried, "What a wretched man I am! Who will rescue me from this body of death?" (7:24).

Hear Paul's agonized frustration. This former ultra-righteous Pharisee had come face to face with his inability to obey the law he claimed to love. And it crushed him, doing exactly what the law was meant to do: it forced him to turn away from himself toward the only One who could rescue him, "Jesus Christ our Lord!" (7:25). Paul recognized that his inability to respond in humility and obedience to God's law could never be overcome by more rules or even more effort.

> Love is the only power that is strong enough to transform us into humble, loving, and kind people. Without the assurance of God's love, the law brings nothing but God's wrath and subsequent spiritual death.

No, his and our only hope is found in the grace of the Son who obeyed the law in our place, forgave all our resistance to his law, and declared us to be righteous rule keepers. Paul realized he needed assurance of God's unconditional love, not more rules. "Thanks be to God" (7:25) is right!

In concert with Paul, we're convinced that any perspective about either who we are as men and women or how we are to relate to men and women that is not based on Jesus' life, death, and resurrection is not only futile, but it will also result in more and more conflict and resistance. That's because rules without the assurance of love and forgiveness are powerless to make us love God and others. Indeed, love is the only power that is strong enough to transform us into humble, loving, and kind people. Without the assurance of God's love, the law brings nothing but God's wrath and subsequent spiritual death (2 Cor 3:7; Rom 4:15; see also Rom 3:20; 1 Cor 15:56; 2 Cor 3:6–7; Gal 2:16;

3:23–25; Jas 2:10). That's because no one obeys it (Rom 3:10–23). As Paul proclaimed, rules are ineffective at transforming our hearts: "If a law had been granted with the ability to give life, then righteousness would certainly be on the basis of the law" (Gal 3:21).

Rules about how to be biblical men and women won't make us love each other. They can't. They won't make us willing to embrace our God-given identities or help us be willing to walk in humble obedience. They can't because they don't have the power to. No, what we need is Someone who will transform our hearts by his love and humility.

THE NEW AND BETTER WORD

We're shaping our model on the incarnation because Jesus is the only one fully qualified to speak a word about who we are and what we are to be. That's because he is both God and man. His new word of love remakes every other word about existence within social structures into a life-transforming gift. He demonstrated what godly authority was when, in the same breath he claimed his Father had given "authority over all people" to him, he also declared that he would not use this authority to rule over and crush his enemies, but rather to give them life (John 17:2). Jesus' new and better word transformed authority into humble service, rulership into servanthood, pride into humility. Then he demonstrated what that looked like when he willingly "poured out his soul to death" (Isa 53:12 ESV), resisting the power and his right to call down legions of angels to rescue him (see Matt 26:53).

> His new word of love remakes every other word about existence within social structures into a life-transforming gift.

Humanity and its endless hunger for power was shamed once and for all by his breathtaking love for the insignificant, weak, and broken. The desire to dominate, to be the boss, was forever swallowed up when, in agony, he said to the Father who had granted him all authority, "not as I will" (Matt 26:39). What does godly authority look like? It looks like using power to lay down your life. He said, "I lay [my life] down of my own accord. I have authority to lay it down, and I have authority to take it up again" (John 10:18 ESV).

THE INCARNATION: A NEW HUMANITY

There is so much about the Christmas season that I love. Sure, there are the cringe-worthy songs, like the one about mama kissing Santa Claus, and the frenetic shopping and stretched budgets we must persevere through, and the overeating we all regret, but still Christmastime remains magical to me. One of the aspects of the season that I find most enjoyable is being able to sing Christmas carols to myself as I wander through stores trying to find that oh so elusive, perfect gift. I particularly love it when "Hark, the Herald Angels Sing" fills the mall's atmosphere and I get to muse on and hum this rich theology:

> Veiled in flesh the Godhead see
> Hail the incarnate Deity

Christmas means that God has been "veiled in flesh." He can be seen. That the invisible God has become visible means that God could be seen for the very first time in all eternity. God was clothed with a human body like ours, becoming incarnate, embodied. The invisible, immortal, omnipotent, and omniscient God fully took on human form and became a visible, mortal, weak human. As a tiny embryo, he gestated in the womb of a young virgin and was born the way we all were: placenta and all. He needed to nurse and be kept from the cold by his mother's body and love. And he needed to be taught how to speak the word "mama," and what it meant to love his neighbors. And he was able to die. That's pretty shocking, isn't it? As the hymn continues, we learn that this newly incarnate Deity has a name: Jesus. And we're told that this divine human has come to complete a particular task: to bow down and dwell with humanity. As one of us … joyfully!

> Pleased as man with men to dwell
> Jesus, Our Emmanuel

The problem we have is that we're not shocked by this all-too-familiar story. But trust me, if you had been one of those shepherds, or the religious elite of the day, or even one who had actually been anticipating his birth, you would have been completely shocked. The Creator took the form of the created? No wonder they killed him: he proclaimed that something entirely new was happening; a novel sort of humanity had just begun. When the Second Person of the Trinity took on flesh, God broke through, into our time and space, into earthly history, and brought about something entirely unique. God became one of us. Never in the history of the world, in all the millions and millions of births that had gone before, had something like this happened. There was, in fact, something new under the sun. *Hail the incarnate Deity!*

Again, we've failed to achieve a joyful consensus about our identity and relationships because we have failed to grasp the significance of Jesus' incarnation and life of self-emptying love. Sadly, because we're not shocked by this story, we've failed to draw out the important implications it forces on us.

What does his taking on our embodied nature as his own mean about each of us as his brothers and sisters? And do those truths impact us practically, particularly as we consider what it means to be male or female? How would it transform the way that we live our lives now, post-Christmas?

Since Jesus Christ is the "radiance of God's glory and the exact expression of his nature" (Heb 1:3), then at the very least we should draw our understanding of gender, and how we are to relate to one another, from the way that Jesus understood and related to both men and women. His story changes the way we view ourselves, each other, and, of course, the way we treat one another. How then could it be that this momentous event, God's voluntary humiliation and condescension to become one of us, would fail to transform everything? Shouldn't humility, condescension, and the desire to be in unity occupy the very heart of every relationship we have, no matter our gender?

Jesus' voluntary relinquishing of rightful authority to become a slave, obedient to his Father's will, his self-emptying love, magnificent act of selfless devotion for the sake of the other, should be the foremost paradigm that informs all of our relationships in whatever sphere they may be: in the home, in the church, and in society. As those who bear his name, the "Christ," Christians should be known as people who refuse to grasp power, even when they think that power could be used for good. We are all tempted to believe that power is best used when it is grasped by us for our purposes. But God, the Son, who really did know how to use power for right purposes, has shown us a different way. He taught us to walk away from positions of power and embrace the life of a servant. He did this from beginning to end. What would Jesus do? He'd walk away from the throne and kneel to wash feet. He really did have *all* authority, and yet he used it only to give life to others.

What has been missing too often from the talk about how men and women, husbands and wives, parents and children, pastors and parishioners should relate to one another is this: the astounding story of humility and good news. The good news reflected in the message of Jesus is actually a message of freedom to serve, not a code of laws and rules about who's in charge or what role one must play in order to be truly masculine or feminine. In fact, these unbiblical rules can harm people. They do so either by making them proud and demanding when they think they're nailing it or by crushing them when they discover they're failing.

Am I a real woman even if I don't love to bake pies? Is Phil, my husband, a real man when he serves me by doing the laundry as I spend my days writing? Man-made rules cause young women to question their gender identity when they find that they love kicking the ball into the net more than dollies; they make young men feel insecure about their masculinity when they love art or dance or are more sensitive than their male friends. These stereotypical rules also breed discontent in men's hearts when they learn what women "should be doing" and look with disfavor on their wives. They cause women to stifle their gifts because they don't want to offend or thwart their husband's masculinity and then, when their husband doesn't perform in expected ways, they're disappointed and frustrated. These rules have also denigrated single men and women by implying that the only way they can truly please God or have value is by getting married—no matter if that is God's plan or even their desire. Rule upon rule about how dads and moms are supposed to parent and how children are to respond have been laid on their backs, all to their deep exasperation and ultimate disappointment.

These teachings have also had profoundly destructive results in Christian churches where men do all the leading and women are viewed as nice but not really necessary, like "throw pillows"—pleasant to look at but not essential to the mission.[1] In some churches, women are viewed with suspicion, charged with being easily deceived or to be avoided because they're out for every pastor's job or, worse yet, his body. They are told the function they have in church is to be quiet or to set up the kitchen for potlucks. In this way, the voices that God has given them are silenced, and the gifts they're given are squandered. This is all to the church's great impoverishment. How can the church flourish if half its army is muzzled? Women are not encouraged to study theology or talk about their studies with their pastors or elders because men shouldn't spend time talking with any woman aside from their wives. And we won't even mention here the ubiquitous emotional, sexual, and institutional abuse that is the fruit of law-driven, gospel-denying structures and the destruction they yield. Think how the church might be strengthened or the world evangelized if the witness of the church were twice as strong and overflowed with the harmonious humble, gracious testimony of both women and men as they outdid one another by showing honor and deference.

RESIST THE WISDOM OF THE WORLD

Many books on "manhood" and "womanhood" claim to be striving to hold the line against the world's influences, and in particular the voice of secular feminism. They say that lines must be drawn marking out

authority and submission in response to the license of feminism. But
feminism isn't the primary problem Christians should resist. That's
not to say that we agree with every form of feminism. We certainly
don't. It's just that the church's response to feminism more closely
resembles the world's structures of authority and subjugation than
the gospel. The problem is this: at their root, both strict feminism and
strict patriarchy are the same, sharing many of the same motivations,
though they claim to have differing origins. They're both motivated
by a desire for power and a fear of loss of control. But this hunger for
power and control didn't originate in the heart of God. And it stands
in stark contrast to Christ's condescension.

Of course, on both sides of this divide, there really are noble motivations. For instance, feminists are right when they say it is good that
women have legal rights to vote, to
own property, to pursue careers, and
to be able to free themselves from abusive situations. It's also good that in the
home and church many patriarchists
seek to understand and follow what
they believe is biblical teaching, even
though they're scoffed at by the world
as antiquated. But Jesus was neither
a feminist nor a patriarchist; nor was
he complementarian or egalitarian. He
simply wasn't interested in trying to

> The problem is this: at their root, both strict feminism and strict patriarchy are the same, sharing many of the same motivations, though they claim to have differing origins.

build a worldly kingdom or attain a position of power for himself.
And he never encouraged anyone else to do so, either. Remember
what he told Pilate: "If my kingdom were of this world, my servants
would fight ... But as it is, my kingdom is not from here" (John 18:36).
In fact, whenever the disciples squabbled about who got to be the boss,
Jesus rebuked them. For instance, when a mom came and asked for
her sons to be granted godlike authority, he told her she didn't know
what she was talking about. His continual refusal to be drawn into
ambitions, power plays, or the disciples' hubris should say something

to us. We should hear his testimony that even the discussion about who gets to demand power over others shouldn't be heard among us. If we're actually following in Jesus' footsteps, we should be running away from the temptation to grasp power, not trying to prove biblically who should wield it, no matter if you're trying to make that point from the right or the left. If you're asking the "who gets to be boss" question, you've already lost.

Jesus didn't have to strive for power because he knew that all power was already his. He didn't have any use for glory-hungry Peter's "may it never be!" proclamation when he told of his upcoming death and apparent loss of status, reputation, and life. Jesus wasn't seeking to exploit what was his, though he had every right to. Instead, he showed us a new way: *a way where authority is willingly relinquished for the sake of the other.* He showed us a new way of love and self-emptying, and we must renovate models of manhood and womanhood based on this new way of love if we want to assign them the name "Christian."

How dare we stake out positions of power in Christ's body when this is his testimony recorded by Paul? Do we believe that peace within the home and church depends on doing life differently than this?

Adopt the same attitude as that of Christ Jesus,

> who, existing in the form of God,
> did not consider equality with God
> as something to be exploited.
> Instead he emptied himself
> by assuming the form of a servant,
> taking on the likeness of humanity.
>
> And when he had come as a man,
> he humbled himself by becoming obedient
> to the point of death—
> even to death on a cross. (Phil 2:5–8)

What do you think "adopt the same attitude" means if not to live a life of self-emptying love?

A NEW WAY TO LOVE

Have you ever wondered about Jesus' words in John 13:34? He said, "I give you a new command: Love one another. Just as I have loved you, you are also to love one another."

Why did he call this command to love *new*? Certainly, the Old Testament was already filled with commands to love and care for one's neighbor (see Exod 22:26; Lev 19:16, 18; Deut 19:14, 27:17). There was nothing new about loving one's neighbor; it was already part of Israel's ethic. So, why did Jesus say this law was *new*? It was new because the way he loved had never been seen before. It was new because it was the first time that someone who had ultimate authority, who held the right to command, control, and punish, opened his hands and let it all go in a magnificent life of service culminating with his death on the cross. The hands that were pinioned to that crossbeam were nailed open. He relinquished it all. Beginning with his incarnation and proceeding all the way through death to his incarnate ascension, and even in his exaltation to the right hand of his Father, Jesus voluntarily renounced all that was rightfully his to give life to us. It's that kind of love that we're called to emulate in all of our relationships.

The war for power between the sexes is driven by a desire that is, at its core, anathema to our Lord. His continual refusal to get drawn into spitting contests about who was greatest was undoubtedly a source of angst and confusion among his disciples who longed to rule over others, who fought on numerous occasions about who was the boss (see Mark 9:34; Luke 9:46; 22:24), and who thought it would be a good idea to call fire down upon their enemies. Like many of us, they simply didn't understand that this desire to be the boss was repugnant to their Lord and testimony to their immaturity and unbelief.

Although Jesus never denied the authority that was truly his, it's instructive to see how he used it. You never see him demanding that others submit to him or acquiesce to his preferences; rather, he demonstrated a better way. For instance, he claimed that he had authority on earth to forgive sins and he healed to prove it (Matt 9:6).

He used his authority to confidently teach truth, something that was unique in his time (Matt 21:23; Mark 1:22). He exercised authority over his enemies: demons and satanic forces (Mark 1:25–27). And he used his authority to bend nature to his will, always for the betterment of those he loved. He changed water into the best wine, calmed storms, walked on water, fed the hungry, healed lepers with a touch, and raised the dead. Then he, the King, let common women worship him and wash his feet with their tears. He praised a destitute widow's generosity and called an unclean outcast, "Daughter" (Luke 8:48). He told the male ruling elite that they would be judged by a female gentile queen (Matt 12:42) because she sought out wisdom. He honored a man who was despised as a traitor and who didn't fit the mold of Jewish masculinity (Luke 19). He had pity on a demon-possessed man who lived in a cemetery and harmed his poor body (Mark 5:1–20). He had sympathy for unclean lepers and blind beggars, and he touched men's unclean bodies to bring them health. And he listened to dads and moms who begged him to have mercy on their children. But he never, ever used his authority to demean those considered in lower status, to ignore their pleas for help (even when the disciples tried to shush them), or to demand that they please him or submit to his preferences by washing the dishes the way he liked. He despised what would have been the "good old boys" club in his day and reserved his harshest criticism for them because they used their authority to close off the kingdom of God from the needy and required obedience to their punctilious demands (Matt 23:13). In the Gospels, the only people fighting for headship are the disciples (pre-resurrection), the religious elite, and the Romans. Jesus never did. He was already the head of the church, and he didn't fight for that place; he died for it.

I AM AMONG YOU AS A SERVANT

Most importantly, he called out the difference between the way he used his authority and the worldly way that was as common in his day as it is in ours. He said,

The kings of the Gentiles lord it over them, and those who
have authority over them have themselves called "Benefactors."
It is not to be like that among you. On the contrary, whoever
is greatest among you should become like the youngest, and
whoever leads, like the one serving ... I am among you as one
who serves. (Luke 22:25–27)

Reconsider that final sentence again: God was among us *as one who
serves*. If you want to know what following Jesus looks like, embrace
servanthood. Even if you think yourself to be something as seemingly
helpful as a "benefactor," one who would use his or her authority for
the betterment of others, embrace servanthood. Jesus warned about
the folly of pursuing anything other than that title and image for
yourself. If you think it's your right to lord your authority over others,
even if you think you're doing so for their benefit, then you're acting
like the world. Jesus said, "It is not to be like that among you" (Luke
22:26). When you claim positions of power for yourself, you're acting
like an unbeliever. It's the world you're imaging, not your humble Lord.

Further, it's important for us to see that these verses are sand-
wiched between a dispute among the disciples about who should be
considered greatest and his warning to Peter, who undoubtedly
thought he had greatness nailed down. This isn't a coincidence. The
disciples were deaf to Jesus' predictions of his humiliation and death
because their desire for power drowned out his voice. And dear Peter is the perfect example of one who would push himself forward because he believed he could handle authority with aplomb. Soon, he found himself weeping bitterly.

> When you claim positions of power for yourself, you're acting like an unbeliever. It's the world you're imaging, not your humble Lord.

Think. Look again at Jesus' words, "I am among you as one who serves" (Luke 22:27). God is not among us claiming to be a benefactor who would lord his authority over others. He is with us as the One who holds all authority and power and yet embraces the life of a servant. He didn't grasp after power; he willingly laid aside his right to demand service and served us instead. With that declaration he should have brought to an end all of our grasping for power. But alas.

ALL AUTHORITY IS MINE, SO GO

At the close of his earthly ministry, Jesus commissioned his followers with these words: "All authority has been given to me in heaven and on earth. Go, therefore, and make disciples of all nations ... teaching them to observe everything I have commanded you. And remember, I am with you always, to the end of the age" (Matt 28:18–20).

Notice that Jesus continued to claim that all authority was his alone and yet, look what he did with this authority. He shared it as he commissioned us all to tell others the good news about his humble love and service. He didn't say that we are to fight for power or decide who's who on some Christian ladder to greatness. He said we're to be like him and we're to love one another in this new way, the way of humility and service. The apostle Paul understood this new way when he wrote to the Corinthians, "For you know the grace of our Lord Jesus Christ: Though he was rich, for your sake he became poor, so that by his poverty you might become rich" (2 Cor 8:9).

In case you're still unclear about what the gospel has to say about men and women and their relationships, here it is: Jesus Christ demonstrated his character, grace, and love by turning his back on his authority, riches, and power and giving them all up for us. Brothers and sisters, let us determine to walk in those same pathways. They are the only way open to the Christian. Every other path leads to only folly and conflict.

CHRISTIC MEN AND WOMEN

Christic men and women? Hmm ... What might that mean? Since this might be the first time you've heard that phrase, here's what we mean by it: First, the word "Christic" probably means what you think it means: "relating to or resembling Christ." So, it follows then that a Christic model would be a way of defining and speaking about gender that is built around and secured to what we know about how Jesus and his followers thought and taught. Of course, it will also include deep consideration of how he related to women and men and what this might mean for us today. This book will stand apart from other books about manhood and womanhood you may have read because we've determined to give you a perspective that insists that this topic, like every other, can be rightly understood only in light of the gospel. So, we've chosen to call this perspective being *Christic men and women.*

In the last thirty years or so, many people have sought to define what it means to be Christian men and women. Using words like "complementarian" and "egalitarian," "biblical manhood and woman-hood," "patriarchy," "hierarchy," and "Christian feminism," both men and women have employed blogs, books, and conferences to prove their favored points. They have chosen sides, divided the territory, drawn lines between the orthodox and the heterodox. Some of this writing has been thoughtful and gracious. On the other hand, too much of it has consisted of mudslinging employing the most unchar-itable assumptions possible. In some spaces in the church, disagree-ment about this topic is analogous to denying first-tier doctrines like salvation by faith, the deity of Christ, and the historic view of the Trinity. To disagree or even differ slightly over the accepted defini-tions automatically places the outlier under a cloud of suspicion. For instance, when my co-author, Eric, posted a list of the Bible's testi-mony about women who were the first persons to participate in the redemption narrative in a particular way,[2] he was accused of worship-ing at the footstool of a feminist goddess. Are all men who hold to a complementarian perspective misogynistic abusers? Are all women who believe in equal value *and* roles guilty of feministic apostasy?

Eric and I have both struggled for some time to find a word that we could use that would be free from the frequently toxic baggage that has attached itself especially to words like "complementarian" and "egalitarian." For a while I was trying to convince him that "reciproci-tarian" would work ... but, alas, it was too heavy to fly—and it didn't quite get to what we wanted to communicate. And then we landed on the word "Christic," and it really does communicate what we want to say: relating to or resembling Christ. Perfect.

We're not the first to use the word Christic, of course. Frequently, however, it has been used has been as an adjective to describe how men (as opposed to women) should act. Certain activities and ways of thinking are considered particularly manly or masculine and have been applied to the way that Christian men are to behave in order to assure themselves of their (1) Christianity and (2) masculinity.[3] Again, although others have used this term before us, we're not aware of anyone who has applied the term to both manhood *and* womanhood. It seems that for some people, only men can be defined as or aspire to be Christic. But we disagree. And here's why: the gospel of Jesus Christ has to be the ultimate and final word on our anthropology (the study of humanity)—on how we define ourselves as women and men and our place in God's world.

We've decided to call the principle of the centrality of Jesus, the gospel, and the incarnation *Christic*. For some, this might be a new term. For others, it might have an unpleasantly narrow definition. That's not how we're using it, though. We're using "Christic" to remind us that every answer to our gender-identity questions has to be related to Jesus—which is, in fact, what "Christic" means.

In the following chapters we'll help you see how this paradigm-shattering perspective transforms the understanding and relationships we have with each other as sisters and brothers in Christ. We'll flesh out the implications of this approach and answer some of those *Yeah, but what about ...* questions that are undoubtedly bouncing around. We'll get there, we promise.

But in the meantime, remember: if you're hoping to find out who gets to be boss, the message of the incarnation is lost. We've lost the gospel. Christ taught us that the boss becomes the slave. He did this for you, and for me, so we can do the same.

At the end of the book you'll find a study guide for individuals and groups. It is meant to challenge you to remember what you've read and process what you learned. We hope you'll take the time to review and respond. At the very least, we've personally found it helpful to try to summarize what we've learned in our own reading by thinking about what we've learned in each chapter.

2

When We Forget

God blessed them, and God said to them, "Be fruitful,
multiply, fill the earth, and subdue it." —Genesis 1:28

I (Eric) was born in the mid-1970s as cassette tapes were overtaking records in popularity. Throughout my childhood, I listened to music on the radio, LPs, cassettes, and (at my dad's office) 8-tracks. As a senior in high school, I'd left that all behind for the compact disc. As I write, I'm listening to Antonín Dvořák's Symphony no. 9 via mp3 on my laptop. Later today, my children will stream music through our television using the Pandora app. Meanwhile, my son—a senior in high school—recently acquired both a turntable and cassette deck. My teenagers are fascinated with this "new" technology.

In the opening chapter, we presented a paradigm for what it means to be Christic men and women—males and females transformed into the image of the Christ. Christ is not Jesus' last name; it is his title. The word "Christ" means "anointed one"; it is the equivalent of the Old Testament title "Messiah." The Old Testament expected a righteous ruler (the Messiah) who would usher in the new order of the kingdom of God. This is why we've said so much about how the Christ used authority and power—the Christ is a ruler.

We see how Jesus Christ exercises authority through the message of the gospel—the life, death, and resurrection of the incarnate Lord, Jesus the Christ. That paradigm of Christic men and women comes with a bold claim—namely, that the gospel changes everything. For the paradigm Jesus introduced is radically new.

When we say this paradigm is new, we mean it in the way that my children are captivated by the "new" technology of a turntable and cassette deck. These are new to them not because this is the first time they've appeared, but because my children have only recently encountered them. Likewise with the paradigm of the gospel. It is "new" because it is in Jesus the God-Man that we first see it in all its glory. No one on earth had ever lived this way without compromise. Nevertheless, this gospel-informed view of gender is not a new concept. It is, in fact, an idea as old as creation itself. It was lost in the fall, when sin changed everything. But through Jesus it is recovered and being restored.

SOMETHING OLD, SOMETHING NEW

In Genesis 1, God created man—male and female—in his own image (Gen 1:26). Each of them—the man and the woman—was fully and completely the image of God in and of themselves, as it is with every human being today (1:27). To be God's image meant representing him on the earth. They would fulfill this calling as they filled and ruled the world (1:28). God did not create men and women to rule one another. He made them to rule the earth together, displaying his character to earth's creatures and the heavenly realms.[1] In this way, their mandate at creation is the same as the mandate of the Christ: to rule creation, exercising authority in a way that reflects the character of God. *Christic* men and women are God's original design.

In Genesis 2, we witness how the Lord created the first man and the first woman individually. The Lord formed the first man from dust and breathed life into him (2:7). Then the Lord placed him in a garden in Eden, tasking him with its care. The first crisis in creation arises when, after a review of the animals, no helper could be found for him. The animals, formed from the ground like the man, were helpful, but they were not helpers (2:19–20). The animals and birds did not correspond to the man; they were a different kind of being. Therefore, they were insufficient to partner with him in filling and ruling the earth.

The Lord's solution was to create a woman for the man. But the first woman is not formed from the dust of the earth as the man and the animals. Instead, the Lord fashions her from the man's flesh and bone (2:22), demonstrating that she was the same kind of being as the man. The man would sing, "This one, at last, is bone of my bone and flesh of my flesh; this one will be called 'woman,' for she was taken from man" (2:23). At last, the man had a strong helper, an ally in the Creation Mandate. Together, they could fill and exercise dominion over the earth. Christic man is impossible without Christic woman.

Before the creation account ends, Moses adds this Spirit-inspired commentary: "This is why a man leaves his father and mother and bonds with his wife, and they become one flesh. Both the man and his wife were naked, yet felt no shame" (2:24–25). These verses give a beautiful picture of the distinct genders united in a common purpose.

Moses writes that "a man leaves his father and mother." Read through the Old Testament, and you'll understand why this statement is remarkable. In marriage, a husband did not leave his family. A woman left her family to join his. Why then does the Scripture say that a man will leave his father and mother? Consider what that would mean for the man. To leave his family meant forfeiting his family's industry and wealth, his brothers' protection, sisters' friendship, and the security of an inheritance. It meant, in short, to sacrifice his life for his bride.

For what cause does the man lay down his life? He "bonds with his wife, and they become one flesh. Both the man and his wife were naked, yet felt no shame" (2:24). Nothing, not even clothing, comes between them. The one-flesh consummation of marriage is a picture of perfect unity between men and women that ought to extend beyond marriage to all partnership in God's purposes.

The man delights in pursuing unity in every sphere of life with the woman, even at the cost of his own life. As a helper, the woman does not pursue her own cause. Instead, she delights in volunteering her strength for this cause, cooperating with him in this mutual pursuit that God assigned *them*. Neither puts their own interest first, but each pursues their joy in a blessed union with the other.

This is our first glimpse of the radical nature of Christic men and women. It does not strive for dominion and authority over other people. Rather, Christic men and women sacrifice security and status to be unified allies in the fulfillment of God's mission.

Genesis 2 is God's picture not only for marriage, but also for humanity itself. The glory of God would be displayed on earth when men and women, through voluntary humility, were united in pursuing God's purposes on earth. The Lord's vision for the earth and humanity was *not* that it would have a "masculine feel" or "feminine flavor." Rather, it would have a Christic shape—it would be shaped into the image of the yet unknown perfect human, the Christ.

The vision painted in Genesis 2 is fulfilled in Philippians 2 as Paul unpacks the glory of Christ Jesus. It would not have been robbery for Jesus to hold on to equality with God, for that was his right by nature. Nevertheless, he took on "the likeness of humanity" (Phil 2:7)—he who was God became the image of God. Having become a human, Jesus displayed the glory of God through a voluntary humility for the sake of shame-free unity with his people (just as the man and woman were to do in Genesis 2). The Christ assumed "the form of a servant" and "humbled himself by becoming obedient to the point of death—even to death on a cross" (Phil 2:6–8).

> Our first glimpse of the radical nature of Christic men and women. It does not strive for dominion and authority over other people. Rather, Christic men and women sacrifice security and status to be unified allies in the fulfillment of God's mission.

How are we, the bride of Christ, to respond to this? We are to "adopt the same attitude as that of Christ Jesus" (2:5). There are not two distinct mindsets—one for the bridegroom and one for the bride. The church's mindset is the same as her bridegroom's. She is to be Christic—to "do nothing out of selfish ambition or conceit, but in humility consider others as more important than yourselves. Everyone should look not to his own interests, but rather to the interests of others" (2:3–4). What is the goal of such a mindset? Perfect unity: "having the same love, united in spirit, intent on one purpose" (2:2). We will discuss this more extensively in chapter three.

So, this Christic paradigm is nothing new. It was God's plan for humanity from all time. And yet, it is new. Before the incarnation, it had never appeared in perfection. For immediately after reading of this glorious creation, we find the image of God rebellious and corrupted. So what went wrong?

WHEN THE FLESH REBELS

In Genesis 3, a serpent—the devil in the flesh—deceived the woman, causing her to eat from the tree that God forbade. Upon eating, she did not die but gave some to her husband, who was with her. When he ate it, "the eyes of both of them were opened, and they knew they were naked" (3:6–7). The man's act of rebellion brought sin, death, and shame into the world and corrupted human nature (Rom 5:12).

Sin also immediately corrupted the shame-free unity between the man and the woman. They realized their nakedness and covered themselves. When the Lord questioned the man, the man shifted the blame to the woman. Then the Lord spelled out the consequences for this sin, which includes a disruption in the union of the man and woman.

The man will still go to the ground, seeking to cultivate it for food. But the land will no longer cooperate. Instead, it will bear thorns and thistles, requiring strenuous labor (3:17–19). The woman will still bear children as they fill the earth. Only now her labor pains will be intensified (3:16a). Do you see the pattern in the poetry? The humans will

> Sin corrupted the relationship between the man and the woman. We see the dire consequences of this disruption play out in the storyline of Scripture, even as they continue today in society, homes, and the church.

still seek to fulfill God's Creation Mandate to fill the earth and rule it, only now the earth and their bodies will refuse to cooperate. With that pattern in mind, read Genesis 3:16b, in which the Lord says to the woman, "Your desire will be for your husband, yet he will rule over you." She will turn toward her husband, desiring to join him in ruling the earth. But now he will not cooperate. Instead of exercising dominion together (unity), he will rule over her. Sin corrupted the relationship between the man and the woman. We see the dire consequences of this disruption play out in the storyline of Scripture, even as they continue today in society, homes, and the church.

DISRUPTION IN THE HOME

Genesis 2–3 describes the relationship between a married couple—the first man and the first woman. Perhaps this is why the first place Scripture records a corrupted relationship between men and women is in the context of marriage. In the latter half of Genesis 4, the culmination of wicked Cain's line is Lamech, who speaks in verses 23–24:

> Adah and Zillah, hear my voice;
> wives of Lamech, pay attention to my words.
> For I killed a man for wounding me,
> a young man for striking me.
> If Cain is to be avenged seven times over,
> then for Lamech it will be seventy-seven times!

Notice first of all that Lamech has wives (plural)—a departure from Genesis 2:24, where a man "bonds with his wife, and they become one flesh."

Lamech calls his wives to him, urging them to pay close attention to what he is about to say. A man wounded Lamech by striking him. In response, Lamech killed him. The punishment did not fit the crime; it exceeded it. The message to his wives is clear: "Wives, listen closely! I respond with lethal violence to those who offend me. You'll bear this in mind if you know what's good for you." Rather than bonding to a wife in the pursuit of shame-free unity, Lamech ruled over his wives with threats of domestic violence. Rather than laying down his life, Lamech warns against offending him with a lethal threat. Lamech is a self-centered murderer set on ruling and abusing others for his own sake. He calls his wives to him and boasts about killing a young man who merely wounded him. He wants his wives to know that he is lethally violent with those who fail to please him. This is the opposite of a Christic man.

We see this today in husbands and wives who see marriage as a means to serve themselves. In the husband who strikes his wife. In the wife whose words demean and destroy her husband. It appears in the husband who rapes or manipulates his wife into performing sexual acts she finds undesirable. We see it in the wife whose jealousy provokes her to constant suspicion or isolates her husband from others.

Sin corrupts parenting, producing mothers and fathers who view their children as a means to glorify themselves. Parents who berate their children for not excelling in sports or academics because it reflects poorly on themselves. A father who calls his daughter "fat" or "ugly," insisting that no one will want someone like her. A mother who molests her children. The parents who will not send their daughter to college because "women don't need an education."

Sin corrupts singleness through views that insinuate a man or woman's worth and purpose are determined by their relationship to a spouse, rather than their relationship to Christ.

What all these examples have in common is that they destroy others while serving the self. They fail to demonstrate a voluntary humility, one that sets aside its own preferences to serve another.

Rather than pursuing the glory of Christ and unity with one another through voluntary humility, they seek the exaltation of the self at the cost of one's neighbor. This is the opposite of Christic.

DISRUPTION IN THE CHURCH

In Genesis 4, we find the first recorded act of worship. Abel and his brother Cain presented offerings to the Lord according to their vocation. Cain, the worker of the ground, presented the land's produce (Gen 4:3). Abel, the shepherd, brought some of the firstborn of his flock (4:4a). The Lord regarded Abel's offering but not Cain's (Gen 4:4b–5a; Heb 11:4). Cain became furious in his jealousy over the Lord's response to his brother. So, he invited Abel into the field, where Cain attacked and killed his brother (Gen 4:8).

Scripture tells us that the Lord approved Abel's offering because Abel offered it by faith (Heb 11:4). This implies that Cain did not present his offering in faith. Consider these contrasting motivations in worship. Abel offered his gift in faith—that is, he trusted in the Lord who promised to send a deliverer to crush the serpent's head. If faith motivated Abel, then what motivated Cain? His response is telling. Cain was furious and downcast that the Lord approved of Abel as a righteous man but did not approve of him. Cain's envy overflowed in murder. Cain offered "worship" for himself, to his own glory and benefit. He did not worship with regard to the promises of God and the glory of the Lord.

Cain was the first person to use an act of worship as a means to glorify himself. When he did not receive the blessing and approval that another worshiper did, he facilitated the first "church split." He and his brother should have labored in unity for the Lord. Instead, because Cain despised humility, he murdered his brother. Cain was the first person to use worship this way, but he would not be the last.

The spirit of Cain flows through the Old Testament in priests who treated worship with contempt, exploiting both worship and worshipers for selfish gain (1 Sam 2:12–17). It appears in the New Testament in those who misappropriated the court of the gentiles as a convenient marketplace, depriving God-fearing gentiles of a place to worship (Mark 11:15–17).

Jesus warned against abusing worship in the pursuit of self-glory. While teaching in the temple, Jesus told the people: "Beware of the scribes, who want to go around in long robes, and who want greetings in the marketplaces, the best seats in the synagogues, and the places of honor at banquets. They devour widows' houses and say long prayers just for show. These will receive harsher judgment" (Mark 12:38–40).

What did the scribes in Jesus' day desire? They coveted elaborate greetings in public places, the best seats in the synagogue, and the places of honor at banquets. Their public prayers were performances and not appeals to God. The scribes were men who used their religious office and acts of worship to exalt themselves.

How did these men treat others? "They devour widows' houses." It is unclear how exactly they did this. J. A. Brooks suggests that "Some may have ingratiated themselves to widows in hopes of being willed their houses, or they may have found technicalities in the law whereby they could lay claim to the houses of defenseless persons, such as widows."[2] J. R. Edwards notes that one man "succeeded in persuading a high-standing woman named Fulvia to make substantial gifts to the temple in Jerusalem. The bequests, however, were embezzled."[3] Whatever the case, Jesus' point is clear—they destroyed widows. To rob a widow of her home was next to delivering her over to death. "Pure and undefiled religion before God the Father is this: to look after orphans and widows in their distress" (Jas 1:27). But these men would kill the most vulnerable to benefit themselves.

Immediately after recounting this teaching, Mark presents Jesus "sitting across from the temple treasury," watching the crowd drop in money (Mark 12:41). While the rich deposited large sums, Jesus notices a poor widow, who "came and dropped in two tiny coins worth very little" (12:42). He says, "Truly I tell you, this poor widow has put more into the treasury than all the others. For they all gave out of their surplus, but she out of her poverty has put in everything she had—all she had to live on" (12:44).

What a contrast this widow was to the scribes! They did not cooperate with God in the pursuit of his purposes. Instead, they co-opted worship to exalt themselves. They did not serve others through voluntary humility. They destroyed others to feed their pride. But this widow "put in everything she had—all she had to live on." Leaving the temple, the widow would have nothing on which to live—nothing but the Lord in whom she trusted. When she offered those two coins, she laid down her life. What motivated her voluntary humiliation? She desired to cooperate with the Lord, giving her life to fund his purposes. No wonder Jesus noticed her. She was conformed to his image.

Sadly, the scribes' spirit still appears in the church and religious institutions—particularly in the relationships between women and men. We find it in churches that cover up sexual abuse, neglecting to report such criminal activity to protect the church's reputation (though not the victims). We see this in a seminary president who urges a rape victim not to report to the police because he cares more for his institution than for the woman.

Women and their gifts are devoured by churches and theologies that promote unbiblical or unbalanced teaching. What happens when seminarians hear that all women, by their female nature, desire to overthrow men? What happens when pastors-in-training are taught only about guarding themselves against temptations, false accusations, and seductresses? What happens when we tell them that friendships with women or coffee with female church members are dangerous and forbidden? Future pastors grow suspicious of their sisters. They will rob the women (and men) in their churches of meaningful partnership and unity in the gospel. The Great Commission and the unbelieving world are underserved when the church prevents men and women from functioning as siblings and allies.

The church is deprived of women's gifts when pastors misapply or overextend biblical principles. A complementarian Bible college president restricts female enrollment to 40 percent to maintain a "masculine feel" on campus. Church elders exclude women from offering the prayer, leading the liturgical readings, or reading the Scripture during corporate gatherings, desiring to promote the appearance of male leadership. Regardless of debates over ordaining women as elders, it is clear that the Bible nowhere commands or commends a "masculine feel" in Christian institutions or worship services. Women are silenced and excluded in corporate worship, even though the New Testament expects women to participate in the worship service through prayer and prophecy (1 Cor 11:5). These are instances of leaders taking what they believe to be biblical principles and overextending them, applying them in ways the Spirit-inspired word does not. What happens in these cases? Theological education is withheld from women. The church is deprived of hearing female voices and being ministered to by their gifts.

The church is harmed when views of manhood and womanhood become functional tests of orthodoxy. For example, say an organization claims it exists to enable Christians of various theological traditions to collaborate around the gospel. It boasts of gladly including cessationists and continuationists, elder ruled and congregational, paedobaptists and credobaptists. They center on the gospel, they claim, even though they divide over "secondary matters" in their local church. Yet, in their statement of faith, we find a statement affirming elder ordination for only qualified males (and *not* females) listed alongside the otherwise "primary matters" of orthodoxy. A cessationist, congregational, Baptist church gladly joins elder-ruled, paedobaptist, and contituationist churches in a city-wide evangelism campaign. It will not, however, partner with or invite the church that has a female pastor.

> These are instances of leaders taking what they believe to be biblical principles and overextending them, applying them in ways the Spirit-inspired word does not.

What do such behaviors imply? They imply that differences over "gender roles" in the church constitute a de facto exclusion from Christian fellowship, if not salvation itself. They make the doctrine of "gender roles" a functional test of orthodoxy. The implication is clear: those who differ from us on a host of "secondary matters" are allies in the kingdom of God—but those who differ on "gender roles" most certainly are not.

DISRUPTION IN THE WORLD

The disruption that sin brings is not limited to home and church. It is prevalent throughout the world and society. It is particularly true in matters of authority. Here, too, the Bible is replete with examples. One is found in the life of King David. David is important because the Christ would be called "the Son of David." There are many ways that David foreshadows the Christ. But in 2 Samuel 11:1–4, David is anything but Christic:

> In the spring when kings march out to war, David sent Joab with his officers and all Israel. They destroyed the Ammonites and besieged Rabbah, but David remained in Jerusalem.
>
> One evening David got up from his bed and strolled around on the roof of the palace. From the roof he saw a woman bathing—a very beautiful woman. So David sent someone to inquire about her, and he said, "Isn't this Bathsheba, daughter of Eliam and wife of Uriah the Hethite?"
>
> David sent messengers to get her, and when she came to him, he slept with her. Now she had just been purifying herself from her uncleanness. Afterward, she returned home. The woman conceived and sent word to inform David, "I am pregnant."

What do we know about David and Bathsheba? David was the king. The story takes place in springtime, "the time when kings go out to battle" (2 Sam 11:1 ESV). Instead of going out to battle with his band of soldiers as he once had, David remained in Jerusalem. His loyal soldiers slept on the battlefield, away from their wives and children. David strolled the roof of the palace. From there, he saw an attractive woman bathing. Instead of protecting her privacy and dignity and returning to bed, David inquired about her. Upon learning that she was the wife of a soldier (and, thus, a woman whose husband was not at home to stand in David's way), he sent men to get her and bring her back. When she arrived, he had sexual relations with her and sent her home. He later learned that she was pregnant with his child.

Bathsheba is depicted as a holy woman. She was keeping covenant through the ritual washing to cleanse herself after her menstrual cycle. Nowhere in the Bible is Bathsheba condemned for sexual relations with David. Given David's elaborate efforts to cover his sin after the fact, he surely did not disclose his intentions when sending for her. Bathsheba is presented as a vulnerable woman. David learned she was the wife of Uriah, a man David knew well. Uriah is listed among "the thirty," an honored group of elite warriors who fought with and for David. Uriah was a man who would have gladly surrendered his life for the sake of David. He was not at home to protect his wife from predatory men. Like her husband, Bathsheba was a loyal subject of the king. She trusted him and honored his summons.

David used his position—one of status, authority, honor, and trust—to manipulate a vulnerable and trusting woman into a situation where he would force her to have sex. There's a word for this—rape. David's behavior is anything but that which we saw celebrated in Genesis 2. Instead of risking his life for the sake of the nation, he declined to go to war. Instead of being in the city to govern and protect it, he used the soldiers' absence as an occasion to prey on their wives. He might have averted his eyes and thanked God for the faithfulness of an Israelite woman. Instead, he lusted after and devoured her.

The situation did not improve when David learned of the pregnancy. He sent for her husband, Uriah. Instead of confessing his evil to Uriah (and Bathsheba) and seeking their forgiveness, David intended to deceive Uriah to protect himself. David repeatedly attempted to send Uriah home in hopes that he would sleep with his wife, even going so far as to get him drunk. This way, Uriah might believe the baby to be his own. But Uriah, being the righteous man that David was not, refused to enjoy sex with his wife while his soldiers and the ark of the covenant camped in the open field (2 Sam 11:6–13).

David could have humbled himself and confessed his evil. But this would have cost David his reputation. It risked provoking the anger of Uriah, for "love is strong as death, jealousy is fierce as the grave. Its flashes are flashes of fire, the very flame of the Lord" (Song 8:6 ESV). Instead of risking his own life to do what was right, David plotted to kill his loyal friend and marry his bereaved wife. So David wrote a letter instructing Joab to "put Uriah at the front of the fiercest fighting, then withdraw from him so that he is struck down and dies." David's murder of Uriah is as cold-blooded and premeditated as his rape of Bathsheba. As much as David was "a man after God's own heart" (1 Sam 13:14), there dwelt within him the corrupted nature of his first father, Adam. Davidesque manhood is opposed to Christic men.

This Davidesque use of authority and societal status to destroy others for self-benefit is alive and well in all levels of our society. It appears in manifold ways—racism, misogyny, misandry, nepotism, favoritism toward the wealthy and influential, prejudice. The list seems to go forever.

American chattel slavery stands out as a particularly egregious example of the abuse of human beings for the sake of status and wealth. Following emancipation, the Jim Crow laws and segregation that codified anti-black hatred illustrate the corrupted flesh's relentless pursuit of its wicked desires. Racism and prejudice are not Christic.

Larry Nassar was a doctor renowned for his ability to treat the unique needs of gymnasts. He served as a doctor to the "Magnificent Seven" at the 1996 Olympic Games. He was subsequently appointed the national medical coordinator for USA Gymnastics. Nassar would serve as an assistant professor at the MSU College of Osteopathic Medicine, volunteer his time with community organizations, receive a US patent, write a textbook, film videos, and receive multiple national awards and recognitions.[4] Needless to say, Nassar positioned himself to receive the trust and respect of organizations, gymnasts, and parents. He endeared himself to those who came to him for care. All the while, Nassar used his position of trust, respect, and expertise to sexually abuse countless underage women, sometimes with their unsuspecting mothers in the room.[5]

Though gymnasts state they reported Nassar's behavior in the 1990s, USA Gymnastics would not take action for almost twenty-five years. The *IndyStar* reported that, amid the USA Gymnastics sex abuse scandal, "at least 368 gymnasts have alleged some form of sexual abuse at the hands of their coaches, gym owners and other adults working in gymnastics." The *IndyStar* reported that "top officials at USA Gymnastics, one of the nation's most prominent Olympic organizations, failed to alert police to many allegations of sexual abuse that occurred on their watch and stashed complaints in files that have been kept secret. But the problem is far worse. A nine-month investigation found that predatory coaches were allowed to move from gym to gym, undetected by a lax system of oversight, or dangerously passed on by USA Gymnastics-certified gyms."[6] Both Larry Nassar and USA Gymnastics served themselves at the cost of harm to young women. Abuse and abuse cover-up are not Christic.

Not all corruption of male-female partnership in society is as evident and stark as what I've described above. It may appear in the subtle denial of differences between the genders. Or it may appear in the overemphasis of differences, in which men and women are presented as two different kinds of being, as different as a semitruck and a racecar. Corruption happens when cultural stereotypes appear as gospel truth. Man and woman are reduced to one's ability with neckties and apple pies, respectively. It occurs when theologies extend concepts of "gender roles" in the church and home to every realm in creation. All men are to lead all women, and all women are to submit to all men. Women should be careful not to snuff out the masculine leadership in their interactions with men, even in the offering of directions. *It happens when Christlikeness is deemed insufficient for discipleship. It is necessary to put on specific masculine or feminine virtues; merely putting on Christ will not suffice.*

Sometimes, it comes in the form of minimizing or downplaying the partnership of women. Consider the example outlined in Sarah Rose's excellent volume *D-Day Girls: The Spies Who Armed the Resistance, Sabotaged the Nazis, and Helped Win World War II.* Winston Churchill knew that winning the war would require a new type of warfare. He authorized the creation of a secret agency for insurgency, what he liked to call his Ministry of Ungentlemanly Warfare.[7] Rose writes, "It would be the dirtiest war, beyond the rules of engagement, outside the protection of courts, contracts, or global political conventions. This was warfare by every available means: There would be murders, kidnappings, demolitions, ransoms, and torture."[8] These insurgents would work behind enemy lines to prepare for the Continental invasion; they would be "bodies on the ground in the occupied countries ... to fuel, fund, arm, organize, train, and command a resistance."

But Britain faced a problem: they had run out of men. So Captain Selwyn Jepson made a bold decision—he would recruit women. Rose writes, "Putting women in the line of fire was obscene, the brass said: War is fought by men for the sake of women and children. What use could women be in combat? Every culture on earth has a taboo against women in warfare; their bodies are purpose-built to create life, not to destroy it. Not since Boudicca led her troops against Rome had an Englishwoman taken up arms against a foreign adversary." Yet women were already serving in defensive combat for the British. "Some seventy-eight thousand women had begun to fire upon Germans, manning the trigger on anti-aircraft (ack-ack) artillery."[9] These included Winston Churchill's own daughter, Mary, in response to which he remarked, "A gunner is a gunner."[10]

But it would be a different matter convincing the higher-ups to send women behind enemy lines. Captain Jepson knew he would need the approval of the prime minister himself. Jepson presented his idea, and Winston Churchill gave his blessing.

Thirty-nine women would be recruited by the British to parachute into enemy territory at night to undertake their top-secret commission. They risked torture, rape, and death—which some suffered—as they bicycled about the country, engaging in espionage and using explosives to destroy infrastructure. How were these strong and courageous heroes honored when the war ended?

> Men won different laurels for their fight. By the end of the war, such sex segregation was a familiar story: Male agents performing the same tasks might be recommended for the Victorian Cross, created by Queen Victoria, the highest honor for military gallantry. While the *Corps féminins* did much of the same work in the same places, they were not technically soldiers and so not eligible for military honors—only civil decorations. It was one of the many ways women were denied equal status. Their salaries and ranks were lower; so too were their war pensions. When it took five parachute jumps to receive paratrooper wings, women were only ever assigned to four jumps and so never received their wings. And though the women of F Section served in combat, government chauvinism dictated they were not eligible for military recognition.[11]

While their valor and service matched that of any male co-laborer, the recognition they received from the British government did not. Commissioning a person to risk and sacrifice for a cause, only to deny them proper recognition, is not the pattern we find in Christ.

The D-Day girls offer a remarkable illustration of the "battle of the sexes." Typically, we use the phrase to refer to conflict and striving between the sexes, each seeking to overcome the other. We certainly find this in the way these war heroes were received and honored below their male counterparts.

But the "battle of the sexes" could be read to mean the battle undertaken by the sexes together, united in one cause. This pattern has been God's purpose from the very beginning. It has been corrupted by sin, attacked by Satan, and resisted by our flesh.

How do we learn to put off the sinful tendency to use, abuse, and divide? Where can we find the power to put on Christ, the true image of God, whose voluntary humiliation served others, bringing unity between persons and glory to God? For that, we must turn to the gospel of Jesus Christ, the incarnate Lord, crucified for our sin and raised from the dead.

3

Brothers, Sisters, Brides, and Sons

Therefore, he had to be like his brothers and sisters in every way. —Hebrews 2:17

What image does the name Crawley invoke? My guess is that many of you just visualized a grand British mansion where the Crawley family and their servants lived and worked in the fictional series *Downton Abbey*. Masterpiece Theater and ITV began airing the show, which lasted for six seasons, beginning in 2011 in the United States. I (Elyse) have to admit I was a rabid fan. I doubt I missed a single episode. From week to week, I couldn't wait to find out what happened to Lady Mary, Mr. Carson, Mrs. Hughes, or Cora. And, of course, I especially enjoyed Violet, the Dowager Countess of Grantham, whose acerbic zingers were always the highlight of the show for me. I relate to her "At my age, one must ration one's excitement" sarcastic humor. Aside from the elaborate sets, gorgeous costumes, all-star cast, and superb writing of Julian Fellowes and others, our collective imaginations were captured by this family with their relationships and customs. We love watching what happens in other families, and the success of *Downton Abbey* proves it.

Of course, if all this is simply too Anglophile for you, how about the "family" from *West Wing*—Josiah Bartlet and Sam Seaborn, C. J. Cregg, Toby Ziegler, and Josh Lyman—who weren't really a biological family but functioned like one over seven highly entertaining seasons. We loved watching the interplay between characters, the way they responded to life, the choices—sometimes very difficult ones—they had to make. And since it seemed like none of them ever went home, the west wing of the White House was their home away from home, their Downton Abbey.

There's something very basic, so intrinsic to our humanness, so familiar about families that we can't help but find them captivating. We're fascinated by them because they're so much a part of who we are. The family is fundamental to who we are as humans, and our interest in them seems inexhaustible. Whether we're spying on the Crawleys or singing "We Are Family" along with Sister Sledge, we seem unable to exhaust our fascination with them. Is it that way for you, too?

In this chapter, we're going to focus in on another family, an utterly unique one. Unlike the imaginary Crawley family and even better than a real-life one I belong to, the Fitzpatricks, this is the oldest, strongest, and truest family there is: this is the family of God. How does Scripture speak of our shared familial relationships? How should a Christic understanding of our relationships as men and women shape our beliefs about how we should think about and relate to one another as brothers and sisters, sons and brides in our Father's house?

Before we answer those questions, let's consider our common ancestry as the writer of Hebrews describes it.

THE EXCELLENT SON AND HIS SIBLINGS

After describing Jesus' superiority over everyone who had come before, the writer to the Hebrews employs deeply relational language. He tells us that Jesus is the heir of creation and the exact representation of his Father. He is the radiance and true reflection of God's glory: he reveals absolutely everything we need to know about his Father's nature. In other words, Jesus looks like his Dad (see 1:1–4). "I will be his Father, and he will be my Son" (1:5) and "Sit at my right hand until I make your enemies your footstool" (1:13) describe the primary relationships in this family: the relationships between the Father, the Son, and the Holy Spirit. If you want to know what God is like, look at Jesus.

After warning the readers not to give up, the writer of Hebrews resorts again to familial language, but now we learn something surprising: this perfect Son has siblings! Notice with me the number of times his family relationships are referenced:

> For in bringing many *sons* and *daughters* to glory, it was entirely appropriate that God—for whom and through whom all things exist—should make the pioneer of their salvation perfect through sufferings. For the one who sanctifies and those who are sanctified *all* have *one Father*. That is why Jesus is not ashamed to call them *brothers* and *sisters*, saying: I will proclaim your name to my *brothers* and *sisters*; I will sing hymns to you in the congregation. Again, I will trust in him. And again, Here I am with the *children* God gave me. Now since the *children* have flesh and blood in common, Jesus also shared in these, so that through his death he might destroy the one holding the power of death—that is, the devil—and free those who were held in slavery all their lives by the fear of death. For it is clear that he does not reach out to help angels, but to help Abraham's *offspring*. Therefore, he had to be like his *brothers* and *sisters* in every way, so that he could become a merciful and faithful high priest in matters pertaining to God, to make atonement for the sins of the people. (Heb 2:10–17, emphasis added)

Isn't that amazing? This Son who is the embodied image of God is *our* brother! Over and over again in this passage we're shown that our salvation is not merely an individual event, but rather something far deeper that has bound us together with other believers from all times, all nations, and all languages. Look again at the way we, men and women, are spoken of: we are *sons* and *daughters* who are brought to glory and have a common *Father*. Jesus isn't ashamed to call us his *brothers* and *sisters* and to join us in song to our Father. You and I are the gift the Father gave to the Son when he assimilated our flesh and blood as his own, so that he is now one of us. Through the incarnation he was forever transformed into the God-Man and joined our family in every possible way. Jesus was made like both his brothers *and* sisters in every way. *In every way.*

SHARING OUR HUMANITY

In his incarnation as a man, Jesus took on every aspect of our shared humanity, excepting sin. He was tempted in every way that I have been tempted. He was tempted in every way that Eric has been tempted (Heb 4:15). Jesus was made like both his brothers *and* his sisters. He took on our common human *nature,* the nature of males *and* females, all his siblings. In every way that I, a woman, have a human nature, he was like me. In every way that Eric, a man, has a human nature, he was like him as well. He knows what it is to be me—not just because he's omniscient, but by personal experience. He experienced every aspect of life as I know it.

> Jesus was made like both his brothers and sisters in every way. *In every way.*

It is crucial that we grasp this truth because, without it, we'll be confused about who he is, who we are, and what he's done. Think again about what this means: "Therefore, he had to be like his *brothers* and *sisters* in every way, so that he could become a merciful and faithful high priest in matters pertaining to God, to make atonement for the sins of the people" (Heb 2:17, emphasis added).

This passage teaches that there isn't a male nature that Jesus assumed and a female nature that he disregarded. There is only one human nature, and Jesus completely incorporated it into himself, temptations and all. Of course, human nature always expresses itself through differently gendered bodies, as we'll consider in chapter five. But before we get there, it's important for us to remember all we share: I am a human who is biologically gendered as a woman. Eric is a human who is biologically gendered as male. Conversely, Jesus was both divine and human, but he was, and always will be, gendered as male. Jesus received his genetic code from his mother Mary through the Holy Spirit, and that genetic code made him one with his whole human family.

BROTHERS *AND* SISTERS

The way we're talked about, especially as brothers and sisters, fathers and mothers, sons and daughters, is highly instructive. Perhaps you've never read passages in your Bible that address brothers *and* sisters like we are now. So let's take a little time now to consider the Greek word *adelphoi* which is the word translated "brothers and sisters."

A Short Excursus into Adelphoi

You may have noticed that we have chosen to use the *Christian Standard Bible* (CSB) in this book. One of the reasons we've done so is the way the CSB translates the Greek plural word ἀδελφοί (*adelphoi*) as "brothers *and* sisters." While this Greek word has traditionally been translated "brethren" or "brothers," sometimes with a footnote that it may also be translated "brothers and sisters" (ESV), modern scholarship dictates that the term actually meant both brothers *and* sisters, *siblings*, and should be translated in that way. As a woman very familiar with the Scriptures, I've found it both surprising and encouraging to see all the places where I, specifically as a woman, a "sister," was being directly spoken to.[1] The CSB translators made the change from the gender-specific "brother" to "brother and sister" not to acquiesce to feminist pressures from the culture, but rather to offer a more accurate translation. In addition, of course, it also pushes back against unnecessarily gendered language that was accepted in the past but is now heard as sexist or dismissive by modern readers. Of course, how we might feel about any given word should never be our primary consideration; rather, accurate translation of the Spirit's intent must be. However, hanging on to antiquated and potentially offensive words just to prove you're not caving to the secular culture is equally wrong, and perhaps more so, because of the harm that some with misogynistic perspectives have caused in the church. It is, in fact, caving to an erroneous church culture.

The adoption of both men and women into God's family is something to be celebrated. Consider now the following verses where our relationships in God's family are made clearer by the proper usage of *adelphoi,* "brothers and sisters":

- "For those he foreknew he also predestined to be conformed to the image of his Son, so that he would be the firstborn among many brothers and sisters" (Rom 8:29). The right of firstborn male privilege, primogeniture, accrues only to Christ. He is the firstborn, but he also shares this right with all of us, both male and female. In addition, this passage shows me that, as a woman, I am being fashioned into the image, nature, and character of my brother, Jesus Christ, gender notwithstanding. To assume that I have an image, nature, or character that is ontologically different from my brothers would cause this passage to lose its impact and transformative power for believing women.

- "My brothers and sisters, I myself am convinced about you that you also are full of goodness, filled with all knowledge, and able to instruct one another" (Rom 15:14). This passage tells us that women, like their brothers, may be filled with goodness and knowledge, which they can employ to teach one another. When Paul wrote to the Romans around seven years *before* writing to Timothy in Ephesus, he certainly did not think that women should never teach anything to men. Rather, he was convinced or completely persuaded that they could and should.

- "What then, brothers and sisters? Whenever you come together, each one has a hymn, a teaching, a revelation, another tongue, or an interpretation. Everything is to be done for building up" (1 Cor 14:26). Paul expected that "whenever" the church at Corinth came together, both brothers *and* sisters would have something to offer that would edify the church. Both male and female voices were necessary for the edification of Christ's body.

• "Therefore, my dear brothers and sisters, be steadfast, immovable, always excelling in the Lord's work, because you know that your labor in the Lord is not in vain" (1 Cor 15:58). In the same way that the brothers in the church in Corinth needed to stand strong without wavering as they excelled in their gospel mission, their sisters did as well. They were all called to work hard in faith for the Lord.

• "Brothers and sisters, if someone is overtaken in any wrongdoing, you who are spiritual, restore such a person with a gentle spirit, watching out for yourselves so that you also won't be tempted. Carry one another's burdens; in this way you will fulfill the law of Christ" (Gal 6:1–2). Both women and men are commissioned to bring gentle restoration to people who are overtaken in wrongdoing. In seeking to help our siblings in this way, we are fulfilling the law of Christ, which is love for one's neighbor. This is not only a ministry that men are called to; rather, both brothers *and* sisters can and should carry one another's burdens.

• "Join in imitating me, brothers and sisters, and pay careful attention to those who live according to the example you have in us" (Phil 3:17). Again, Paul isn't concerned about women only acting like women. Rather, Paul wants women *and* men to imitate him and to live according to his example.

- "So then, my dearly loved and longed for brothers and sisters, my joy and crown, in this manner stand firm in the Lord, dear friends" (Phil 4:1). It's not surprising that Paul refers to the women and men in Philippi as his "dearly loved and longed for ... joy and crown," his "dear friends." Remember that this church began with the baptism of Lydia, the first convert to Christianity in Europe. The church was birthed in her home, and she was undoubtedly one of the main sources of support for Paul. Lydia and the entire church that met in her home were encouraged to stand firm against both the worldly influences and the persecution they were facing. Paul loved Lydia and the rest of the brothers and sisters there dearly.

Here's why this is so important: if there is a male nature that differs in essence from a female nature, and if Jesus assumed a male nature but not a female one, then I, as a woman, can't be saved. The ancient theologian Athanasius (AD 296–373) rightly understood that if there were any part of human nature that hadn't been assumed by Jesus in the incarnation, then that part of our nature, whatever it might be, could not be part of his record of perfect law-keeping and substitutionary death in our place. Jesus had to be like me in every way or I can't be saved in any way. Jesus is the perfect human, which means he stands in as both the perfect man *and* the perfect woman. He is not merely my example, he is also my brother, my righteousness. He fulfilled all God's law perfectly in my place and died for breaking the law in my place so that I, as a woman, can be both forgiven and counted completely righteous. The importance of this truth can't be overstated: We share the same humanity.

In addition, I wonder how relationships between men and women in the church would be

> Jesus is the perfect human, which means he stands in as both the perfect man *and* the perfect woman. He is not merely my example, he is also my brother, my righteousness.

transformed if, before responding to a female parishioner's concerns or questions, a male pastor or elder would remember that Jesus is her older brother who feels every filial impulse to protect and cherish her as any good brother does. As I've listened to stories about how certain pastors and Christian leaders have responded to hurting women who have come to them for help, I wonder if they would have been more respectful and understanding had they realized her big Brother was standing there in the room with her.

FEMALE SONS

Not only do we have many passages about our relationship as brothers and sisters in God's family, but there are also passages where women are referred to and given the same rights of inheritance as sons: "Now you too, brothers *and* sisters, like Isaac, are children of promise" (Gal 4:28, emphasis added). Just like Isaac, the promised son who would inherit the blessing, all believers, women *and* men, inherit the promised blessing as sons.

As with Paul's use of the word *adelphoi* to describe brothers and sisters, his employment of the use of "son" when speaking of female believers would have shocked his Roman hearers to their core. Even though God had approved the principle of Israelite daughters inheriting from their fathers who had no sons (see Num 27), the Romans didn't practice it. In fact, female infants were considered a burden and were frequently exposed to die. They had no civil rights or any value aside from childbearing. No one would want to adopt a useless female ... no one but God our Father. The gospel changes everything; it turns believing women into sons with the same rights as firstborn sons (primogeniture).

- Addressing the brothers and sisters in Rome, Paul writes: "all those led by God's Spirit are God's sons" (Rom 8:14).

- "You received the Spirit of adoption, by whom we cry out, '*Abba,* Father!' ... we are God's children, and if children, also heirs—heirs of God and coheirs with Christ"

(Rom 8:15–17). Don't miss the import of this: In Ancient Rome, women had no rights of inheritance as sons. But now, women are adopted, call God their Father, and inherit with Christ.

- "You know, then, that those who have faith, these are Abraham's sons ... for through faith you are all sons of God in Christ Jesus" (Gal 3:7, 26). Paul goes so far as to say that the dividing lines between Jew and Greek, slave and free, male and female are done away with through baptism, which takes the place of gender-specific circumcision, into Christ. As a believing woman, I am an heir of the promise given to Abraham and his male heirs.

- "To redeem those under the law, so that we might receive adoption as sons" (Gal 4:5). Roman adoption practices were legally binding agreements wherein a favored slave could be granted all the rights of primogeniture, including inheriting the status and name of the benefactor. Women were never given these rights in secular society— before the gospel, that is.

- "And I will be a Father to you, and you will be sons and daughters to me, says the Lord Almighty" (2 Cor 6:18). Unlike the misogynistic heads of households in the Greco-Roman world, women are precious to the Father and are welcomed as part of the family.

Believing women have all the rights of primogeniture. In what ways would our practice toward women in the church change if we saw them as daughters with all the rights of firstborn sons in the Father's family?

THE MALE BRIDE

At the end of time, all believers, both men and women, will be part of the Son's bride. In fact, that's what we all are right now. If you want to talk about the nature we will take into eternity, we're all more like a bride than anything else.

> At the end of time, all believers, both men and women, will be part of the Son's bride. In fact, that's what we all are right now.

- In one of Paul's primary passages on marriage, he refers to the whole church as Christ's bride. While we will look at this passage later in the chapter on marriage (chapter eight), the primary point of it is not the household codes laid out there, but rather the relationship between Christ, the husband, and the church, his bride.

- "Christ is the head of the church. He is the Savior of the body. Now as the church submits to Christ ... Christ loved the church and gave himself for her to make her holy, cleansing her with the washing of water by the word. He did this to present the church to himself in splendor, without spot or wrinkle or anything like that, but holy and blameless ... For no one ever hates his own flesh but provides and cares for it, just as Christ does for the church, since we are members of his body. ... This mystery is profound, but *I am talking about Christ and the church*" (Eph 5:22–32, emphasis added).

     Did you notice Paul's summary sentence there? All that he had written was actually about the relationship between Christ and his bride. That's the point.

- "For I am jealous for you with a godly jealousy, because I have promised you in marriage to one husband—to present a pure virgin to Christ" (2 Cor 11:2). Not only are men and women Christ's bride, but we are also considered spiritually pure virgins betrothed to him.

- "'Come, I will show you the bride, the wife of the Lamb.' He then carried me away in the Spirit to a great, high mountain and showed me the holy city, Jerusalem, coming down out of heaven from God, arrayed with God's glory. Her radiance was like a precious jewel, like a jasper stone, clear as crystal" (Rev 21:9–11). The church in eternity will be unimaginably beautiful, clothed with God's glory. She will be composed of both brothers and sisters, men and women from all time and all ethnicities.

- "For in the resurrection they neither marry nor are given in marriage but are like angels in heaven" (Matt 22:30).

When we are finally clothed with our resurrection bodies on the new earth, our gender will not mean to us then what it means to us now. Yes, we will remain male and female, but we will not have the same perspective on gender that we have now. We know that there will be gender there because the angels appear to be gendered and Jesus was resurrected as a male. What life there will be like is unknown, but we do know this: Although we will indeed be gendered, we will not be sexual in the way that we think of our sexuality now. We will be brothers and sisters.

BROTHERS AND SISTERS, SONS AND BRIDES

The reason that men are called to be brides and women are called to be sons is that, in God's kingdom, the things that separate us, like gender, are far less significant than the many things we share. As we saw above, on the new earth, we won't live out gender roles. We'll all be the bride, siblings, together.

Jesus' incarnation foreshadows this sameness as he was made "like his brothers and sisters in every way" (Heb 2:17), even including the way we're tempted. "For we do not have a high priest who is unable to sympathize with our weaknesses, but one who has been tempted in every way as we are, yet without sin" (Heb 4:15).

There isn't a particular sort of masculine temptation that is unknown to women. There aren't uniquely feminine temptations that men never face. No, Jesus faced every temptation that is "common to humanity" (1 Cor 10:13), common to his brothers and sisters. He was tempted like us all—in every way. Of course, that doesn't mean that Jesus was biologically androgenous. Nor does it mean that he wasn't masculine. Because he was a man, he couldn't be anything other than masculine. And because I am a woman, I can't be anything other than feminine. But my femininity does not mean that I have a different human nature than my husband, Phil, or my co-author, Eric, nor that I face a uniquely feminine set of temptations.

BE LIKE JESUS ... OR NOT ...

Historically, Christian men have been told to strive to be like the man, Christ Jesus, which is why recent discussions about being Christic men always focus on male manliness. But being a Christic woman has not been explored . That's because Christian women have many times been viewed as deficient and different in nature, a "deformed man"[2] in intellect, emotions, strength, capacity, and morality.[3] Therefore, it has been considered inconceivable that women should strive to be like Jesus, a man. Because Jesus was male, he was the exemplar for men.

One might imagine that the view that women are inferior in nature is confined to the past but that would be a mistake. Although very few teachers are willing to say exactly what Aquinas said— "Woman is naturally subject to man, because in man the discretion of reason predominates"[4]—they come close. Here's Wayne Grudem on the topic:

> God gave men in general, a disposition that is better suited to teaching and governing in the church, a disposition that inclines more to rational, logical analysis of doctrine and a desire to protect the doctrinal purity of the church, and God [made women] less inclined to oppose the deceptive serpent.[5]

Although Grudem uses the word "disposition" instead of "nature," he is in fact echoing what Aquinas said in the thirteenth century: women are by nature less rational, less able to resist temptation—that is, spiritually defective. They must be led. Joseph Pipa, president emeritus of Greenville Presbyterian Theological Seminary, puts an even finer point on it:

> God has not made her [woman] to exercise the kind of hard, judgmental discernment that is necessary in theological and Scriptural issues. *By nature, a woman will more likely fall prey to the subtleties of mental and theological error.*[6]

According to Grudem and Pipa, women are in fact the inferior sex when it comes to discerning and obeying the truth. And, shockingly, that means that Adam was justified in accusing God about "the woman you gave me" (Gen 3:12), if in fact he had made the woman "less inclined to oppose the deceptive serpent" or "more likely to fall prey to error." If what Grudem and Pipa (and others) write is true, then it is difficult to see how we can call God or his creation—specifically the woman—good. By this logic, in creating Eve as defective, he set Adam up to fail. In addition, if God made Eve less inclined to rational, logical analysis of doctrine and desire to protect the church and oppose Satan, then she would hardly be culpable for her sin. This "differing natures" falsehood undermines belief in God's goodness and wisdom, in Christ's once-for-all atonement, and in true ontological equality.

In reality, many contemporary writers who proclaim differences between male and female natures or inclinations would not so blatantly say women are defective per se, but they come to the same historic conclusions: by nature, men are more capable than women to lead, to think rationally, to understand theology, and to make hard decisions. In Raymond C. Ortlund Jr.'s words,

> This "differing natures" falsehood undermines belief in God's goodness and wisdom, in Christ's once-for-all atonement, and in true ontological equality.

"A man, just by virtue of his manhood, is called to lead for God. A woman, just by virtue of her womanhood, is called to help for God."[7] Therefore, by nature, women are not suited to teach or lead.[8]

Contemporary writers who consistently insist that they believe in ontological gender equality *and* distinctions in created nature always end up inadvertently attacking the goodness of God, the efficacy of the atonement, and ultimately our shared creation in the image of God. In addition, many who propose that women are intellectually, emotionally, and spiritually weaker than men use physiological differences between female and male bodies to bolster their presuppositions about gender roles.

FORM FOLLOWS FUNCTION

The fact that the male body is generally larger and stronger is assumed by some to prove that men were created to be leaders, protectors, and warriors and should therefore be in authority. From this misapplication of what we see in nature, or what is commonly called "natural law," gender roles about masculinity and femininity are assumed. Men are generally bigger and, therefore, it is thought, they are to rule. Women are usually smaller; therefore, they are to be subordinate. But, when we draw these kinds of assumptions from nature as we observe it today, we neglect to recognize that nature is not only created, it is also fallen. None of us know what Adam or Eve looked like before their fall and banishment from the garden of Eden. It's presuming too much from the way things appear to us right now to conclude that the male's larger, stronger body would have been necessary in the sinless garden—where there were no enemies or wars. The garden of Eden was a place of deep peace where both the man and the woman were equally tasked to work as brother and sister, husband and wife.

So, while men are physiologically stronger in certain ways than women, that doesn't necessitate the conclusion that man was created with a different nature than woman, and particularly not one that is meant to be dominant. When we seek to understand the roles that men and women are to fill, we should never go beyond Scripture by looking at natural law,[9] nor should we forget that our understanding of what life was like in Genesis 2 is undoubtedly limited.[10] Because these statements are ubiquitous in Christian gender discourse, damaging assumptions about the nature and appropriate roles of men and women are drawn.

A more God-honoring, Christ-exalting, scripturally faithful hermeneutic about men and women is desperately needed in our day. This Christic perspective would counter falsehoods about women having been created as weak-minded and easily deceived and would open the door for both women and men to discern and fully follow their calling, whether those callings fit stereotypes or not. Whenever we make broad-brush assertions about eight billion unique persons, none of whom are exactly the same (though we share a common humanity), we're bound to err. In addition, forcing men to deny an artistic, nurturing gifting or forcing women into the mold of the 1950's American housewife causes great damage, and perhaps the transgender movement is just one aspect of that.

The teaching that women are defective, or that men are by nature superior, is harmful to both women and men and is erroneous. This teaching has no foundation in Scripture, and it denigrates God's goodness and Christ's value. And, sadly, it is a perfect example of the tail wagging the dog. When one comes to the Bible searching for weapons to be employed in fighting the culture wars, nothing good happens. Rather, we need to come to Scripture, and particularly to the message of the New Testament, and let it direct and guide our conclusions about who we are and what we are to do. We are brothers and sisters, sons and brides, united together for one purpose—the glory of God and the betterment of the world.

THE CREATION MANDATE

When the Creation Mandate was given, there weren't two different commands, one masculine command for Adam and a feminine one for Eve. No, God issued just one Creation Mandate. Here it is:

So God created man in his own image; he created him in the
image of God; he created them male and female. God blessed
them, and God said to *them*, "Be fruitful, multiply, fill the earth,
and subdue it. Rule the fish of the sea, the birds of the sky, and
every creature that crawls on the earth." (Gen 1:27–28, emphasis added)

There was only one command given to them both because they
were both equally created in the image of God. Both sisters and
brothers together are commanded to *be* fruitful, to multiply, fill the
earth, *subdue* it, and to *rule* over it
together as co-regents. We are to
have dominion over all of creation—
not as a leader and a follower, but
rather as co-heirs and co-rulers.

> We need to come
> to Scripture, and
> particularly to the
> message of the New
> Testament, and let it
> direct and guide our
> conclusions about
> who we are and
> what we are to do.

If you want to know what
Adam was like before the fall, look
at Jesus. Jesus wasn't a he-man, nor
did he ever tell women to stay home
because they were too soft, emotional, and vulnerable. In fact, he
welcomed married women to itin-
erate with him (Luke 8:1–3). He didn't assume that their feminine
nature was different from his or that they couldn't understand his
teaching or love him as their rabbi. Nor did he tell them that life on
the road was too hard or dangerous for them and they should stay
home and make sandwiches. He treated them with love and respect,
just like he treated the men, because they were his beloved sisters and
brothers. His natural inclination was to love and welcome them all.[11]

Remember our fascination with the Crawleys? We love to think
about and explore family relationships. That's because being part of
a family is what is most basic about us. We know who we are as we
learn about those around us. Aside from our fascination with fictional

families, perhaps we're enamored with picture taking (and posting) because it tells us something essential about who we are: these are our brothers and sisters; these are our parents and children. No wonder social media has exploded in recent years—it's a perfect vehicle to talk about family.

We've spent time considering our relatedness as brothers and sisters, sons and brides in this chapter. We've considered the amazing truth that Jesus took on our shared nature, faced all of our temptations, loved his neighbors perfectly, died shamefully, and rose bodily in our place. In the next chapter, we'll consider what God's purpose is in our shared human nature.

4

One Family,
One Calling

*Go, therefore, and make disciples of all nations,
baptizing them in the name of the Father and of the
Son and of the Holy Spirit, teaching them to observe
everything I have commanded you. —Matthew 28:19–20*

In a 2018 opinion piece, Clay Routledge noted the concerning 25 percent increase in death by suicide since 1999. He commented, "These numbers clearly point to a crisis, but of what kind?" His answer: "As a behavioral scientist who studies basic psychological needs, including the need for meaning, I am convinced that our nation's suicide crisis is in part a crisis of meaninglessness."

Routledge, a professor of social psychology at North Dakota State University, went on to argue that "in order to keep existential anxiety at bay, we must find and maintain perceptions of our lives as meaningful." A life without purpose leaves people "psychologically vulnerable," he argues, noting empirical studies linking meaninglessness to substance abuse, depression, anxiety, and suicide. "And when people experience loss, stress or trauma, it is those who believe that their lives have purpose who are best able to cope with and recover from distress."

Routledge argues that humans find purpose in relationships with other people in which they know they are valued. America is experiencing decreasing interaction with neighbors and decreasing family size. Likewise, he notes, young adults are less likely to identify with a religious faith and community. All this combines to foster a sense of meaninglessness and a loss of purpose. Moreover, he posits, it may contribute to America's "rancorous political divisions" and "fractious political culture."[1]

Fortunately, the Bible offers an answer to this crisis. It not only tells us that we have value, but it also gives us purpose. The gospel tells us our purpose—given to us in creation, redeemed and transformed in Christ, and extending into eternity through our resurrection with Jesus. Knowing our purpose not only provides us with a sense of meaning as individuals, but it also builds and preserves unity between men and women as they share it in Christ.

OUR SHARED PURPOSE: FROM THE CREATION MANDATE TO THE GREAT COMMISSION

In Chapter Two, we discussed that God created women and men in his image to rule the earth together in a way that displays God's character to every creature in heaven and on earth (see Gen 1:26–28). This collaborative rule—the Creation Mandate—is summarized in four simple commands: "be fruitful, multiply, fill the earth, and subdue it" (1:28). Simply put, the image-bearers were to make more image-bearers—so many that they would fill the earth. Together, they were to rule the earth, to bring it under their dominion as the royal, priestly children of God. In this way, God's glory would be displayed everywhere. Christic men and women were to produce more Christic men and women.

Sadly, as we saw in Chapter Two, sin entered the world and disrupted every realm on earth and in human life. Human flourishing would be painful, frustrated by thorns and thistles (both literally and figuratively). Ultimately, flourishing as image-bearers would be disrupted—*ended*—by death. But death would not be the end of God's story, nor of his plan for human image-bearers to exercise his rule on earth. The very last use of the word "reign" in the Bible speaks of God's people—human image-bearers—reigning on earth (Rev 22:5). That is his purpose for us and the earth.

God promised the man and woman a Savior. With the Lord's help, the woman would conceive and give birth to a son who would rule and reign (Gen 3:15; 4:1). As we explained in the last chapter, that son was Jesus of Nazareth, the Christ. Jesus became like his brothers and sisters in every way (Heb 2:17)—that is, he was born in the image and likeness of God, tasked with filling the earth and subduing it. Likewise, he was not "a high priest who is unable to sympathize with our weaknesses, but one who has been tempted in every way as we are, yet without sin" (Heb 4:15). That means he faced every frustration brought to the world by sin but never failed to reign. He responded to all things in a manner that perfectly displayed the glory of his Father (John 1:18).

After conquering sin, death, and the devil in his death and resurrection, Jesus appears as a "second Adam" tasked with filling and ruling the earth (1 Cor 15:49). And, just as it was not good for the first Adam to be alone, the last Adam (Christ) will not carry out this mandate alone. He declares that he will fill the earth and rule it through and with his bride, the church (Matt 28:18–20; Rom 16:20; Rev 21:2; 22:5).

All Scripture points to Jesus.[2] All God's purposes find their true meaning and fulfillment in the Christ. That is true of the Creation Mandate, which Jesus fulfills and transforms in the Great Commission found in Matthew 28:18–20:

> Jesus came near and said to them, "All authority has been given to me in heaven and on earth. Go, therefore, and make disciples of all nations, baptizing them in the name of the Father and of the Son and of the Holy Spirit, teaching them to observe everything I have commanded you. And remember, I am with you always, to the end of the age."

The Creation Mandate said, "Be fruitful, multiply, fill the earth" (Gen 1:28). The first man and woman were to fill the earth through procreation. In the kingdom of Christ, he and his bride will fill the world with new image-bearers by making "disciples of all nations, baptizing them in the name of the Father and of the Son and of the Holy Spirit" (Matt 28:19). Through the proclamation of the gospel, people are born again by God to bear the image of Christ (1 Pet 1:3; Rom 8:29; 1 Cor 15:49; Phil 3:21; Col 3:10; 1 John 3:2). Christ is the "firstborn among many brothers and sisters" whom God "predestined to be conformed to the image of his Son" (Rom 8:29). That is, God transforms depraved men and women into gospel-centered, Christic men and women.

The Creation Mandate also called image-bearers to subdue and rule. In the Great Commission, Jesus presents himself as the one authorized to rule: "All authority has been given to me in heaven and on earth. Go, therefore" (Matt 28:18–19). People are subdued by Christ through the gospel message. When they believe in Jesus' death for sins and his resurrection, they are born again into his kingdom. Through his teachings, they are ruled by Christ, who calls them to "observe everything I have commanded you" (Matt 28:20). The kingdom is ruled by "the law of Christ," which consists of love, gentleness, compassion, humility, generosity—all that Christ was and taught (Gal 5:22–6:2). Through the Holy Spirt, evangelism, and discipleship—the work of the church—Christ and his bride fill the earth and subdue it.

The Creation Mandate said to *them* (plural, the male and the female), "Rule." It was a collaborative effort—male and female image-bearers filling the earth and subduing it. In the Great Commission, Jesus does not task his bride with multiplying and subduing the earth only to sit back and watch her do the work. Nor does he tell her, "Stand back and let the Last Man handle this!" No, the Great Commission is a collaborative effort—"I am with you always, to the end of the age" (Matt 28:20). The bridegroom and the bride will be one flesh, bound together in perfect unity (John 14:23; 17:20–26; Col 1:27; 3:3). Together the Last Man and his bride—Christ and the church—will reign forever (Rev 21:2; 22:5).

The kingdom of Christ is unlike any other kingdom. In the kingdom of the beloved Son, every citizen and subject is family. We are adopted as sons, with God as our inheritance-bestowing Father (Gal 3:27–4:7). That makes Christ our older brother—one that we look like (Rom 8:29)! We—men and women of faith—are not at enmity or estranged, nor are we competing. We are related to one another as siblings—brothers and sisters, fathers and mothers, sons and daughters (1 Tim 5:1–2).

In this kingdom, we are the bride of Christ (Eph 5:28–32; Rev 19:7; 21:1–2). The Son left his Father in heaven to bond with his wife, and the two became one flesh, a union in which there is no shame (Gen 2:24–25; Eph 5:29–32; Ps 25:3). As his bride, the church is Christ's body, bone of his bone and flesh of his flesh, for it was made from him (Gen 2:23; Eph 5:30; Col 1:18). As such, he ministers through us bringing his reign to its completion (1 Cor 12:27; Rom 16:20). What God has joined together, none shall ever separate (Rom 8:38–39). This King and his bride will reign forever and ever (Rev 22:5).

Simply put: as men and women in Christ, our shared purpose is to reign with Christ as his image-bearing body and bride, both now and forever. Before we go any further, let us encourage you to pause to rejoice and thank God for this good news. Our purpose finds its fulfillment in Christ. If you've ever wondered what your purpose is, there it is: to fill the earth and rule it for the glory of God. Of course, you and I have failed at that. But Christ obeyed that mandate on our behalf. He bore the curse of death for our disobedience. He rose from the dead, destroying the enemies of sin, death, and the devil. When we put our hope in Christ, God forgives our sins, rescuing us from the domain of darkness and transferring us into the kingdom of the Son he loves (Col 1:13). In that kingdom, you are united with Christ, who sends you and goes with you to fill the earth, extending his kingdom through the preaching and teaching of his gospel. It's all yours in Christ, by grace through faith (Eph 2:1–10).

HOW SHOULD WE THEN REIGN?

As men and women in Christ, our shared purpose is to reign with Christ as his image-bearing body and bride, both now and forever. The questions before us now are: What does that look like? What does it look like as men and women in Christ fulfilling this purpose? How should we reign? The answer is: as Christic men and women.

In the Creation Mandate, being the image of God meant living together in a way that displayed God's character. It follows then that being the image of Christ means living together in a way that displays the character of Christ. *We carry out our shared purpose by living in a way that shows the world how Christ lived on earth.* That sentence summarizes the ethical teaching of the New Testament. It also captures the substance of Christic men and women. That is what it means to follow in his steps (1 Pet 2:21) and "fulfill the law of Christ" (Gal 6:2). We are to live in a way that shows others what the Christ is like.

In his letter to the Philippian church, Paul paints a remarkable picture of saints—men and women—carrying out their shared purpose in Christ. Here's our summary of what we see in Philippians:

> In Christ, believing men and women are to glorify God by cooperating for the advance of the gospel and imitating Christ in voluntary humiliation, reciprocal benevolence, and mutual flourishing.

That's our shared purpose in Christ. That's Christic men and women. We'll look at what that means for unique relationships—the church and family—in later chapters. For now, we'll spend the remainder of the chapter looking phrase by phrase at this summary as it is fleshed out in Jesus and the book of Philippians.

> We are to live in a way
> that shows others what
> the Christ is like.

IN CHRIST ...

No hope of a successfully shared purpose for men and women exists outside of Jesus Christ. God divides humanity between those "in Adam" and "in Christ"—Adamic humanity and Christic humanity—"as in Adam all die, so also in Christ all will be made alive" (1 Cor 15:22).

Adam had a unique role as the head of humanity; he represented all humans. Thus, when he sinned, all those in him were born sinful, and death reigned over his successors—all human beings (Rom 5:12–14a). But there is good news: Adam was "a type of the Coming One" who would reverse the curse (Rom 5:14b).

The Coming One is Jesus Christ, who stands as the head of God's new people. Jesus was perfectly righteous; he was without sin. Thus, death could not reign over him. Instead, he reigned over death. Jesus represented his people in his life, death, and resurrection (Phil 2:6–11). Faith unites his people with him in crucifixion and death, resurrection and life (Rom 6:4–10). Just as death reigned over those born in Adam, life reigns over those who receive the gift of grace and righteousness from Jesus by faith (Rom 3:21–28; 5:15–17).

Adam failed and brought us frustration, corruption, and death; Christ succeeded as God's true image (Col 1:15). Christ is now our head, the first-born of the new humanity who is setting everything right (Col 1:18–20). Before you read any further, pray

> Continually grasp and believe this truth: there is no true, ultimate, satisfying, good, and eternal purpose for our lives outside of Jesus Christ.

that you will continually grasp and believe this truth: there is no true, ultimate, satisfying, good, and eternal purpose for our lives outside of Jesus Christ. Those who turn from sin to hope in Jesus are in him and have a life of true and lasting meaning. May we trust in Christ alone!

... BELIEVING MEN AND WOMEN ...

Our shared purpose is in Christ. Therefore, we must believe, for it is only through faith that we are united with Christ and in Christ. Men and women cannot share a purpose in Christ unless both are in Christ. Therefore, we must be "believing men and women."

Paul recognizes that men and women equally share God's purpose in Christ. He writes this letter "to all the saints in Christ Jesus who are in Philippi" (Phil 1:1). A saint is a person in Christ by faith, for

Christ Jesus is our sanctification (1 Cor 1:30). Both believing men and
believing women are equally saints, as evidenced by Paul's inclusion of
instruction to particular women (Phil 4:2). Therefore, Paul writes to his
"brothers and sisters" (Phil 1:12; 3:1, 13; 4:1, 8) "every saint in Christ Jesus"
(Phil 4:21), even as all the saints with him send greetings (Phil 4:22).

Faith is more than a requirement to be in Christ. It is an indispens-
able means through which we carry out our shared purpose. Fulfilling
our shared purpose is not merely a matter of understanding correct
information. It is certainly not accomplished by our works. We cannot
flourish as women and men in the image of Christ by merely trying
harder in our own power. The flesh cannot make us Christic women
and men.

The power to pursue and accomplish our shared purpose is found
only in the good news of Jesus Christ. The gospel "is the power of
God for salvation to everyone who believes" (Rom 1:16). Salvation is
not merely our justification and forgiveness. It includes all that God
intends to do in and through us as Christic people—including the
shared purpose discussed in this chapter. Our access to and reception
of this gracious power begins and ends with faith (Rom 1:17). We are
only transformed by looking at God's glory in the face of Jesus Christ
brought to us in the gospel message (2 Cor 3:18–4:6).

So, Paul reminds the Philippians that God has granted us our faith
(Phil 1:29). His readers suffer, strive, and struggle to work out God's
purpose only because "it is God who is working in you both to will and
to work according to his good purpose" (2:12–13). How do we will and
work according to his good purpose? "By holding firm to the word of
life" (2:16)—that is, by believing the good news of Christ's life, death, and
resurrection on our behalf (see 2:14–16). Paul puts himself forward as
an example of one who finds his righteousness and the power of Christ
only through faith in Christ (3:7–10). Our final and perfect transformation into the image of Christ happens only by Christ's final appearance
(3:21). So, we wait for him in faith (3:20, 22). Until that day, God guards
our hearts and minds through faith in Christ (4:4–7). From beginning
to end, we truly receive God's power only by faith in Jesus (Rom 1:17).

... ARE TO GLORIFY GOD ...

If our renewed purpose in Christ and the power to accomplish it are by God's grace received by faith, then we have no reason to boast (Rom 3:27–28; Eph 2:9). All the glory goes to God. That is why Paul thanks *God* for the Philippians' faithfulness—and trusts God for the completion of that good work (Phil 1:3–6). Their fruit of righteousness is an answer to prayer "that comes through Jesus Christ to the glory and praise of God" (1:9–11). So, Paul's hope for his life is that "Christ will be highly honored" (1:20). Likewise, he urges his readers to live a life that reflects the worth of Christ in the gospel (1:27a).

"*Glory*," according to D. A. Carson, "commonly refers to the manifestation of God's character or person in a revelatory context."[3] So, to glorify God means to reveal God and what he is like. When the eternal Son of God took on flesh and dwelt among us, he neither sought his own glory nor glorified himself (John 8:50, 54). When Jesus did pray for God to glorify him, it was for the sake of glorifying the Father (John 17:1–2). For when Jesus' character and person were revealed, the Father's glory would be manifest in him. As a human (the image of God), the Christ's work was to glorify God, a work he accomplished fully (John 17:3–4). The glory of the Son on earth was to be the perfect image of the glory of God. To be Christlike or Christic is to glorify God.

It is good to think about men and women in the workplace, academy, government, military, community, church, and home. But if we focus our concern and efforts on who is getting more glory—men or women—then we fail at the start. Competition between the sexes is not God's purpose; it is a distraction from and enemy of God's purpose. We are to "do nothing out of selfish ambition or conceit" (Phil 2:3). God did not create men and women to compete for glory amongst themselves but rather to cooperate together for his glory.

The ultimate concern of cooperation between the sexes is to manifest "God's glory in the

> God did not create men and women to compete for glory amongst themselves but rather to cooperate together for his glory.

"face of Jesus Christ" (2 Cor 4:6). That happens when we proclaim the gospel and it transforms us by it through faith. If we genuinely care about the glory of God, then we will care for one another as valuable glory-displayers, nurturing one another's faith so that we all may be transformed in the image of Christ and reach the world for him.

... BY COOPERATING FOR THE
ADVANCE OF THE GOSPEL ...

At the start of the chapter, we observed how the Creation Mandate given to the first man and woman finds its fulfillment in the Great Commission given by Christ to the church. Likewise, in the last section, we saw how the person and work of Jesus Christ perfectly displays God's glory. It is no wonder then that our central purpose is to glorify God through the advance of the gospel (the charge of the Great Commission). The advance of the gospel is at the heart of Paul's concern for the saints in Philippi.

With joy, Paul thanks God for the Philippian saints every time he prays (Phil 1:4–5). Why? "Because of your partnership in the gospel from the first day until now" (1:5). What does such a partnership consist of? "You are all partners with me in grace, both in my imprisonment and in the defense and confirmation of the gospel" (1:7). The brothers and sisters there supported Paul when he was imprisoned for preaching the gospel. They stood beside him in defending and confirming the message of Jesus Christ. Paul constantly rejoiced over these saints because they consistently cooperated with him to advance the gospel message.

Because he knows of their concern for the gospel's spread, Paul wants them to know that his imprisonment "actually advanced the gospel" (1:12). Because of his imprisonment (and their support), the entire imperial guard knows Paul is in chains for Jesus (1:13). As a result, other believers' confidence grew so that they proclaimed the word with greater boldness (1:14). Paul does not mind that some preach the gospel hoping to make trouble for him. Why would he complain about this? The gospel is being proclaimed (1:17–18). Paul longs to see believers "standing firm in one spirit, in one accord, contending together for the faith of the gospel" (1:27).

Paul writes the Philippians to encourage their alliance in furthering the gospel. His joy will be complete if they are "intent on one purpose" (2:2). In this way, they imitate the focused cooperation of God the Father and the Lord Jesus Christ (see 2:5–11). Christ humbled himself to exalt the Father in his death. Therefore, the Father exalted Jesus in his resurrection and enthronement in glory. As a result, every knee will bow, and every tongue will confess the lordship of Jesus Christ to the glory of the Father.

The Father, the Son, and the Holy Spirit are an eternal alliance, working together to glorify God through the whole creation confessing that the crucified and risen Son is Lord. At creation, men and women were to pursue God's glory in perfect unity—the high point of the man and woman's creation, something worthy of leaving father and mother to pursue (Gen 2:23–25; see Mark 10:29; Luke 18:29). To be godly (godlike) is to devote yourself in the same way to the same cause in unity with others. Unity in gospel ministry is a sign of salvation (Phil 1:27–28).

Sin hinders our godly concern to work together to advance the gospel. Euodia and Syntyche had worked side by side with Paul, contending together for the gospel in their God-glorifying shared purpose (Phil 4:2). But now, Paul is concerned because some unnamed disagreement threatens their unity and partnership (4:1). So Paul urges a mutual friend, a true partner, to help them reconcile in the Lord.

The partnership with Euodia and Syntyche that Paul recalls fondly is a model for male-female relationships in the church. "These women … have contended for the gospel at my side, along with Clement and the rest of my coworkers whose names are in the book of life" (Phil 4:3). Paul and Clement labored side by side with Euodia and Syntyche, redeemed co-workers advancing the gospel. Paul, Clement, Euodia, and Syntyche model the partnership of Christic men and women. They imitate Christ, who traveled about preaching the gospel accompanied by the Twelve and a sizable group of women (Luke 8:1–3).

In the local church (and beyond!), believing men and women should see one another as co-workers in the service of Jesus. We are not to contend against one another, opposed to each other. Rather, we are each to labor at the other's side, contending together as sisters and brothers for the gospel. When sin or disagreement interrupts the partnership of men and women, we should address it with the aim of unity and agreement in Christ (Phil 4:2).

If men see women in the church as temptations, deceptive usurpers, overly emotional liabilities to ministry and intellectual inferiors, true partnership will never occur. If women see men in the church as lords to obey, threats to avoid, or obstacles for advancing their own agendas, they will never be co-workers. We must strive to be what the apostle celebrates—partners who labor side by side for the gospel. For that to happen, believing men and women must view each other as both Jesus and Paul do. We are not enemies, threats, or competitors. We are siblings in Christ, allies in God's mission.

> Believing men and women must view each other as both Jesus and Paul do. We are not enemies, threats, or competitors. We are siblings in Christ, allies in God's mission.

... AND IMITATING CHRIST ...

We discussed above that the message about Jesus Christ is God's power for our salvation. We are saved and changed by receiving this grace through faith. While receiving the gospel brings and empowers salvation, the good news is not merely for believing. God calls us to imitate it. The gospel is the source and power of our salvation. It is also our new covenant instruction, what Paul calls "the law of Christ" (Gal 6:2). That is why Paul exhorts the Philippian saints to think and act like Christ. He encourages Christic lives.

At the heart of his letter, Paul appeals to his friends. If they have received encouragement, comfort, fellowship, affection, and mercy from God through the gospel, then they should treat each other the same way God treats them in the gospel (Phil 2:1–2). They are to act like the God who is revealed in Christ. And to act like him, they must think like Christ. "Adopt the same attitude as that of Christ Jesus" (2:5), Paul urges them.

The eternal Son of God had an attitude—and what an excellent attitude it was! Paul describes it this way (2:6–11):

> [Christ Jesus], existing in the form of God,
> did not consider equality with God
> as something to be exploited.
> Instead he emptied himself
> by assuming the form of a servant,
> taking on the likeness of humanity.
>
> And when he had come as a man,
> he humbled himself by becoming obedient
> to the point of death—
> even to death on a cross.
>
> For this reason God highly exalted him
> and gave him the name
> that is above every name,
> so that at the name of Jesus
> every knee will bow—
> in heaven and on earth
> and under the earth—
> and every tongue will confess
> that Jesus Christ is Lord,
> to the glory of God the Father.

What glorious good news! We were created in the likeness of God, children who were to look like our Father. But we failed, bringing a curse upon ourselves. So, for our sake, the Son of God, though equal with the Father from all time, became the servant of God we were not. He took on "the likeness of humanity" (Phil 2:7), which was made in the likeness of God. Though he was God, he became the image of God to fulfill the mission at which we failed. As a man, he lived humbly, obeying until he became both sin and a curse (Phil 2:8; 2 Cor 5:21; Gal 3:13). Imagine that! His obedience was to become our sin and curse in death on a cross so that in him we might become righteousness and receive the life-giving Spirit (see 2 Cor 5:21; Gal 3:14).

There is no being—supernatural or human—more beautiful than the one described in those verses. For those words describe the Christ, whose life revealed and explained God (John 1:18). This means that if we want to see God, then we have to look at Christ. In the same way, if we want to glorify God, then we must be Christic. Because we are assured of Jesus' loving character, we can be freed from seeking to grasp our own glory. We can leave everything in God's hands. We can humble ourselves, becoming Christlike, assuming the lowly status of a servant, obeying God in service to others until it costs us our lives. "Carry one another's burdens; in this way you will fulfill the law of Christ" (Gal 6:2).

Christian men are not handsome when they perform feats of strength and strut around like cocks. Christic men are not about outward displays of strength and pompous boasting on Twitter. Christic masculinity is an internal matter of the heart (2 Cor 5:12). Christic men make themselves little. It looks like weakness and foolishness to the world (1 Cor 1:18–31). It is lowly and humble in heart (Matt 11:29). Like a lamb led to the slaughter, it is quiet (Isa 53:7; 1 Tim 2:2). Christic men willingly die for the sake of others.

> We can humble ourselves, becoming Christlike, assuming the lowly status of a servant, obeying God in service to others until it costs us our lives.

Christian women are not beautiful when they are adorned with the latest clothing, hair, and jewelry styles or when covering themselves with plain and unfashionable garments. Christic women are not about the outward appearance of beauty or Instagram posts that influence millions. Christic femininity is an internal matter of the heart (2 Cor 5:12).

Christic women make themselves little. It looks like weakness and foolishness to the world (1 Cor 1:18–31). It is lowly and humble in heart (Matt 11:29). Like a lamb led to the slaughter, it is quiet (Isa 53:7; 1 Tim 2:2). Christic women willingly die for the sake of others.

... IN VOLUNTARY HUMILIATION ...

The dominant theme of Christ's attitude is voluntary humiliation. "He emptied himself by assuming the form of a servant" (Phil 2:7). "He humbled himself by becoming obedient to the point of death—even to death on a cross" (Phil 2:8). Jesus, of course, was humble and humbled. But notice who was behind his humiliation—he was. Jesus emptied himself. He humbled himself. Jesus' ultimate act of voluntary humiliation is his choice to die under God's curse (Phil 2:8; see John 10:17–18; Gal 3:13). Out of love for God and his people, the Good Shepherd laid down his life for the sheep (John 10:14–15).

Jesus said the Father loves him because he voluntarily dies for his people (John 10:17). Likewise, Paul says that Christ's voluntary humiliation results in his glorious exaltation. Because he humbled himself, God exalted him. The Father gave Jesus a name above every name—he made him Lord and Christ (Phil 2:9; Acts 2:36). This name comes with enthroned power so great that every person in all creation will bow before him and confess that Jesus the Messiah is Lord (Phil 2:10–11; Acts 2:33–35).

The voluntary humiliation and subsequent exaltation of Christ illustrates an important biblical principle: "God resists the proud but gives grace to the humble" (Jas 4:6; 1 Pet 5:5). James and Peter learned this from their Lord, who taught:

> But when you are invited, go and sit in the lowest place, so that when the one who invited you comes, he will say to you, "Friend, move up higher." You will then be honored in the presence of all the other guests. For everyone who exalts himself will be humbled, and the one who humbles himself will be exalted. (Luke 14:10–11)

If you exalt yourself, God will humble you. If you humble yourself, God will exalt you (Luke 18:14). Jesus said that "the greatest among you will be your servant" (Matt 23:11). Christ is exalted above all others because he humbled himself by becoming a servant below all others.

Paul shared the attitude of Christ. While he wanted to be with Jesus, he was willing to continue in humility, remaining in the flesh to serve the Philippians and help them flourish (Phil 1:21–26). "But even if I am poured out as a drink offering on the sacrificial service of your faith, I am glad and rejoice with all of you" (2:17). He expects them to do the same. "Do nothing out of selfish ambition or conceit, but in humility consider others as more important than yourselves" (2:3). Paul can give this command with confidence since he has already benefited from their voluntary humiliation in service to him (4:10–20).

If we are to cooperate with Christ and one another to advance the gospel, we must follow Christ, deny ourselves, and take up crosses (Matt 16:24). This means that men do not see women as servants given to them by God to fulfill their every desire and need. Nor do women see men as people to manipulate to get what they want. Neither men nor women should look only to their own interests but rather to the interests of others (Phil 2:4). They should serve Christ together in gospel-shaped thinking and love, united in spirit, intent on accomplishing the same goal (Phil 2:2). This would mean that we see when the other stumbles and kneel to help them up. We recognize each other's weaknesses and bear with them. We hear the other groan under their burdens and volunteer to carry them.

... RECIPROCAL BENEVOLENCE ...

Voluntary humiliation does not exist for its own sake. God does not command us to humble ourselves by living in a cave and practicing self-flagellation. God does not call us to pain for pain's sake. Christ's voluntary humiliation sought the good of others—our salvation and God's glory. Jesus died to redeem us and cause us to flourish as his image-bearers. He died to see the glory of God spread to the ends of the earth. We can't fulfill the call to voluntary humiliation alone; it must happen in a community shaped by love.

Benevolence—the disposition to act kindly for another's good—is the proper motivation of voluntary humiliation. Christlike love is a genuine and affectionate concern for another, so great that it would die for the good of the other (John 13:1–20, 34–35). Paul urges us to adopt this attitude.

Paul certainly had this attitude toward the Philippians. He opens and closes his letter with evidence of his benevolent desires, praying they would receive grace and peace from God through his letter (see Phil 1:1–2; 4:23). He prays for them constantly as they are always in his heart (1:4–7). He remains in the flesh and determines to continue with them so that they would progress and have joy in the faith (1:21–26). Paul hopes to send them

> We can't fulfill the call to voluntary humiliation alone; it must happen in a community shaped by love.

Timothy, who exemplifies benevolence (2:19). "For I have no one else like-minded who will genuinely care about your interests; all seek their own interests, not those of Jesus Christ" (2:20–21).

The benevolence of Christ is not one way. Love given calls for love in return. "We love because he first loved us" (1 John 4:19). So, Paul calls the church to have the same love as Jesus (Phil 2:2). "Everyone should look not to his own interests, but rather to the interests of others" (2:4). We see this modeled in a small way as Paul expresses the love of the saints he is with for the Philippians (4:21–22).

Christic men and women are genuinely concerned for the good of one another. That means that male faculty and students do not mock and question female students for pursuing theological education. Rather, they support and encourage their learning! Genuine concern means that men and women are not focused solely on men's ministry or women's ministry, respectively. Instead, the men want to know how to serve the women, even as the women desire to serve the men. A pastor who is genuinely concerned for the good of all does not focus his attention solely on training men for ministry; he values talking to, listening to, and teaching his sisters. He welcomes their reciprocal benevolence as they talk to, listen to, and teach him!

... MUTUAL FLOURISHING.

The aim of our benevolence is the flourishing of the other. Christ humbled himself in the incarnation so that his people would "have life and have it abundantly" (John 10:10 ESV). In response, believers now are to do everything to see God glorified through Jesus Christ (1 Pet 4:11; 1 Cor 10:31). Paul aims to see Christ's glory flourish, whether by his life or death (Phil 1:20). Christ pursued our good; we pursue Christ's glory.

A concern for mutual flourishing should characterize all our churches. Paul prays for the Philippians to flourish and is eager to hear that they are (1:9–11; 2:19). He is willing to die to serve their faith (2:17). Likewise, the Philippians were concerned to know that Paul was flourishing and to help him do so (4:10–20).

Epaphroditus is a remarkable illustration of concern for mutual flourishing (2:25–30). The Philippians sent him to Rome to serve Paul and care for him (2:25). On the way, Epaphroditus became "so sick that he nearly died" (2:27). Epaphroditus was sent and risked his life to help Paul flourish (2:25, 30). But Paul cared so deeply about Epaphroditus's flourishing that he would have had "sorrow upon sorrow" had Epaphroditus died (2:27). Likewise, the Philippians so cared for Epaphroditus's flourishing that they were sad when they heard of his sickness. But it doesn't stop there! Epaphroditus so cares about the Philippians' flourishing that he becomes distressed upon knowing they know that he is sick—he doesn't want them to worry about him (2:26)! And now, Paul is anxious about the Philippians being sad over Epaphroditus's condition. So, to minister to the Philippians, Paul sends back to them Epaphroditus, the very man they sent to Paul to minister to him. Everyone in the paragraph seems to be concerned about how the other is doing! Moreover, everyone is acting for the flourishing of others. When humility and benevolence characterize a community, everyone flourishes. That is Christic humanity.

Christic men and women must be concerned about the flourishing of one another. That means they move beyond small talk in the church foyer to show a sanctified curiosity for one another's well-being. Men will ask their sisters where they are rejoicing or what is causing them sorrow. Women will ask their brothers what truths are encouraging and what doubts plague them. A brother will rejoice to hear his sister is flourishing and offer help when he learns how she struggles. A sister will show interest in what her brother is learning and doing, offering her advice and counsel when he lacks wisdom. Christic men and women are happy to serve and be served by one another.

Here, then, is our shared purpose in Christ as believing men and women: Christic men and women glorify God by cooperating for the advance of the gospel and imitating Christ in voluntary humiliation, reciprocal benevolence, and mutual flourishing. That is what God made us for. That is what Christ redeemed us for. That is what the Spirit fills us for. May the grace of God transform our hearts and minds so that we might work together for his glory.

5

Sisters and Brothers in God's Image

It is not good for the man to be alone.—Genesis 2:18

I (Elyse) am an introvert. I would imagine that's hard for some of my readers to believe, since I am also a public person who is quite comfortable speaking before groups of people. But the truth I've come to realize about myself is I'm happiest when I'm quiet and alone with my thoughts. But, alas, it seems like truly alone time has been harder to come by since we were locked in our houses during the pandemic. That my husband and I definitely got to know each other better would be a bit of an understatement. We went months without spending any time with anyone else, and it really was a hard time. I can't imagine how difficult it must have been for my poor husband, Phil, who loves to chat people up and was simply dying for someone who hadn't already heard all his jokes. I've just about decided that I'm only an introvert when it's voluntary. Otherwise, I really don't want to be alone.

In this chapter we'll discover why God made the announcement that being alone isn't "good" (Gen 2:18). That announcement, though I'm coming to agree with it more and more, is particularly surprising because Genesis 1–2 reverberates with an exactly opposite sentiment. Over and over again God looks at his handiwork and judges it "good."

84

The light was good, the heavens and the earth were good, the seas and the dry land were good, vegetation was good, the sun, the moon, and the stars were all good; birds, fish, and all living creatures were good; and, finally, humanity was *very good*. Reading over that list seems almost redundant: Good? Yes! Good? Yes! Good, good, good? Yes! Yes! Yes! Next? Good? Nope! Wait! What's that you say?

In the days when we used to listen to vinyl records (yes, I'm that old), if I wasn't careful to lift the needle cautiously, I would end up hearing a dreaded scraping sound that meant I had just ruined my latest Beatles record. Imagine that you're listening to a song that keeps repeating our lovely "Good? Yes!" theme over and over, and then, suddenly, you hear something that sounds like you're dragging the needle across the vinyl. Yikes! The words in Genesis 2:18 resemble that horrible scraping noise. Good, good, good ... "not good"! What? In God's perfect and perfectly balanced and beautiful world, there's something that's not good? Adam's fresh new life is not good? How can that be?

As shocking as Adam's negative situation is to our ears, God's pronouncement of Adam's "not good-ness" is even more startling in the original language because the full meaning is missed in English translations. Here's why: In Hebrew there are at least two ways of saying something is "not good." You can say that something is lacking in good (*en tob*), like a meal without salt, for instance. "In this usage, something is missing, without which the thing is not as good as it could be."[1] Or you can say that something is positively bad (*lo tob*), which is the case with the Hebrew used here. In other words, it wasn't that Adam's aloneness was just lacking something that would have made it better. Rather, it was that his aloneness was positively bad. Why would the Lord say that being alone was so awful? Why was the perfect man living in the perfect place actually in a terrible situation just because he was *alone*? Wasn't Adam's relationship with the Lord enough to make his

> It wasn't that Adam's aloneness was just lacking something that would have made it better. Rather, it was that his aloneness was positively bad.

life good? And if Adam needed company, why didn't God just create another man? How did the woman's creation transform a terrible situation into something "*very good indeed*" (Genesis 1:31, emphasis added)? Another way to ask this question is, *Why was it necessary for God to create woman?*

LOVE CREATES

In order to understand the Lord's purpose in creating two genders, male *and* female, we need to look first to our Creator, for it is "by means of your light we see light" (Ps 36:9).[2] And when we look at him, what do we see? We see that God is not solitary. He is a Trinity: he is a Father, he is a Son, and he is a Spirit. Before the world was created, God existed in unbroken, joyous, and unified diversity within himself. Unlike Allah, the Christian God is not alone, which should change everything we understand about him. Yes, he is one God, but that one God exists as three distinct and co-equal persons united by love. In fact, love is the definition of God's essence, for as John wrote, "God *is* love" (1 John 4:8, emphasis added). God is so infused with love he could not *not* love.[3] Before the worlds were spoken into being, that holy love was shared between members of the Godhead who were completely happy, satisfied, joyous, and who existed in harmonious bliss with one another. Even before the creation, God was not solitary, which is why it's silly to say God created humanity because he was lonely. God never was and never could be lonely because he was never alone; he is three persons in one. But then, in his wisdom, the unbounding love the members of the Trinity had for one another simply exploded in glorious life-giving creation. Everything we see is the outworking of the exuberant love shared by the Trinity throughout eternity.

> Being perfectly loving, from all eternity the Father and the Son have delighted to share their love and joy with and through the Spirit. It is not, then, that God *becomes* sharing; being triune, God is a sharing God, a God who loves to include. Indeed, that

is why God will go on to create. *His love is not for keeping but for spreading.*[4]

Working in unison within himself, the Three-In-One created worlds and then commanded that our world be filled with unique persons upon whom he could joyfully shower his love. These persons would then in turn come to experience his joy, the joy of creating others to pour their love on.

IN OUR IMAGE

Then God said, "Let us make man in our image, according to our likeness." ... So God created man in his own image; he created him in the image of God; he created them male and female. (Gen 1:26–27)

Many theologians have sought to define what being made "in the image of God" means. Many have said that God's image in humanity has to do with human beings' "knowledge, righteousness, and holiness, with dominion over the creatures."[5] Theologian John Calvin wrote, "God's image was visible in the light of the mind, in the uprightness of the heart, and in the soundness of all the parts"[6] of a person. Others find the image of God in human beings as we function as sons, in royal dominion, representation, glory, and prophetic witness.[7] And still others believe that the image of God in humanity primarily means that we are relational beings, especially since it is in their relationship with each other, as an "us" in "Let *us* make man," that Adam and Eve were created.[8] Each of these perspectives are certainly true. But don't they seem dull in comparison to the jubilant love song that was heard when "let us make ... in our image" was first sung?

Remember with us what was going on when God spoke the words "Let *us* make man in our image" (Gen 1:26, emphasis added). Recall, if you will, the occurrences of the previous five days: God's love had been exploding out in one creative act after another, creating worlds filled with life and beauty and harmony and love. Wouldn't it follow then that part of what it means to be created in the image of God is that humanity would love and then, out of that love, create? Remembering that humanity's creation occurs at the very climax of this exuberant celebration of astonishingly joyous activity, doesn't it seem logical that the image of God in us is primarily seen in the godlike impulse to love and to partner with others to create even others to love? The mutual cooperation between the Father, Son, and Spirit was so joyful, so beautiful, so satisfying that being made in God's image means, at least in part, that we image him most closely when we delight in creatively partnering with others like he did. As brothers and sisters who love one another and rule together for the glory of God, we learn to embrace our differences and strive toward the unity that will reflect God's creative nature to the world.

> As brothers and sisters who love one another and rule together for the glory of God, we learn to embrace our differences and strive toward the unity that will reflect God's creative nature to the world.

IN BOTH UNITY AND DIVERSITY

The Trinity displays both unity *and* diversity, Three-In-One: Father, Son, and Spirit. In the same way, males and females who work together in loving creative partnership image him. The persons of the Trinity are completely unified as one without any difference of will or purpose (John 14:9–11; 17:21), but also without the blurring of their natures into some sort of amorphous blob. So, in the same way, man is not woman, nor woman man, and yet together, in unity as human beings, they originate from the same source and are both equally human. Adam's aloneness was positively bad because, as a solitary human being, he would never know the joy of the Trinity when the Father, Son, and Spirit worked in alliance to lovingly create. And wouldn't that creative love of an *other*, a love of one who is *like* but *different*, be why, when God made human beings in his image, "he created them male and female" (Gen 1:27)? Perhaps the best and most biblical way for us to understand being male and female in God's image is this: God created a being, "man," in his image and then divided that being, "man," into male and female image-bearers.

God created male and female so that they could love and through that love image him as life-givers! How can we miss the truth that being made in God's image means that we are most like him when we are loving life-givers? Don't be confused here. We're not only talking about sexual union producing biological children, though certainly that is part of it. There are as many ways to lovingly create as there are people in relationships. We partner to create in the way we love one another and cause life to flourish as we serve in joyful alliances. We were literally made for this. As Michael Reeves states:

> Because we live in a world created by a triune God, it makes sense that different notes can sound together pleasantly, that different colors can complement each other, that things can cohere.[9]

So, again, why was it positively bad for Adam to be alone? It was bad because without Eve as his partner/sister, Adam couldn't experience God's supreme joy of loving another with whom he is one and yet different. No wonder then that Adam's song, after falling asleep as one and awakening as two, was, "This one, *at last*, is bone of my bone and flesh of my flesh; this one will be called 'woman,' for she was taken from man" (Gen 2:23, emphasis added). Adam, who had tasted the "not good-ness" of a solitary existence, had become two persons who were of equal value and of the same origin by God's creative act. This diversity coupled with unity is why a man "leaves his father and mother and bonds with his wife, and they become one flesh" (Gen 2:24). "As God is not alone, so a human in his image should not be alone."[10]

THE BLESSED ALLIANCE

Upon their creation, God's blessing rested on the man and the woman together. Together, their relationship became, in Carolyn Custis James's words, a "Blessed Alliance":

> The clear message of the Bible is that God intended for men and women to work together. He *blessed* them before presenting them with their global mandate (Genesis 1:28). They are a *Blessed Alliance.*[11]

He declared to them that together, as equal co-regents in his world, they were to "rule ... the whole earth" (Gen 1:26) and "be fruitful, multiply, fill the earth, and subdue it" (Gen 1:28). Because they were made to be like God, they would find their ultimate satisfaction in partnering together. Of course, if all God wanted was to have a population explosion, he could have made more than one Adam, or he even could have made the man asexual and able to reproduce without a woman. But he didn't. He made something that was nearly the same thing ... but not. The Lord made a woman, a necessary helper (*ezer*), for the man whose aloneness was not good. Together they were to rule over the good world God had made. Together they would know, love, and bless the creation through one another and image God in that way.

Now, this doesn't mean *at all* that the only reason females were created was to produce children, though of course that is a part of it. Notice that the Creation Mandate was not only to multiply and fill the earth with biological children but was also to be fruitful, to subdue the earth, and to "rule ... the whole earth" (Gen 1:26). The man was to bond[12] or join together with the woman in this unified purpose. Male and female were created so that they could rule together and experience the satisfying harmony of different voices blending together that would produce a symphonic song of loving rule and creative acts in worship to their Creator. They were to be one in unity while maintaining their distinctiveness. They, like the Three-In-One, were to know *unity in diversity*.

Sadly, much of what has been written about Eve being a "helper" has been restricted primarily to marriage. Even the Hebrew phrase *ezer kenegdo* has unfortunately been historically translated "helpmeet," which I've heard twisted into "helpmate." Rather than "helpmeet," which is antiquated and confusing at best, let's look more closely at what this definition actually portends.

THE *EZER KENEGDO*

The first Hebrew word in the phrase *ezer kenegdo,* "*ezer*," actually means "a strong help" and is used especially of God giving military aid to Israel in times of trouble (e.g., Ps 28:7; 1 Chr 5:20).[13] It is then coupled with "*kenegdo*," a word that means "in front of or facing" him.[14] When God created the woman, he created her to be strong help to her brother. She is a warrior who stands with him and is like him. She's his valiant sister in the battle, who is in an alliance with him to rule and subdue the earth. In the movie *Black Panther*, the elite forces who protected the kingdom of Wakanda are called the *Dora Milaje*. Whether you're a superhero buff or not, those strong female warriors get a lot closer to the true meaning of *ezer kenegdo* than the Victorian perspective of the woman as a fainting weakling who'd pass

> Male and female were created so that they could rule together and experience the satisfying harmony of different voices blending together that would produce a symphonic song of loving rule and creative acts in worship to their Creator.

out at the sight of blood. I mean, blood and pain are usually part of the majority of a woman's life. The Victorian view of women who need servants who do their dirty work while they learn to string seashells, embroider, and play the pianoforte, like the women in Jane

Austen's novels, are a perverted view of the necessary help the man needs. By the way, do the *Dora Milaje* remind you of all the passages we considered about brothers and sisters who are working in the Great Commission together?

SO ... WHAT IS IT? NATURE OR NURTURE?

What makes you who you are? Why are you unique, or different from your siblings or friends, even if they are the same gender as you? That's a question that philosophers, psychologists, and theologians have tried to answer through the ages.

Nature

People who choose the "nature" side of this debate think that most everything depends on your DNA. You're born with particular physical and personality traits, and that's why you are what you are. I can see this perspective when I get together with my half-sister, Julia. We weren't raised in the same environment, nor did we have the same relationships, education, or opportunities. But when we're together, you'd swear we spent our whole childhood together. We're so much alike, it shocks my kids! If you've ever said, "The apple doesn't fall far from the tree," you're speaking the language of nature. Believing in nature or genetic determinism will breed either pride or despair in our hearts: pride when our children are successful or despair when we recognize that no one in our family tree has ever been anything more than a failure.

Nurture

Others choose the "nurture" perspective. They believe that people are shaped primarily by their environment: our home life, our schooling, our relationships. This perspective got a big boost from a type of psychology called "behaviorism" in the early 1900s. Behaviorism teaches that people are determined solely by the kind of environment they live in, particularly as children.

Behaviorism, also known as behavioral psychology, is a theory of learning which states all behaviors are learned through interaction with the environment through a process called conditioning. Thus, behavior is simply a response to environmental stimuli.[15]

People who believe in behaviorism think that a person is formed almost exclusively through the input of those around them. Many people, particularly Christians influenced by Dr. James Dobson (among others), believe this explains why people are the way they are. For instance, have you ever wondered what a parent did wrong when you hear that her son has left the faith? If your automatic response to a report like that is to blame the mother, you've chosen "nurture" over "nature." A lot of guilt and condemnation has been heaped on spouses and parents when relationships, especially with children, aren't what we expect them to be. Here's the bottom line in this puzzle: Nurture is too much of an ask. Nature is a hopeless luck of the draw. Neither one of them is good news.

We discovered that the Bible teaches both nature and nurture. We recognize the importance and power of our genes, but we also know that God frequently does shape us through our environments, which is why it's important to live in a Christian manner in our homes. Nevertheless, each person has a unique soul in a unique body that cannot be fully explained by either their DNA or by their environment. God's unique calling and gifting in individuals is a mystery (Jer 1:5), which is why it's important to avoid stereotypes and assumptions and walk in humble dependence on Jesus alone.

> We are not automata, able to do nothing but react mechanically to our genes, our environment or even God's grace. We are personal, responsible beings created by God for himself. ... Moreover, what God has given us is not to be regarded as a static endowment. Our character can be refined. Our behaviour

[sic] can change. Our convictions can mature. Our gifts can be cultivated ... We are free to be different.[16]

Each unique physical body, female or male, has varying levels of strength and hormones and expresses its gender in shockingly differing ways. Everyone grows and matures in wildly differing homes, interacting with parents, siblings, teachers, and friends who each shape how we see ourselves. And finally, and most importantly, the Spirit calls us and gifts us with unique abilities and oversees our life in his sovereign plans that sometimes complement our nature and other times surprise us. To then say that there is only one way of being masculine or only one way of being feminine is myopic and condemning to those who don't fit that crushing stereotype.[17]

While eschewing every stereotype, we do need to say that women and men have distinctly different experiences because of their bodies. As Prudence Allen explains:

> The differences are deep, running all through ... personality and mode of self-expression, but they are not because [we have] a different kind of soul, but because the human soul in each case has to operate and express itself through this particular body, which allows some of its many potentialities to develop, others not, or some more than others. Thus, a human soul operating in a male body just cannot conceive, bear in its womb, and give birth to a human child, because it has no womb with which to do so.[18]

Most women know what it is to menstruate, which means that from their early teen years until menopause, they deal monthly with blood, pain, and hormonal fluctuations that really are no laughing matter. Their breasts grow, and they learn that there is a good possibility that they will produce, within them, a food that will sustain their children. For some women this is very satisfying; for others it is painful and exhausting. Some will also learn what it is to nurture life within themselves, to be totally responsible for the life of another and to have their very own blood and oxygen nurture another being who lives within them. And they're well aware of the danger and agony that pregnancy and childbirth will foist upon them.[19] Once a woman has conceived, she knows she has probably taken on a lifetime of labor and pain. Because of this, women are trained early through their bodies to be aware of the needs of the people around them and to learn what it is to nurture others. "This 'predisposition' in women to pay attention to another person is there whether or not a woman gets pregnant and gives birth to a child."[20] This part of the human experience is unique to women alone, and it shapes them in ways that men don't experience. Any stereotype that fails to recognize the courage and deep impulse to give life to others at all costs fails to understand the true nature of a woman.

Men, on the other hand, know what it is to be physically stronger than their female counterparts:

A study in the Journal of Applied Physiology found that men had an average of 26 lbs. (12 kilograms) more skeletal muscle mass than women. Women also exhibited about 40 percent less upper-body strength and 33 percent less lower-body strength, on average, the study found.[21]

Ideally, this means from an early age (before their strength develops) young boys are to taught to use their bodies to help and protect girls, not to hurt them. When puberty hits, testosterone surges and muscle develops along with his libido. A young man becomes aware of the temptation to use his strength to take what he wants regardless of consent. He must learn restraint and servanthood. Properly developed, he desires to use his size and strength to serve and protect those in his company. He is aware of those who are in danger or in need of assistance; he longs to help those in his sphere of responsibility. "A man has the disposition, after accepting responsibility for particular persons in his sphere of activity, to protect and provide for them."[22]

So then, because we are created in the image of God, both women and men are made to nurture and protect life, to fulfill the Creation

Mandate. Some women do so by nurturing life within themselves and then sustaining that life through nursing. Some men father children and then choose to protect and provide for them. Both can choose to sacrifice their life for the sake of others, of those who need care and protection. But biological life-giving isn't the only way we image God. Not by a long shot. Neither masculinity nor femininity are defined solely, or even primarily, by means of marriage roles. A woman is a human being made in the image of God whether she is married or a mother or not. A man is a human being made in the image of God whether he is married or a father or not.

> A woman is a human being made in the image of God whether she is married or a mother or not. A man is a human being made in the image of God whether he is married or a father or not.

Furthermore, whether we are married or single, parents or not, male or female, we are all called by the Lord to nurture life in others because we are created in the image of God to love and to create. Deborah, for example, is called a mother in Israel, and Paul described himself as a father to his son Timothy. Paul even took on the voice of a pregnant mother laboring that Christ would be formed in the Galatians: "My children, I am again suffering labor pains for you until Christ is formed in you" (Gal 4:18–19). Paul was comfortable referring to himself as both a father and a mother—that's because he saw beyond the Greco-Roman and Jewish stereotypical roles that had crushed both men and women. He recognized that his calling was the same as his Lord's: to love and to give life:

> Just as Moses lifted up the snake in the wilderness, so the Son of Man must be lifted up, so that everyone who believes in him may have eternal life. For God loved the world in this way: He gave his one and only Son, so that everyone who believes in him will not perish but have eternal life. (John 3:14–16)

Women and men are called to partner together in the Blessed Alliance to lay down their lives for the life of the church.

THE BLESSED ALLIANCE ... EVEN HERE

Jesus represents both men and women because he is both the valiant warrior who fought throughout his entire existence to bring us true life and because he is the true life-giver. He willingly took upon himself the role of a pregnant, nursing mother who nourished his people from his own body:

> For the bread of God is the one who comes down from heaven and gives life to the world ... I am the bread of life ... No one who comes to me will ever be hungry, and no one who believes in me will ever be thirsty again. (John 6:33, 35)

Our valiant warrior husband gave us his life so that we might live. The words he used to describe his life-giving mission were shocking:

> This is the bread that comes down from heaven so that anyone may eat of it and not die. I am the living bread that came down from heaven. If anyone eats of this bread he will live forever. The bread that I will give for the life of the world is my flesh. (John 6:50–51)

In response to these astounding words, the Jews argued, "How can this man give us his flesh to eat?" (John 6:52). And then Jesus dropped the atomic bomb on them:

> Truly I tell you, unless you eat the flesh of the Son of Man and drink his blood, you do not have life in yourselves. The one who eats my flesh and drinks my blood has eternal life, and I will raise him up on the last day, because my flesh is true food and my blood is true drink. (John 6:53–55)

However you might want to try to soften Jesus' nearly cannibalistic sounding words, you must admit that in his alliance with his Father and the Spirit, the Son's sole purpose was to image the Three-In-One by creating new life out of an abundance of love using both his body and soul. And then, during the Last Supper, he said, "This is my body" and "this is my blood" given so that you may have eternal life. Like a mother, Jesus created new life from his body. Like a father, he used his strength to provide for and protect his sisters and brothers.

And while his atoning sacrifice is utterly unique in its redemptive power, let's not forget the other strong helper, Mary, who basically made his life possible. When Mary said "yes" to Gabriel, what that meant was this *ezer kenegdo* would offer lifeblood, oxygen, DNA, and nourishment from her body to the body of her Savior, so that he would live. Like Jesus, she would give her body and blood so that he could ultimately give his body and blood for the life of the world.

Both men and women are to use their physical bodies, in whatever way their souls are inclined, called, or gifted by God, whether they fit masculine or feminine stereotypes or are completely out-of-faze with Elizabeth Bennet or Mr. Darcy, to partner together in creative love for the life of the world. Some men and women will be called to full-time ministry. Others will image God in their daily vocations, in both private and public spheres. Nevertheless, in whatever way they fulfill God's design for their lives, they are to strive to find unity in diversity as they partner together in creativity, filling the earth with fruit, all for the glory of God.

A CHRISTLIKE NATURE

Eowyn Stoddard rightly points out that "desirable qualities that are pleasing to God, such as the fruit of the Spirit, are not couched in terms of virility or femininity."[23] As you read over the character qualities listed below, which are masculine, which are feminine? Does one need a certain sort of disposition or nature to be considered spiritual?

> But the fruit of the Spirit is love, joy, peace, patience, kindness, goodness, faithfulness, gentleness, and self-control. (Gal 5:22–23)

Certainly, if Paul were trying to uphold the Roman status quo, he would have indicated that these qualities were primarily for the women. Then, he should have listed other more "masculine" traits for the men who were to go out into the public, take initiative, and conquer. But that's not what he did, is it? No. Rather, these characteristics are to be part of both male *and* female redeemed human nature as members of the spiritual family because we're all being recreated into the image of Jesus, who certainly possessed them all in full.

> The qualities that are usually considered feminine are actually the qualities of both Christian men and women. This is to be the nature of all those in God's family. This is our shared spiritual DNA. *Godliness is not gendered.* Imaging God is not gendered.

Consider the following verses that describe the characteristics of a godly woman *and* man:

- "Therefore, as God's chosen ones, holy and dearly loved, put on compassion, kindness, humility, gentleness, and patience, bearing with one another and forgiving one another ... Above all, put on love" (Col 3:12–14).

- "Be kind and compassionate to one another, forgiving one another ... as dearly loved children, ... walk in love" (Eph 4:32; 5:2).

- Women and men are to seek to be poor in spirit, to be those who mourn, to be humble, to hunger and thirst for righteousness, to be merciful, pure in heart, peacemakers, to be those who respond in gracious patience when persecuted or reviled (see Matt 5:1–11).

The qualities that are usually considered feminine are actually the qualities of both Christian men and women. This is to be the nature of all those in God's family. This is our shared spiritual DNA. *Godliness is not gendered.* Imaging God is not gendered.

In his marvelous book *Gentle and Lowly*, Dane Ortlund shows that in the one instance in which Jesus spoke of his nature, his heart, he said, "I am lowly and humble in heart" (Matt 11:29).[24] *Lowly* and *humble.* When he chided his disciples for their ambitious grasping after authority, he was speaking in harmony with his true nature. He simply wasn't enticed by a lust after power. In his masculinity, the Son of God destroyed every stereotype about male dominance.[25] Instead, he bent down and washed feet.

What does being Christic men and women look like? It looks like brothers and sisters who partner together as image-bearers. We are one, and yet we are different. We are co-equals with the same callings. Christic women nurture life and use their strengths for the sake of others. Christic men nurture life and use their strengths for the sake of others. Together they are discovering the joy and blessing of being life-givers who learn what it is to find unity in their diversity. Together they share in God's delight as they discover their similarities and differences and grow in love for one another.

As I said earlier, I am by nature an introvert, and although that's not sinful, it does mean that I want to grow in finding joy as I partner with my sisters and brothers. Jesus himself needed time away, but he was also intent on building relationships with the men and women whom he drew to himself. He loved being around them and wanted them to grow in understanding that they were beloved and that their relationships with one another were more holy than they ever realized.

6

Siblings Serving Together

And we have this command from him: The one who
loves God must also love his brother and sister.
—1 John 4:21

This is God's command: "The one who loves God must also love his brother and sister" (1 John 4:21). At its very core, our relationship with one another as women and men has just one overarching tenet. It isn't authority and submission, it's not gender roles, femininity or masculinity. No, it is love. Brothers are commanded to love their sisters. Sisters are commanded to love their brothers. Shortly, we'll help you define what love looks like specifically in the church and in the home, but in the meantime, let's remember that one command: We must love.

In this chapter we're going to define what this kind of loving Christlike or Christic relationship looks like in action. We'll learn about our identity as men and women who each have a call as brothers and sisters to deeply desire and pursue the mutual flourishing of one another and our communities. We'll talk about what it means to speak "Let there be life" into one another and how that fulfills the image of God and is, in fact, the goal of being made in God's image as male and female.

Remember that a distinctly Christic model of male and female is a way of viewing gender that is built on and around the gospel. God the Son has taken on our flesh (Heb 2:17) and isn't ashamed to call us his brothers and sisters (Heb 2:11). He has laid down his life for ours, and we are to treat one another in the same way. Contrary to some popular teachings, our highest calling isn't marriage or childbirth—though both are good. No, our highest calling, our Christic calling, is to love our male and female neighbors as ourselves and, by doing so, to be conformed more and more into the likeness of our brother, Jesus (Rom 8:29). Christic men and women pursue:

> Our highest calling, our Christic calling, is to love our male and female neighbors as ourselves and, by doing so, to be conformed more and more into the likeness of our brother, Jesus.

- *Recognizing and respecting* others' value as made in God's image: "Outdo one another in showing honor" (Rom 12:10 ESV) because "God created man in his own image; he created him in the image of God; he created them male and female" (Gen 1:27).

- *Welcoming* one another into loving familial relationships because we are his sisters and brothers, members of one family: "Love one another deeply as brothers and sisters" (Rom 12:10) and "Therefore, my brothers and sisters, when you come together to eat [communion], welcome one another" (1 Cor 11:33).

- *Humbling* ourselves before one another, joyfully relinquishing the desire for authority and control: "Do nothing out of selfish ambition or conceit, but in humility consider others as more important than yourselves" (Phil 2:3) because "you were called to be free, brothers and sisters; only don't use this freedom as an opportunity for the flesh, but serve one another through love" (Gal 5:13).

- *Pursuing* unity with one another: "There is no Jew or Greek, slave or free, male and female; since you are all one in Christ Jesus" (Gal 3:28), so make "every effort to keep the unity of the Spirit through the bond of peace" (Eph 4:3) and "put on love, which is the perfect bond of unity" (Col 3:14) because "he is our peace, who made both groups one and tore down the dividing wall of hostility" (Eph 2:14).

- *Devoting* ourselves to the flourishing of all: We are to "pursue … what builds up one another" (Rom 14:19), "encourage one another and build each other up" (1 Thess 5:11), and "seek to excel in building up the church" (1 Cor 14:12).

What does it mean to be Christic men and women? Nothing more than *recognizing and respecting, welcoming, humbling, pursuing, and devoting ourselves to one another for the glory of God.* Certainly, there are ways those five categories play out in differing relationships (which we will talk about), but if we claim to hold to a gospel-informed worldview, we'd better be careful not to add preconceived ideas about gender "natures" or "roles" that go beyond Scripture and bind men's and women's consciences to man-made rules and ideas.

CHRISTIC MEN AND WOMEN IN ACTION

Let's look at each of those points briefly now, and then in the chapters to come you'll see how they work out in specific contexts like the church, home, and society.

Recognizing and Respecting Others' Value

- Recognizing and respecting others' value as made in God's image: "Outdo one another in showing honor" (Rom 12:10 ESV) because "God created man in his own image; he created him in the image of God; he created them male and female" (Gen 1:27).

It will be impossible to enter respectful relationships that show that you believe others have value if you presuppose that because of their gender they are flawed and unworthy. For instance, if you believe that all men are power hungry and objectify women or that they are lazy and irresponsible, your words and actions will be disrespectful and unkind. If, on the other hand, you believe that by nature women are easily deceived seductresses or that they are out to usurp positions of power, you will fear having relationship with them and will be tempted to objectify or ignore them. The false teaching we've mentioned previously has severe real-world consequences, and even though lip-service is given to ontological equality, the way much of the "gender role" theology has played out has harmed both men and women.

Welcoming One Another

- Welcoming one another into loving familial relationships because we are his sisters and brothers, members of one family: "Love one another deeply as brothers and sisters" (Rom 12:10) and "Therefore, my brothers and sisters, when you come together to eat [communion], welcome one another" (1 Cor 11:33).

Since the publication of *Worthy: Celebrating the Value of Women*, we have heard from countless women whose experience within the church has been anything but welcoming. One woman said that her experience with men in the church has been to either be ignored or objectified. Rather than viewing one another as loving members of the same family, both men and women are viewed as completely other—strangers not to be welcomed or trusted.

*Humbling Ourselves and Relinquishing the
Desire for Preeminence and Control*

- Humbling ourselves before one another, joyfully relinquishing the desire authority and control: "Do nothing

out of selfish ambition or conceit, but in humility consider others as more important than yourselves" (Phil
2:3) because "you were called to be free, brothers and
sisters; only don't use this freedom as an opportunity for
the flesh, but serve one another through love" (Gal 5:13).

Far too much of what has been written about men and women
on both sides of the debate has been concerned with who gets to be
boss. As we've said previously, throughout his life Jesus consistently
refused to buy into the world's perspective about power. While everyone around him was fighting for authority and power, he was walking toward Calvary. Rather than
pursuing the best seats at banquets or respectful greetings in
the marketplace, Jesus made himself "of no reputation." And so, we
"preach Christ crucified, a stumbling block to the Jews and foolishness to the Gentiles" (1 Cor 1:23)
because "God's foolishness is wiser
than human wisdom, and God's
weakness is stronger than human
strength" (1 Cor 1:25). Those who
watched him die were sure he was

> Throughout his life Jesus
> consistently refused to
> buy into the world's
> perspective about
> power. While everyone
> around him was fighting
> for authority and
> power, he was walking
> toward Calvary.

a fool. They saw his weakness as he hung there in agony and thought it
was folly. In fact, however, his humility proved his wisdom and power.
Christ calls us to put aside the struggle for control over others and
freely lay down our lives as he did.

Pursuing Unity with One Another

- Pursuing unity with one another: "There is no Jew or
  Greek, slave or free, male and female; since you are all one
  in Christ Jesus" (Gal 3:28), so make "every effort to keep the

unity of the Spirit through the bond of peace" (Eph 4:3) and "put on love, which is the perfect bond of unity" (Col 3:14) because "he is our peace, who made both groups one and tore down the dividing wall of hostility" (Eph 2:14).

On the night Jesus was betrayed by power-hungry Judas, he prayed for himself and his disciples. He also prayed for all of us. What did he pray for? Our unity.

> May they all be one, as you, Father, are in me and I am in you. May they also be in us, so that the world may believe you sent me. I have given them the glory you have given me, so that they may be one as we are one. I am in them and you are in me, so that they may be made completely one, that the world may know you have sent me and have loved them as you have loved me. (John 17:21–23)

Jesus taught that unity is the key to evangelism. When the world observes us fighting to attain power, whether that's through politics or gender debates, the world won't think there's anything different about us. They'll think we're just a bunch of power- and glory-hungry fools who want to make everyone else do what we want.

Aside from the commonly proclaimed (but rarely observed) pursuit of unity called for in the church, the relationship between husbands and wives in marriage is to be defined not primarily by authority and submission but rather by unity as Genesis 2:24 explains: "This is why a man leaves his father and mother and bonds with his wife, and they become one flesh" (more about this later). As Michelle Lee-Barnewall wrote in her groundbreaking book *Neither Complementarian nor Egalitarian: A Kingdom Corrective to the Evangelical Gender Debate*, "The importance of the motif of unity between the first man and the first woman should not be underestimated, especially since it reappears in Ephesians 5, not only in relation to Christian husbands and wives but also as part of the 'mystery' of Christ and the church."[1] Barnewall continues,

"If God commissioned Adam to promote the unity of the marriage, then it is difficult to imagine that 'authority' would be a main characteristic of his responsibility since power relationships tend to separate rather than create unity."[2]

Her conclusion that "power relationships tend to separate rather than create unity" is spot on. No matter which side of the gender debate you're on, as soon as one person demands de facto authority over another, unity will be broken. That's not to say that unity between leaders and subordinates is impossible. As you'll see in the chapters to come, it is possible to partner together in unity when every member of the relationship has agency to choose and every member is striving toward humility, respect, welcome, and the flourishing of the other.

> No matter which side of the gender debate you're on, as soon as one person demands de facto authority over another, unity will be broken.

Devoting Ourselves to the Flourishing of All

- Devoting ourselves to the flourishing of all: We are to "pursue ... what builds up one another" (Rom 14:19), to "seek to excel in building up the church" (1 Cor 14:12), and to "encourage one another and build each other up" (1 Thess 5:11).

In the next chapter, we'll look more deeply at what devotion to the flourishing of others entails. But just to whet your appetite, perhaps you might ask yourself whether you consciously pursue what builds up or edifies the sisters and brothers in your life. The word "pursue" (διώκω) there means "to do something with intense effort and with definite purpose or goal—'to do with effort, to strive toward.' "[3] Do you seek to excel[4] in the building up and strengthening of others more than the exaltation of yourself? Are you intent on encouraging, consoling, building up the men and women around you? If those questions make you uncomfortable, or if you're thinking, *But that might mean I'd have to spend time with people of the other sex,* and you're not sure about the propriety of that, the next chapter will help you. While it is wise to know your own propensities and weaknesses, too many women have been ignored or left without encouragement or consolation because their pastors are afraid of spending time with them. Our perspective is this: If you think that by spending time encouraging a woman you might fall into sin, you probably shouldn't be in the pastorate.

Let's remember that the apostle John says that anyone who does not love his brother or his sister does not know or love God: "If anyone says, 'I love God,' and yet hates his brother or sister, he is a liar. For the person who does not love his brother or sister whom he has seen cannot love God whom he has not seen" (1 John 4:20).

John's reasoning here is clear, and the CSB's translation makes it even more evident: Sisters and brothers have both been created in God's image. Together they mirror, reflect, and represent him. John's point is that it's impossible to love God and not love those whom he created to be like him. We know that we have passed from death to life because we love our brothers and sisters. The one who does not love remains in death. As Danny Akin writes,

> This statement serves as a stern warning for anyone at anytime who finds an absence of love in his heart. For those in the community of faith, it should be an occasion for soul searching and careful examination "to see whether you are in the faith" (2 Cor 13:5).[5]

The apostle John's teaching about God's image and loving others is like my saying that I love Phil and yet, every time I see a picture of him, I want to burn it. Of course, maybe I don't like a particular pose or light, but because I love him, I look at pictures of him with fondness and they engender in me an affection that softens my heart. Phil has a sweet picture in his office of us a few years ago at Disneyland. He's standing there smiling away, and I've got my arms draped around his neck. I love that picture of him—and I love what that picture means about us. I love pictures of him because I love the person he is. It would be impossible for me to love him and hate everything I can see about him. Here's John again:

> We know that we have passed from death to life because we love our brothers and sisters. The one who does not love remains in death. Everyone who hates his brother or sister is a murderer, and you know that no murderer has eternal life residing in him. This is how we have come to know love: He laid down his life for us. We should also lay down our lives for our brothers and sisters. If anyone has this world's goods and sees a fellow believer in need but withholds compassion from him—how does God's love reside in him? Little children, let us not love in word or speech, but in action and in truth. (1 John 3:14–18)

Christic women and men shower others with compassion and lay down their lives. Being Christic means doing everything within your power to care for and protect his image-bearers, to listen carefully and seek to understand their concerns, and not turn them away empty handed (see Rom 12:13; Jas 2:15).

IMPARTIALLY LOVE ONE ANOTHER

We would imagine that most of our readers would respond to the verse above with a *Hold on! I don't hate anybody!* We understand that response, but let us push back against it for a moment. If you've ever ignored or neglected the needs of another person because of his or her gender, you've hated them. If you've ever listened to cries for help and thought, "Typical," that's hatred. If you've ever closed your heart to the needs of another because of their gender, that's hatred, too, and this kind of hatred is called sexism, which is "prejudice or discrimination based on sex or gender."[6] While sexism usually refers to prejudice or discrimination against women, it can also affect men. Imagine for a moment that the last time you ignored or disbelieved someone, how would you have responded if the person had been a different gender? For instance, if you've ignored a woman who says she's being abused, how would you have responded to a man who said the same thing? If you've elevated the concerns of pretty women because of their beauty, that's sexism. If you've assumed that the man you're talking to couldn't possibly understand your concerns because he is a man, that's sexism. If you've paid a woman less than you would have paid a man for the same work, that's sexism. It's also favoritism.

James wrote, "If ... you show favoritism, you commit sin and are convicted by the law as transgressors" (Jas 2:9). Favoritism is "the practice of giving unfair preferential treatment to one person or group at the expense of another."[7] In James's day, he was primarily referring to honoring people who had more wealth. And while that's certainly a concern in our time, we should also think about how we give unfair preferential treatment to men or to women at the expense of ignoring the needs, gifting, or desires of the other. Of course, everyone has people they feel more comfortable around. But that's not what favoritism is. Favoritism is seen when you promote a woman instead of a man simply because she's a woman. It's also seen when you invite only men into studies of theology or assume that women should oversee the coffee service at a meeting while the men discuss the "important" things. How imperative is this concern? Here's the apostolic warning: "I solemnly charge you before God and Christ Jesus and the elect angels to observe these things ... doing nothing out of favoritism" (1 Tim 5:21). That's a solemn charge before God, the Son, and even the elect angels given by the apostle by the Spirit. Pretty imperative, it seems. As John says,

> The one who loves his brother or sister remains in the light, and there is no cause for stumbling in him. But the one who hates his brother or sister is in the darkness, walks in the darkness, and doesn't know where he's going, because the darkness has blinded his eyes. (1 John 2:10–11)

I have no doubt that both men and women can feel shocked when they realize that the way they've responded to a particular situation is decried as favoritism or sexism. For instance, when a woman comes to her leader and reports a sexual assault, and he ignores her concerns and then is ultimately fired from his position, he'll probably say he didn't see that coming. Or, if a man is judged more harshly by his female employer simply because he is a man, that's sexism. And if she's reported to HR because of that, she might feel surprised as well. This experience of feeling surprised is sometimes called being "blindsided." To be blindsided is to be unaware or blind in an area where you then experience an attack or assault. The apostle John says that one reason we may be blindsided is because we have hatred toward others.

There are some people who automatically denigrate or dismiss the opposite gender, and these people are walking in darkness. They're blind to the fact that the others are their neighbors, people who have been created in the image of God, brothers and sisters they are called to love. And because of that, they're walking in darkness. "The one who says he is in the light but hates his brother or sister is in the darkness until now" (1 John 2:9). How important is it for us to learn to consistently love both our brothers and sisters? It's the difference between light and darkness. It's the difference between walking in sexism and favoritism. It's the difference between hatred and fulfilling "the royal law prescribed in the Scripture, 'Love your neighbor as yourself' " (Jas 2:8). James reaffirms his concerns when he says that if you love your sisters *and* brothers in an unbiased way, "you are doing well." Indeed, to fail to do so is sin.

Even before those who were accusing him, Jesus' witness was that he didn't show partiality but rather taught truthfully the way of God (Luke 20:21). To show partiality is to "make unjust distinctions between people by treating one person better than another."[8] Jesus didn't kowtow to any group or faction or try to curry favor or glory by shading the truth or failing to speak out against untruths (see John 8:50; 1 Thess 2:6). What does it look like to be Christic brothers and sisters? It looks like treating one another equally in love. We would recognize it if our testimony before the watching world was, *My how they love one another.*

BUT THE BIBLE SAYS

Of course, it's easy to excuse what may actually be favoritism, sexism, or hatred by wrapping it with a cloak of biblical inerrancy. It might surprise some of our readers to learn that on both sides of the gender divide claims of orthodoxy are made. Among egalitarians and complementarians, patriarchists and feminists, are those who are concerned about being faithful to the Scripture. The truth is that many are indeed faithful believers who assent to the supremacy of the Bible but interpret what they read there differently. As we've read over and considered much of the literature (on all sides) and have then observed how their doctrines are lived out, how their teachings become the "shoulds" of gender faithfulness, we must wonder. When people construct teachings that denigrate or dismiss an entire gender, isn't there a possibility that this is sexism, favoritism, partiality, or hatred, whether it's cloaked in supposed "biblical" truth or not?

What does it look like to be Christlike or Christic sisters and brothers? It looks like believing and teaching the truth, holding on to clear passages of Scripture, interpreting unclear passages by clear ones, saying only what the texts actually say, and resisting the temptation to pile on more and more rules that find no basis in the Bible. It looks like fashioning your beliefs about gender by observing the beliefs of Jesus. For instance, generalizations about masculinity or femininity that claim to find their genesis in the Bible, but actually do not, may very well be sexism or partiality cloaked in pop American evangelicalism. What does it mean to be Christic? It means daily walking out your beliefs by living the way Christ did.

> Generalizations about masculinity or femininity that claim to find their genesis in the Bible, but actually do not, may very well be sexism or partiality cloaked in pop American evangelicalism.

Perhaps some of what we've said might seem new or unusual to you, but let us assure you that it's not. Yes, we're talking about being Christic brothers and sisters, and that may be a new way to frame this discussion, but the idea that we are all one in God's image and are called to live together considering that is nothing new.

THE COMMUNION OF SAINTS

When I was an early teen, I was sent to catechism in the Lutheran church. I'm thankful for the time I had there, though the truth is that I can't recall understanding what we learned. I must have been able to recite back the right answers because I was confirmed and welcomed as a communing member. Part of what I had to memorize was the Apostles' Creed. In case it's been a while since you recited it (or even heard it), here you go:

> I believe in God, the Father almighty,
> creator of heaven and earth.
>
> I believe in Jesus Christ, his only Son, our Lord,
> who was conceived by the Holy Spirit
> and born of the virgin Mary.
> He suffered under Pontius Pilate,
> was crucified, died, and was buried;
> he descended to hell.
> The third day he rose again from the dead.
> He ascended to heaven
> and is seated at the right hand of God the Father almighty.
> From there he will come to judge the living and the dead.
>
> I believe in the Holy Spirit,
> the holy catholic [Christian] church,
> *the communion of saints,*
> the forgiveness of sins,
> the resurrection of the body,
> and the life everlasting. Amen.[9]

Part of what was shattered at the fall was the communion, the fellowship, and the mutual devotion and love for one another between Adam and Eve and their Lord. While every part of the creed is tremendously important to our faith, the phrase that we want to focus in on now is "the communion of saints" because that phrase really gets at what we've been trying to say in this chapter about our calling to image Christ in our relationships.

In essence, the communion of saints is "The universal fellowship of Christians and the solidarity they have with one another."[10] Adam and Eve knew fellowship and solidarity until their sin shattered their souls and bodies and nearly destroyed their relationship. They were naked and ashamed of themselves, and so they covered themselves up and lived lives of hatred, self-interest, and self-protection. The sad truth is that we're just like them unless the Spirit reminds us of our oneness and remakes us into the image of Christ. Because we're continually faced with the pull to isolate ourselves, hide, and ignore our call to love our neighbor, we need to confess frequently that we are saints living in communion.

Simply put, a saint is someone who has been made holy by the work of God by grace through faith. Every believer in Christ's body is a saint (see Rom 1:7 1; Cor 1:2–4). Augustine used the word "communion" "in belief that the word was derived from *com-* 'with, together' and *unus* 'oneness, union.' "[11] When we confess that we believe in the communion of saints, we're saying that we're in union together with every other member of the church. Indeed, in its essence, the church is the communion of saints, the union all forgiven people have in the Spirit with one another. We are one body, one family. We are sisters and brothers.

This communion or fellowship we have with each other mirrors or images the communion between the Three-In-One and our communion with him. It is part of the *imago Dei* that we can have communion with him; he has created us to be relational (1 John 1:3). Speaking of both himself and his Father, Jesus said, "We will come to him and make our home with him" (John 14:23). Think of that—Jesus said he and the Father would actually move in with us! But that's not the only communion we have. John said, "If we walk in the light as he himself is in the light, we have fellowship with one another" (1 John 1:7). The word "fellowship" there, κοινωνία, denotes an association involving close mutual relations and involvement—"close association, fellowship,"[12] a communion of saints.

If one were to understand the communion of the saints by mere observation of the state of the church today, it might be a good idea to scrub that phrase from the creed. Although that seems sadly true, the truth is that there's never been a time when the church wasn't torn apart in some way. Whether it was deep disagreements about theology or politics or what sort of music should be played in church or the gender wars, the one thing that most impartial observers would say about us is that we Christians love to fuss more than fellowship. It's not hard to understand why the watching world questions the veracity of our truth claims. After all, Jesus said that the way the world would know him was through our love ... and it seems to be sorely lacking in our day.

While that is true, it is also true that there still is something very real about our communion as saints. Luther writes that it is sensed by the believing heart and

> is "impalpable" and "intangible." Nevertheless ... [it] is a communion in spirit linking believers from every tribe and nation. Empirically the church is a community of sinners. This is why the communion of saints, like the incarnation and resurrection of Christ, can only be believed.[13]

While the truth is that outwardly we seem to be nothing more than a community of sinners who love to fuss with each other, the truth is that we're saints bound to one another by our common faith in our Savior, regeneration by the Spirit, and adoption as brothers and sisters in one family.

Being Christic means that we define ourselves as brothers and sisters shaped by Christ and called to love each other. We're called to

recognize, respect, and welcome one another. We're to humble ourselves and pursue unity. We're to be utterly devoted to the flourishing
of one another all because we've been loved by Christ.

In the next chapter, we'll look more closely at what this kind of
flourishing means, but in the meantime, why not pray now for the
Lord to show you how you love and whether there are any places
where sexism, favoritism, or partiality have sown seeds of hatred in
your heart. And then rest in the righteousness of the Christ who forgives you and loved perfectly in your place.

7

The Pursuit of Mutual Flourishing

I have no greater joy than this: to hear that my
children are walking in truth. —*3 John 4*

I've (Elyse) had the great privilege of sitting in a counseling room with one of my pastors as he seeks to help couples grow in their marriage. I've been blessed to hear his wise counsel to them, but the aspect of our time together that is the most meaningful to me is listening when he speaks about his wife. With a smiling face he says, "I want her to thrive. I love to watch her blossom and flourish. Her walk with the Lord is her walk, not mine, but I want to make a way for her to grow. I love hearing her laugh. As I've changed from trying to control her to just loving her, I've watched her blossom and bloom and thrive."

I love those words. Together, let's examine what it looks like when the men and women around you, your Christian brothers and sisters, are committed to your flourishing. We'll begin by defining our terms so we're sure we're on the same page. In this usage, being devoted means that one is committed or dedicated to a task or purpose, having single-minded loyalty. We might say that this would be a top-tier issue or a life goal. It's what John meant when he said, "I have no greater joy" (3 John 4). Being devoted means that you aren't apathetic or indifferent.

FLOURISHING

To flourish is "to grow, thrive, prosper, do well, develop, burgeon, increase, multiply, proliferate, spring up, shoot up, bloom, blossom, bear fruit, burst forth, run riot, put on a spurt, boom, mushroom."[1] I really love some of those words. To flourish means to grow or develop in a healthy or vigorous way, especially as the result of a particularly favorable environment. My pastor's wife is in a particularly favorable environment for her growth and development. He's doing all he can to help her prosper and blossom. On the other hand, to fail to flourish means to die or wither. Here's how the psalmist described this process:

> The righteous *thrive* like a palm tree and *grow* like a cedar tree in Lebanon. Planted in the house of the Lord, they *thrive* in the courts of our God. They will still *bear fruit* in old age, healthy and green, to declare, "The Lord is just; he is my rock, and there is no unrighteousness in him." (Ps 92:12–14, emphasis added)

In November of 2020, my ninety-seven-year-old mother died. Although she had been treated for metastatic breast cancer for years, the underlying cause of her death was "geriatric failure to thrive." Her body was simply ceasing to function as it once did. She didn't flourish. No matter what we did in trying to interest her in food or her favorite goodies, she was simply wasting away, and we were powerless to stop it. Failure to thrive can happen to anyone from birth to old age. And it can happen spiritually, too.

We're convinced that what it means to be Christic brothers and sisters is to be committed to the cause of the thriving of others. To put it in opposite terms, it means that we're *not* indifferent to the withering or wasting away of one another. That's why my pastor's words about his wife are so nourishing to me. He's devoted to his wife's flourishing, intent on her thriving, and would do practically anything to help her grow and blossom. That's what it means to be devoted to flourishing, and it's certainly what it means to walk in Christic ways as men and women.

Our prayer is that every person in our churches will be able to say, "But I am like a flourishing olive tree in the house of God; I trust in God's faithful love forever and ever" (Ps 52:8).

Lest you think that this idea of flourishing is restricted to the Old Testament, listen to how the apostle Paul rejoiced about his friends: "We ought to thank God always for you, brothers and sisters, and rightly so, since your faith is flourishing and the love each one of you has for one another is increasing" (2 Thess 1:3). Paul's word "flourishing" (ὑπεραυξάνω) there means that their faith was growing abundantly or wonderfully,[2] and it was doing so in the context of the mutual love of each brother and sister.

FIGHTING INDIFFERENCE AND APATHY

Let's consider what would stop us from being devoted to others' flourishing. To begin with, we cannot and will not be devoted to anyone else's thriving unless we are convinced that Jesus is devoted to our own. If you believe that you must work to secure God's, your own, or others' good opinion, you'll find it impossible to live a life dedicated to others. You will only find the desire to love as you understand how you've been loved. You will only be inclined to forgive because you've been forgiven. And your motivation to lay down your life, your desires, or your rights will grow when you know that you've already been given everything you need by the Lord. We can only overcome the lie of self-protection, self-sufficiency, and self-righteousness with the truth of the gospel. The truth is that our identity and the security it brings frees us to live for the flourishing, thriving, blooming of others— even those who are not our gender, whom we might be tempted to distrust. For instance, this truth is beautifully portrayed in the first chapter of Ephesians:

> If you believe that you must work to secure God's, your own, or others' good opinion, you'll find it impossible to live a life dedicated to others.

- Because we have been blessed with every spiritual blessing by our union with Christ, we are free to seek to be a blessing to others (1:3).

- Because we have been singled out to be recipients of the Father's love, we are free from keeping the "who is being the most loving" score (1:4).

- Because we have been declared holy and blameless before him, we don't have to keep track of other's performance (1:4).

- Because all of us, both men and women, have been adopted as sons and given the rights of inheritance, we don't have to envy the status or resources of others or worry about whether we'll have enough to make it.

- And finally, though we could go on and on for pages, because we have the forgiveness of our sins by the grace he has richly poured out on us, we can forgive (1:7).

If we fail to remember the glorious riches bestowed on us through the gospel, we'll not have the power or inclination to be welcoming, generous, and loving with others.

Here's an illustration that might help: Let's say that a woman has learned, either through painful experience or teaching (or both), that she should not trust men, that they will fail to respect her and will objectify her. Her whole experience with men might be summed up this way: Rather than loving and protecting her, they have hated and abused her. Now, she may know that she has an obligation to love her neighbor (which she already feels guilty about), but it will still feel utterly contradictory to care about his flourishing. In addition, she'll feel that she must fight to protect and provide for herself and won't be free to work for her brothers' well-being. Instead, she'll feel enchained to fear, self-protection, and the desire for control.

Now we assume that there are some women who just read the above and felt a visceral response that might be summed up in, "Sorry ... That's never going to happen. I'm never going to be concerned about whether any man is thriving." We understand. We know that some of you have finally gotten out from under an abusive relationship, and we would *never* tell you to go back into it. Please understand this: loving your neighbor *and* working for his flourishing doesn't mean allowing him to sin against you. Ever. In fact, sometimes loving your neighbor means that you start holding him accountable for harm he has done to you; sometimes that means detaching yourself from him and letting the consequences of his wrongdoing hit him with the full force of justice. What's surprising is that it is the gospel itself that will make you strong enough to stand against evil and for your brothers' flourishing. It is only as you find your identity bound up in the courage and goodness of Jesus that you'll find yourself growing progressively toward the desire and ability to be devoted to the flourishing of others, even your brothers. Remember, you are forgiven, you are loved, you are precious in his sight (Col 3:13; Rom 9:25; Isa 43:4). And because that is true of you, you are freed from the fear that loving others might bring. And you can lay down your life because Jesus laid down his life for you and you believe that everything that you need has already been granted to you in Christ.

OUR SAMARITAN SISTER

In the story of the Samaritan woman (John 4), we meet a woman who certainly knew what it was to be ignored, objectified, and misused.

Frequently her story is told as though she is the immoral one (I've even done this myself.). But the truth about her five husbands and the man she's living with when she meets Jesus isn't quite what we've assumed. In those times, a woman did not have the right to initiate divorce. Even if, in fact, her marriages had all ended in divorce (though we don't know that), those divorces weren't her decision. In addition, because there were no social safety nets for an unattached woman, she only had one of three choices after her last marriage fell apart. She could hope to get married again or she could just live with someone. Or she could become a prostitute. Those were her options. So, she shunned the oldest profession while trying to protect and provide for herself as a woman without power or privilege.

What's really amazing about this story is that she is the first gentile to whom Jesus revealed himself as the Messiah. When he said, "I, the one speaking to you, am he" (John 4:26), she had finally met a man who loved her unselfishly and honored her above every other gentile (male or female) he had met. Get that. Jesus was devoted to her flourishing, so he honored, respected, and welcomed her. And that interaction with Jesus transformed her. By the way, in the Eastern Orthodox Church, this woman is venerated as Saint Photine, who eventually migrated to North Africa with two of her sons, where she was martyred in AD 66 under the reign of Nero for preaching the gospel. I'm so thankful that Jesus didn't have any scruples about talking with a woman privately or about sullying his reputation. In fact, it might be assumed that he purposely sent the disciples away so he could have time alone with her.

St. Photine's conversation with Jesus changed the very trajectory of her life and transformed her relationship with all her brothers, for whom she would pour out her life in service of their flourishing. Think about what he might do for you.

OUR ABUSED BROTHER

Again, if a man believes that most women are dangerous, seductive, and out to usurp authority, he'll find it very difficult to enter deep, healthy, and mutually beneficial relationships with them—but the Lord can transform a man's heart, too. Some men have experienced terrible destruction in their relationships with women, perhaps a mother or wife who misused, abused, maligned, or crushed them. If that's been your experience with women, the story below might help you.

Think for a moment with me about the life of Joseph (Gen 39). You'll remember that Joseph was sold into slavery by his jealous brothers. Even though he begged them for mercy, they used their power to exile him from his father, family, and homeland. He ended up in the house of Potiphar, who was the captain of Pharoah's guards. Day after day, he faithfully served his master, who left everything in his charge. In this land of his captivity, the Lord's blessing (Gen 39:5) was on Potiphar because of Joseph. But also, day after day, Joseph suffered sexual harassment from the hands of an unnamed woman: Potiphar's wife. Listen to this description of his harassment,

> After some time his master's wife looked longingly at Joseph and said, "Sleep with me." But he refused … "How could I do this immense evil, and how could I sin against God?" Although she spoke to Joseph day after day, he refused to go to bed with her. Now one day he went into the house to do his work, and none of the household servants were there. She grabbed him by his garment and said, "Sleep with me!" But leaving his garment in her hand, he escaped and ran outside. When she saw that he had left his garment with her and had run outside, she called her household servants. "Look," she said to them, "my husband brought a Hebrew man to make fools of us. He came to me so he could sleep with me, and I screamed as loud as I could. When he heard me screaming for help, he left his garment beside me and ran outside." … When his master heard the story his wife told him … he was furious and had him thrown into prison. … So Joseph was there in prison. … *But the LORD was with Joseph and extended kindness to him.* (Gen 39:7–15, 19–21, emphasis added)

Although there are numerous abuse and sexual assault stories in Scripture, this one is unusual because it involves family members and ultimately a woman who had authority over a man. Joseph suffered deep abuse at the hands of his brothers—men who should have loved and protected their younger sibling from harm. He also suffered sexual harassment and assault at the hands of a powerful woman. She sought to seduce him and exploit his deep loneliness and pain. And then she lied about him to cover up her sin against him.

How on earth could Joseph become a man who was devoted to the flourishing of another? Notice the last sentence of the passage above: "The LORD was with Joseph and extended kindness to him" (Gen 39:21). I'm sure you know how this story ends. In the concluding verses, we find Joseph living a life of dedication to the flourishing of his oppressors in Egypt and even his wicked brothers. How could that happen? It happened because, over the years, God had shown kindness to him repeatedly, so he knew he could make it through anything. Which was how he could name his sons Ephraim, because God had made him "fruitful in the land of [his] affliction" (Gen 41:52), and Manasseh, because God had made him "forget all [his] hardship and [his] whole family" (Gen 41:51). In addition, his recognition of and belief in God's kindness had made him kind and forgiving. He forgave the wickedness of his brothers and welcomed them, saying, "I am Joseph, your brother ... the one you sold into Egypt. And now don't be grieved or angry with yourselves for selling me here, because God sent me ahead of you to preserve life" (Gen 45:4–5). Think of that. "I am Joseph, your brother." *I'm here devoted to your life, your flourishing, your care.* How could anyone who had been treated like that say those words? Only because he recognized the loving-kindness and care of his heavenly Father. And that's the only way any of us could be freed from revenge, hatred, or unforgiveness. The only way.

Many women have learned to believe that every man is out to subjugate or abuse them. Likewise, some men assume that every woman is out to seduce or humiliate them. In some quadrants of the church, these assumptions are inevitable because Christ's condescension and devotion to each member's flourishing has been so relegated to insignificance that it has failed to build mutual love and respect. When brothers and sisters feel unloved, insecure, abandoned, or fearful, they won't have the desire or strength to devote their lives to the betterment of others.

This is the most important truth about us: We are adopted, beloved, and justified. Because of this, we are freed from trying to prove we're better than others. We can be utterly devoted to the flourishing of each other. It is only then that we can rejoice with those who rejoice and weep with those who weep (Rom 12:15). Once we are freed from the inner slave driver who insinuates that we can never rest or be at peace, and once we're unchained from the craving for reputation or status, we can love one another deeply, no matter our gender. Once we know how trustworthy the Lord is, we can begin to walk out of fear and the desire to control. We can give ourselves to our *imago Dei*: to partner with others and work for the flourishing of our communities. We can learn to partner together and to speak "Let there be life!" into every relationship. We no longer need to fear that we will lose something we think we need. As a woman, I don't need status or to be in charge to know that I'm okay, to know that I'm beloved and have value. As a man, Eric doesn't need status or to be in charge, either. He knows that he is the beloved of God and that his life has meaning and value. Now that doesn't mean that we are never in any sort of position of authority. Of course, we are. What it does mean, though, is that we don't *need* to be in control at some sort of psychological level. This kind of need says, *I have to be respected/ honored/powerful in order to breathe.*

> This is the most important truth about us: We are adopted, beloved, and justified. Because of this, we are freed from trying to prove we're better than others. We can be utterly devoted to the flourishing of each other.

This is the trap that Jesus warned against when he said, "Whoever wants to save his life will lose it, but whoever loses his life because of me will save it. For what does it benefit someone if he gains the whole world, and yet loses or forfeits himself?" (Luke 9:24–25).

When Jesus was talking about losing one's life for his sake, he was talking about the cost of Christic discipleship. He calls us to follow him, deny ourselves, and take up our cross daily. Frequently, what that means is that, first, we strive to find our identity solely in him. That means that we ask him to help us grow in trusting that everything we need for our own flourishing has been and will be given to us. What makes you feel you're okay or that you have value? If the answer to those questions is anything other than the love of God shown through the perfect obedience and substitutionary death of Jesus Christ, then you'll find it hard to freely give your life away.

Of course, now that we're talking about people who have been sinned against and yet, by faith, lived for the flourishing of others, we would be utterly remiss if we failed to mention the Man who

> ... bore our sicknesses and carried our pains ... we are healed by his wounds. We all went astray like sheep; we all have turned to our own way; and the LORD has punished him for the iniquity of us all. ... After his anguish, he will see light and be satisfied. By his knowledge, my righteous servant will justify many, and he will carry their iniquities. (Isa 53:4–6, 11)

From the moment of his incarnation and especially at the end, Jesus had "determined to journey to Jerusalem" (Luke 9:51, 53), to the cross which meant death for him but life for us. He was utterly devoted to loving us and paying the ultimate sacrifice for our flourishing. Thank God.

Please don't misunderstand. Again, we are not saying that being devoted to another's flourishing means that you allow them to habitually sin against you or that you suffer in silence. In fact, just the opposite is true. Sometimes devotion to the good of another means that you refuse to be the target of his or her attack. King David couldn't learn what it was to be concerned about the flourishing of others until he knew what it was to be called out publicly and to mourn (see 2 Sam 12:7, 18–23; Pss 32; 51).

WHEN DEVOTION GOES WRONG

The pressure to have bragging rights, to be seen as together, valuable, and loved, played out recently in the American college admission scandal. Netflix's *Operation Varsity Blues* tells the sad story of high profile, wealthy parents who paid thousands of dollars to college counselor Rick Singer so their children would be accepted in elite colleges. Singer would bribe contacts at these universities to accept his clients' sons or daughters into athletic programs that they weren't qualified for or to take entrance exams for them so their scores would be high enough. Fifty parents and numbers of college employees, especially heads of athletic departments, were charged with conspiracy to commit fraud. Many of these parents ultimately pled guilty and had to serve sentences (though light) for their crime.

In this case, the parents would have said they were sacrificing so their children would flourish. But is that what was really going on? As I listened in on the dramatized conversations parents had with Singer, I can hear a love for their children for sure. But that's not all

> We are not saying that being devoted to another's flourishing means that you allow them to habitually sin against you or that you suffer in silence. In fact, just the opposite is true. Sometimes devotion to the good of another means that you refuse to be the target of his or her attack.

I heard. I heard parents who were desperate to be able to approve of themselves, to know that they made the grade, and to have bragging rights about how successful their children were. These parents were looking for a way to save their life (ambition, pride, self-righteousness), and they ended up losing everything.

Whenever you look at someone as a stepping-stone to your "okay-ness" or as proof of your value, you are using them for yourself and not loving them. I can't imagine the shame those children must feel, knowing that their parents were willing to break the law to get them into a school, an accomplishment they couldn't achieve on their own. It appears the only entity that ended up profiting from this scam was the universities themselves—universities who continue to accept overly privileged, underachieving students through the "back door" of enormous monetary gifts.[3] This is the opposite of what an authentic commitment to flourishing looks like.

VALUING OUR GIFTEDNESS

What would it look like in daily life to be genuinely devoted to the flourishing of each other? It would look like seeing the value in one another and doing all we can to help one another grow in their giftedness. Here's how Paul saw it:

> Now concerning spiritual gifts: brothers and sisters, I do not want you to be unaware. ... Now there are different gifts, but the same Spirit. There are different ministries, but the same Lord. And there are different activities, but the same God works all of them in each person. A manifestation of the Spirit is given to each person for the common good. ... One and the same Spirit is active in all these, distributing to each person as he wills. For just as the body is one and has many parts, and all the parts of that body, though many, are one body—so also is Christ. ... But as it is, God has arranged each one of the parts in the body just as he wanted. (1 Cor 12:1, 4–7, 11–12, 18)

Can you hear Paul's heart to encourage both brothers and sisters in recognizing and valuing one another's giftings? God is the one who gives gifts, and the Spirit has given gifts to each person. That means that our brothers and sisters each have precious gifts that God has bestowed just as he wanted. There are different gifts, ministries, and activities, but each one comes from the hand of the Lord in just the way he has planned.

VALUING OUR FAMILY

Later in the passage, Paul writes that there should be no divisions among us and that we should have the same concern for each other, no matter if we think our own or another's gifts are superior. It is only in this way that we will be inclined to both suffer and rejoice together (see 1 Cor 12:24–26).

In his letter to the church at Rome, Paul reiterates the same ideas about giftedness and makes it plain that we are one body or family, "members of one another":

> Now as we have many parts in one body, and all the parts do not have the same function, in the same way we who are many are one body in Christ and individually members of one another. According to the grace given to us, we have different gifts. (Rom 12:4–6)

But then he brings his readers back to the primary point of all he's been saying. We are one family, and because of that, we are to "love one another deeply as brothers and sisters" (Rom 12:10a), and we are to "outdo one another in showing honor" (Rom 12:10b ESV). Think about those words again: because God is the one who has made us unique and members of one another, we are to love each other "deeply as brothers and sisters," recognizing our diversity and yet pursuing unity.

During Holy Week this year, I was introduced to the concept of Tenebrae. Tenebrae, which is Latin for "darkness," is a visual representation of the death of Christ by candles being extinguished followed by a

> Because God is the one who has made us unique and members of one another, we are to love each other "deeply as brothers and sisters," recognizing our diversity and yet pursuing unity.

loud noise, symbolic of the earthquake when Jesus died.[4] To accompany this remembrance, I listened to the Tenebrae Choir and was so blessed as I heard the harmonies of the whole group and soloists glorifying God through the differing ranges of their voices. Each gendered body had differing ranges and strengths. They were beautiful both alone and when they blended in harmonies. There was a special blessing when no one voice stood out ... but then there was also the blessing of hearing the soloists. The women didn't need to try to sing the men's parts nor did the men try on the women's. Because their vocal cords reflect their gender, their song to the Lord was beautifully different and yet the same. And once again I remembered that it wouldn't have been good for either the men or the women to be alone.

Sure, you may have different gifts than me, but I need to outdo you in showing you honor as one who has been loved and gifted by God. That really sounds like being devoted to mutual flourishing to me. The kind of love that Paul is referring to here in Romans 12:10 is to be "tenderly loving, being devoted."[5] Paul goes on to command us to eagerly honor one another. We are to be devoted to the flourishing, the blossoming of one another's gifts, the welcoming of our different callings, and in humility consider others as better than ourselves (Phil 2:3).

FINDING AND FULFILLING YOUR CALL

Part of what Eric and I do for the flourishing of men and women in the church is host the *Worthy* podcast. In these weekly discussions we seek to foster respectful conversations about the value of women and men in the home, church, and society. One of the topics that we find ourselves discussing frequently is how the women we interview understood their call to ministry. What we have heard over and over again is something that sounds like this: *I didn't know that what I was experiencing was an actual call. I just felt disturbed about a particular need ... almost haunted by it ... and I just couldn't get away from it.*

We've also heard that a lifelong vocation or call was only understood "in the rearview mirror." In other words, understanding the gifting and purpose the Lord had in mind wasn't something that was immediately obvious to them but rather was something that just wouldn't go away, some niggling feeling that something needed to be answered. And then, when their life of faith was viewed from a down-the-road perspective, it became beautifully clear what God had been doing all along.

For the man or woman who is blessed enough to live in a culture of flourishing, finding one's giftedness is a joyous lifelong journey. Because my husband Phil has consistently been my biggest cheerleader, I've been able to seek out and discover God's plan for my life. Here's how it looked for me: Although I didn't become a Christian until adulthood, I frequently found myself in two different situations. First, it seemed as though people were always asking me for advice, and usually I had no idea why or even what I was supposed to say, which eventually pushed me to get training in biblical counseling. And, secondly, I was consistently haunted about the lostness, confusion, and brokenness that I saw in others and knew something needed to be done about it. These concerns led to writing and speaking.

We've heard others describe God's call as both inward and outward. What they mean by that is one has an inner sense that they want to do a specific ministry for the Lord and then that sense is outwardly confirmed by others, usually people already in that ministry. While this is a time-honored way for men to discern a vocational call to ministry, it's frequently lacking for women. Unless a woman is in a church devoted to her full flourishing, she won't hear those confirming sentiments. In that case, she might just need to prayerfully consider where her ministry heart "itches" and then pursue it while God opens doors. This disparity between male and female confirmation of gifting is one of the reasons there are so many parachurch ministries run by women these days. They see that a specific work needs to be done, they see that no one else is doing it and that no one in their church is interested, so they just go ahead, because they can't not, and God blesses them. This is certainly the case with women like Christine Caine, whose global ministries include A21, which seeks to free women from sex trafficking, and Propel Women, a ministry that strives to help women find and flourish in their calling. It's also true of Beth Moore, who has lived a life of devotion to the flourishing of Christian women everywhere. It is also the case with men like Raleigh Sadler, who heads up the Let My People Go ministry, whose purpose is to identify people who are vulnerable to exploitation and to offer them options that will lead to their freedom and flourishing.

It is our hope that each church will develop a Christic devotion to the flourishing of all its members. What this will look like in each one may be somewhat different, but it should be evident that from the leadership on down, this is a place where *all* people are encouraged to find and fulfill their calling.

We know that many churches focus on training men for ministry, which is good. But we'd also love to see that same kind of dedication to the growth and flourishing of women. Part of what it means to be Christically devoted to the flourishing of each other is that we diligently pursue both women and men and assist them in finding where their heart of ministry is. For instance, instead of just having a leadership class for the men, so that future leaders might be identified, you should invite women in also. That wouldn't mean that women would automatically be given ministries that are limited in your local congregation—even if your tradition doesn't ordain women, that doesn't mean women don't have gifts given to them by God that need to be honored and cultivated. Our churches need to begin to take seriously Paul's other words about gifting and ministry—and not just those in certain limiting passages.

> We know that many churches focus on training men for ministry, which is good. But we'd also love to see that same kind of dedication to the growth and flourishing of women.

I have accomplished what I have because I've known consistent devotion to my flourishing in my home and elsewhere. I've been able to pursue God's gifts in my life and rarely felt like I should pursue some other path because of my gender. I've been blessed, and I know it. Only in eternity will I begin to understand how the love and devotion of my family and friends has been multiplied out to others.

In the chapters to come we'll talk more specifically about how Christic devotion to flourishing looks in the home, church, and society, but for now consider how you might pursue your own giftedness and the flourishing of others.

8

Husbands, Wives, and the Gospel

*For this reason a man will leave his father and mother
and be joined to his wife, and the two will become
one flesh. This mystery is profound, but I am talking
about Christ and the church. —Ephesians 5:31–32*

Gender roles. Headship. Submission.* Some of you picked up this book and immediately flipped to this chapter to see what we have to say about these matters. If that's you, you're welcome to start here; we don't mind (though we'd encourage you to read the whole thing). In fact, we (sort of) applaud you. You've drawn a conclusion—the end of the matter. You want to see if a work agrees with you in the end before you invest in its beginning. You might be surprised to find we're (sort of) doing the same thing.

Marriage—like our gender—is best understood with the end in mind. So, we start with our understanding of what it means to be Christic men and women and ask what it looks like for *Christians* in a marriage. We are not presenting a theology of marriage in general—one that applies to all marriages. As we think of *Christic* marriage, we consider how Christ shapes and informs a Christian as a husband or a wife. To that end, we're beginning with the end—the purpose of gender as informed by Christ.

In Chapter Four we defined the purpose of Christic gender this way: "As men and women in Christ, our shared purpose is to reign with Christ as his image-bearing body and bride, both now and forever." Reigning with Christ means filling and ruling the earth in a way that shows the world what God is like. We image forth his glory as the gospel transforms us into the image of Christ. That purpose became more specific as we saw how Christ transformed the Creation Mandate into the Great Commission. We now fill the earth with new believers and teach them to obey Jesus. With that in mind, we narrowed the definition of our purpose as follows:

> In Christ, believing men and women are to glorify God by cooperating for the advance of the gospel and imitating Christ in voluntary humiliation, reciprocal benevolence, and mutual flourishing.

This purpose defines what men and women work toward. But how do men and women interact as they collaborate toward that shared goal?

In Chapter Six, we considered how Christic men and women should work together. We said that Christic gender should be characterized by the following:

> Recognizing and respecting each other's value, welcoming one another, humbling ourselves before one another, pursuing unity with one another, and devoting ourselves to one another's flourishing—and all of this for the glory of God.

If the above definitions of our shared purpose and characteristics of Christic gender are correct, then our definition of Christic marriage should sound almost identical. The following is our definition of Christic marriage:

> Christic marriage is a covenantal display of Christ's glory by both the husband and the wife, through which they cooperate to display the gospel, imitating Christ in voluntary humility,

reciprocal benevolence, and mutual flourishing as they recognize and respect one another's value and pursue unity with
one another.

Let's unpack that statement a phrase at a time.

A COVENANTAL DISPLAY OF
CHRIST'S GLORY ...

There is one aspect of marriage that differentiates it from relationships
between Christic men and women in general. *Marriage is a covenant
relationship between one man and one woman.*

A covenant is a solemn agreement between two parties, especially
as it outlines their obligations to one another. A biblical example is the
covenant between God and Israel made at Mount Sinai. God promised
to be their God and show them faithfulness; Israel was to be a nation
that reflected the image of God.[1] In marriage, a man and a woman solemnly vow to be husband and wife, obligating themselves to mutual
love and faithfulness. Such a vow does not characterize the relationship between men and women in general. So, our relationships with
our respective spouses are markedly different than our relationship
with one another as co-authors.

Throughout the Bible, the Lord speaks of his *covenant relationship*
with his people in terms of husband and wife. So, for example, the Lord
says to Israel, "I remember the loyalty of your youth, your love as a
bride" (Jer 2:2). And later, speaking of the Israelites' unfaithfulness, he
says, "because unfaithful Israel had committed adultery ... I had sent
her away and had given her a certificate of divorce" (Jer 3:8). Likewise,
the end of the Bible depicts the *covenant relationship* between Christ
and the church as husband and wife:

> Let us be glad, rejoice, and give him glory,
> because the marriage of the Lamb has come,
> and his bride has prepared herself. (Rev 19:7)

Similarly, the Lord speaks of the *marriage covenant* as an illustration of Christ and the church. The apostle Paul writes, "For this reason a man will leave his father and mother and be joined to his wife, and the two will become one flesh. This mystery is profound, but I am talking about Christ and the church" (Eph 5:31–32).

This predominant use of marriage to illustrate God with his people leads to this conclusion: *God created the marriage covenant as a living parable of his covenant relationship with his people.* Note that we have highlighted the word "covenant" in the above paragraph; it is of utmost importance. God chose the particular *covenant relationship* of marriage to illustrate his relationship with his people because *marriage* illustrates unity, love, and faithfulness as no other relationship could.

That means that *marriage is a unique aspect of Christic gender identity.* We may not extrapolate principles from the *marriage covenant* and apply them to the relationships between men and women in general. Whatever "headship" and "submission" might mean in marriage, they are unique to marriage. They say *nothing* about the relationship between men and women in general. There is no warrant to say that *every man* is the head of *every woman* or that *every woman* must submit to *every man.* Nor should we even imply that these concepts should incline every man and every woman to act these ways. Implying that all male-female relationships in general model Christ and the church only obliterates the meaning of marriage and the gospel.

> That means that marriage is a unique aspect of Christic gender identity. We may not extrapolate principles from the marriage covenant and apply them to the relationships between men and women in general.

The glory of the relationship between the Lord and his people is its uniqueness (see Amos 3:2; Exod 19:5–6). The Lord is not a polygamist; he does not have multiple brides. The Lord has *one people*—and, therefore, they are to have *one God.*

When we state that all men should be inclined to lead or protect all women or state that all women should draw out male leadership and be inclined to submit to it, we obfuscate the relationship between Christ and the church. Defining male and female along the lines of covenant marriage, applying it even in a limited capacity to all male-female relationships, blurs or denies what is unique about marriage. Applying these principles to all men and women presents a picture of soft universalism, which is heresy. Such a theology implies there is nothing unique about Christ's relationship to the church—that he relates to all people the same. He does not, as his wrath falls on those who will not become a part of his bride, but only his redeeming love falls on his bride.

The marriage covenant is an utterly unique relationship that typifies the relationship between Christ and the church. So, what does that look like? Let's continue with our definition.

... BY BOTH THE HUSBAND AND THE WIFE ...

"Christic marriage is a covenantal display of Christ's glory by *both the husband and the wife.*" That phrase—"both the husband and the wife"—is essential to marriage but too often overlooked. Because the Bible speaks of the relationship between God and his people in marriage terms, it is often wrongly assumed that *only* the husband displays the glory of Christ. The wife *only* pictures the church. Such an assumption is detrimental to both the marriage and the individual.

In Christic marriage, both the husband and the wife display *Christ's* glory; both are a picture of Christ. Let's consider an understanding of marriage in which "the husband is the head of the wife as Christ is the head of the church." It is easy to see how a husband would picture Christ—he is called to love his wife "just as Christ loved the church" (Eph 5:25). But what would it mean for a wife to be a picture of the church? To answer that question, we need to understand what the church is.

The church is the collective people of God. We have the *universal church*—all God's people from all times and all places. And we have the *local church*—a local assembly of believers in a particular place. In short, the church is Christ's people, which is described in several ways.

A prominent description of the church is that of Christ's body: "He is also the head of the body, the church" (Col 1:18; see also Rom 12:4–5; 1 Cor 12:12–27; Eph 3:6; 4:15–16; 5:23; Col 1:24). God calls the church, as his body, to "grow in every way into him who is the head—Christ" (Eph 4:15). This language typifies the commanding theme of sanctification: the church is to "put on the Lord Jesus Christ" (Rom 13:14), to "be imitators of God" (Eph 5:1), Christ in particular. In sum, God calls the church to look like Jesus. If the church is the living body of Jesus, then a wife picturing the church is a woman picturing Jesus. As the church is to display his glory, so is she. Therefore, being a wife is a *Christic* calling; its ultimate aim is to look and act like Jesus.

... THROUGH WHICH THEY COOPERATE TO DISPLAY THE GOSPEL ...

As mentioned above, God often uses marriage to illustrate his relationship with his people. In the New Testament, we see this predominantly at the Bible's end. The book of Revelation presents Jesus as the bridegroom (see Matt 9:15; 25:1–13; Mark 2:19; Luke 5:34; John 3:29). Correspondingly, the church is presented as his bride (see Rev 19:7; 21:2, 9–10; 22:17).

It is no mistake that the storyline of the Bible both begins and ends with a marriage. In Genesis 2, we have the woman presented to the man, and they become one flesh—a marriage. In Revelation 19:7, we find the same scene: "Let us be glad, rejoice, and give him glory, because the marriage of the Lamb has come, and his bride has prepared herself." In the beginning, God commissions a man and woman (husband and wife) to rule on the earth. In the end, a husband and wife rule on the earth forever—Christ and the church.

> In the beginning, God commissions a man and woman (husband and wife) to rule on the earth. In the end, a husband and wife rule on the earth forever—Christ and the church.

It is no surprise then that God would call for marriages to imitate and display this good news.

"Christ and the church" is a beautiful picture of the best news ever. Unfortunately, what that means and looks like has been interpreted and applied in ways that are anything but beautiful. They are certainly not *Christic*. Much of this flows from how one understands "headship and submission," as presented in Ephesians 5:22–33:

> Wives, submit to your husbands as to the Lord, because the husband is the head of the wife as Christ is the head of the church. He is the Savior of the body. Now as the church submits to Christ, so also wives are to submit to their husbands in everything. Husbands, love your wives, just as Christ loved the church and gave himself for her to make her holy, cleansing her with the washing of water by the word. He did this to present the church to himself in splendor, without spot or wrinkle or anything like that, but holy and blameless. In the same way, husbands are to love their wives as their own bodies. He who loves his wife loves himself. For no one ever hates his own flesh but provides and cares for it, just as Christ does for the church, since we are members of his body. For this reason a man will leave his father and mother and be joined to his wife, and the two will become one flesh. This mystery is profound, but I am talking about Christ and the church. To sum up, each one of you is to love his wife as himself, and the wife is to respect her husband.

Much ink has been spilled in debates over the two terms. Some see "head" to mean "source," others as "authority." Naturally, these interpretations influence how one understands "submit." So what do headship and submission mean? What do headship and submission look like?

In all doctrine and practice, we must be cautious not to go beyond what we find in Scripture. Many confessions of faith, such as the Westminster Confession of Faith and the Baptist Faith and Message, contain a line to this effect: "God alone is Lord of the conscience, and He has left it free from the doctrines and commandments of men which are contrary to His Word or not contained in it." That means that no church, council, denomination, or other Christian "authority" is allowed to bind a believer's conscience with teaching that contradicts the Scripture or is not found in it. This is not only biblical but also important to what it means to be men and women—marriage included. What the Bible has not said about being a husband or a wife, we may not say. We may not insist that husbands or wives behave in ways not taught in Scripture. That is true whether they are traditional, cultural, or appear to be a conclusion of "natural revelation." The word alone is God's final source of authority over his people.

When the New Testament gives general instructions to wives and husbands, it is devoid of specific details. The New Testament does not give us a cookie-cutter model for marriage. It does not tell us in detail how every wife and husband should act. Theologies and resources that present one-size-fits-all instructions beyond what the Bible says tend to create terrible pain in marriages.

Scripture does not give us a cookie-cutter for marriage because it knows something important: individuals are different; therefore, every marriage is unique. In some marriages, the husband and wife cooperate best with him working full time and her working as a homemaker. In other marriages, the couple thrives as witnesses to Christ with her working fifty hours a week as a CEO, while he puts in his forty hours a week as a mechanic and runs the kids to and from school. How any particular couple best displays Jesus to the world will depend on those who make up that household.

> The New Testament does not give us a cookie-cutter model for marriage. It does not tell us in detail how every wife and husband should act. Theologies and resources that present one-size-fits-all instructions beyond what the Bible says tend to create terrible pain in marriages.

What does Paul mean by the husband being the "head" of the wife? He simply doesn't define it—he displays it. He tells us what it looks like. So, whether one holds to an egalitarian or complementarian interpretation of "headship," the husband in a healthy marriage ought to look the same—that is, *Christic*. (In fact, if a marriage is genuinely Christic, an outside observer will not be able to discern whether it is egalitarian or complementarian.)

The first thing we should note is that the Scripture never tells the husband to "be the head of your wife." Not even close. Nor is the husband ever exhorted to "lead" his wife or be the "spiritual leader" in the family. Some extrapolate "lead" from the wife's call to submit. But that is simply an extrapolation. Others extrapolate "spiritual leader" from Paul's admonition to love one's wife as Christ loved the church "with the washing of the water by the word" (Eph 5:26). But again, these are merely extrapolations, not the clear intent of Paul's letter.

Paul's simple command to husbands is:

> Husbands, love your wives, just as Christ loved the church and gave himself for her to make her holy, cleansing her with the washing of water by the word. He did this to present the church to himself in splendor, without spot or wrinkle or anything like that, but holy and blameless. In the same way, husbands are to love their wives as their own bodies. He who loves his wife loves himself. (Eph 5:25–28)

Love is the command and description of headship. This love is sacrificial. Christ gave himself for the church's good. Jesus did not condemn or punish his bride. Instead, he sacrificed himself to satisfy God's wrath for her sin and give her abundant life. All that Christ does to, for, and with his bride is for the flourishing of both. Therefore, headship calls for a husband to sacrifice himself for her flourishing. We see the seeds of this in Genesis 2:24: "This is why a man leaves his father and mother and bonds with his wife, and they become one flesh." Contrary to the norm of a wife leaving her family for his, the *man* will sacrifice the fellowship and security of father and mother to go and bond with his wife. If headship means anything, it means the husband is the first to die for the sake of the marriage. He will sacrifice his dreams, ambitions, reputation, and potential for the sake of being one with her. The husband who refuses to do this refuses to picture and glorify Jesus.

> All that Christ does to, for, and with his bride is for the flourishing of both. Therefore, headship calls for a husband to sacrifice himself for her flourishing.

The husband's love is mutually beneficial—"He who loves his wife loves himself" (Eph 5:28). They are one flesh, so he must be as concerned for her flourishing in Christ's purposes as he is for himself. Christ's concern for the church's flourishing is a concern for his own glory, just as much as his concern for his own glory is manifest in his inexhaustible love for the church. That is Christic headship. The husband who neglects his wife so that she withers while he is away building a ministry teaching sound theology to the masses (or a workaholic pursuing material wealth) is not Christic; he is anti-Christ. Not only that, he is anti-self. No matter how much he thinks what he is doing is suitable for his interests, the neglect of his wife's flourishing will result in his own destruction.

For these reasons, husbands should not be bitter toward their wives (Col 3:19). Christ is never bitter toward his bride, the church. Instead, Christ is perfectly patient, gentle, and understanding of his bride (1 Cor 13:4–7). Jesus volunteered to be made like his bride in every respect so that he could be merciful and faithful (Heb 2:17). Because he entered into his bride's experience, the bridegroom is able to sympathize with her weaknesses and extend her "mercy and … grace to help" her (Heb 4:15–16). Christ is the bridegroom who humbled himself to become an understanding and merciful helper to his bride.

That is why Peter exhorts, "Husbands, in the same way, live with your wives in an understanding way, as with a weaker partner, showing them honor as coheirs of the grace of life" (1 Pet 3:7). Terry L. Wilder reminds us, "Weaker partner denotes physical weakness and should not be taken to mean that wives are morally or intellectually inferior to their husbands. Husbands are typically stronger physically."[2] As the one who could leverage his physical strength to abuse his wife and force her to serve him, he is to resist this temptation to rule her. Instead, he should understand the experience of being the physically weaker partner. Through that understanding, like Christ with the church, he should be gracious to her. He should honor her as someone who inherits salvation and all its privileges in the same way that the bridegroom shares his inheritance with the bride.

The husband who refuses to enter into his wife's experiences (thinking empathy to be a worthless pursuit) is not Christic—he is anti-Christ. The husband whose pride prevents him from becoming like her in every respect so that he can be merciful and faithful is not a model of Christ—he is playing with being a picture of Satan. The husband who seeks to rule over his wife is not a picture of the Christ; he is a picture of the consequence described in Genesis 3:16.

In light of this, what does it mean for the wife to "submit to" (Eph 5:22; Col 3:18; 1 Pet 3:1) her husband? Before moving any further, we should note that the instruction is in reference to *their* husbands—that is, to her own husband, not any other. Women, and wives in particular, are nowhere called to obey all husbands or all men. Nothing in the New Testament even hints at the idea that Christian women should be inclined to defer to, obey, or be led by all men in general. That is not a biblical concept.

We find help from another passage that incorporates the word submit. In Hebrews 13:17, the author exhorts Christians to "obey your leaders and submit to them." In this sentence, the Greek word translated "submit" is the same as that used in the wives' instruction in Ephesians 5:22, Colossians 3:18, and 1 Peter 3:1. The author of Hebrews uses two words together "obey ... and submit." These words are used as near synonyms, each informing the meaning of the other. The word "obey" contains the idea of "be persuaded by."

In Hebrews 13:17, how these Christians submit to their leaders is by being persuaded by them. Submission here is being persuaded. The leaders mentioned are those who keep watch over their souls, most likely referring to local church elders. So, how do these leaders persuade and win submission? We see this in Hebrews 13:7: "Remember your leaders who have spoken God's word to you." They persuaded them by teaching them the word of God.

Elders rule a congregation through—and only through—persuading with God's word, the Bible. The authority of church elders is their teaching of the word alone. If it is not in God's word, they may not insist on submission in any way. Elders have no biblical grounds for forcing the submission of any Christian nor the church as a whole. They may appeal from the word but not demand and insist. The individual Christian and the gathered church always have free agency—the right and liberty to decide based on their understanding.

Therefore, if the elders' simple reasoning from the word of God does not persuade the individual Christian or the congregation, they have no obligation to submit. The attitude of the church ought to be that of Martin Luther at the Diet of Worms: "Unless I am convinced by Scripture and plain reason ... my conscience is captive to the word of God. ... for to go against conscience is neither right nor safe." Luther refused to submit to church leadership's demands if they failed to convince him by plain reasoning from the Scripture.

The call to submission in Hebrews 13:17 is almost identical to Ephesians 5:22, Colossians 3:18, and 1 Peter 3:1. As she is one flesh with her husband, she should be open to being persuaded by him, to join him as an ally in the purpose of marriage—to display the glory of Christ in the gospel. The call to submission is nothing more than what God describes in Genesis 3:16: "Your desire will be for your husband." The wife should want to partner with her husband in doing what God has called his people to do. Insofar as his intentions are wise and consistent with Christ's mission for his people, she should be inclined to join him. Her inclination is fitting, Peter insists, even when a husband is not a believer.[3] But as with the church (and Luther), the wife always maintains free agency. That is why the command is given to the wife and not the husband. She has no obligation to submit to anything that would contradict Scripture and plain reason. He is never allowed to "make her obey and submit." Her submission is always free and voluntary. Because she has been assured of her value and knows she is worthy of respect, she knows that she is free to walk alongside her husband and, in humility and love, to seek his flourishing. This is what Christic submission looks like: it comes from a place of strength and free agency.

That tells us that a wife is not allowed to submit to a demand or request that violates her conscience, contradicts God's word, or is adverse to her flourishing. A wife should never consider a husband's request that she join him in sin; in such a case, she should be inclined to disobey him fully and immediately. A wife ought never to be encouraged to endure abuse from her husband in any form; in such a case, she should remove herself to safety as soon as possible. A husband who is an unrepentant abuser in any category has forsaken the marriage covenant; she is not obliged to remain in it.

… IMITATING CHRIST IN
VOLUNTARY HUMILITY …

Both the words in this phrase are essential. Both the husband and the wife are called to humility—and that humility is voluntary, not forced.

For the husband, voluntary humility looks like Jesus surrendering his desires ("Father, if you are willing, take this cup away from me—nevertheless, not my will, but yours, be done," Luke 22:42) to sacrifice himself for the good of his bride ("Christ also loved us and gave himself for us, a sacrificial and fragrant offering to God," Eph 5:2). His desires, interests, and dreams do not determine the marriage's direction; *her flourishing does.*

Likewise with the wife. She is voluntarily inclined to be persuaded by him and cooperate with him to fulfill God's mission. She is not required to do anything and everything he wants. Here, someone may object that Paul says that "wives are to submit to their husbands in everything" (Eph 5:24). Doesn't "everything" mean *everything*? No, it doesn't. "Everything" cannot mean *everything*, as this would require her to sin, something that is never allowed. We understand "everything" in the context of the entire sentence: "Now as the church submits to Christ, so also wives are to submit to their husbands in everything."

What does it look like for the church to submit to Christ "in everything?" We can learn much by recognizing what the church submitting to Christ *is not*. Christ does not micromanage the church. Have you considered how much free agency Jesus gives us? Most often, we have very general commands to live in a way consistent with his character. But we're never told precisely what that looks like. For example, God's word tells us, "Whether you eat or drink, or whatever you do, do every-

> Doesn't "everything" mean *everything*? No, it doesn't. "Everything" cannot mean *everything*, as this would require her to sin, something that is never allowed.

thing for the glory of God" (1 Cor 10:31). Christ tells us to eat for his glory, but he does not tell me whether I order steak, chicken, or tofu in my burrito. He tells me to dress modestly, but he does not tell me which fabrics or color combinations to choose. Scripture offers a general principle, "Glorify God in your eating," that comes with vast freedom to choose according to our desires. Therefore, to be called to submit to everything "as the church submits to Christ" can never mean "submit to being micromanaged." God does not call a wife to submit to a husband who tells her what she may and may not wear, eat, listen to, etc. He should encourage her to glorify God in those activities and then take joy as he watches her make these decisions according to how God designed her as an individual.

Likewise, Jesus persuades his bride through his word with great patience, understanding, grace, and mercy. He never forces obedience, nor does he manipulate or abuse the church to get his way. The church can never submit to manipulation, abuse, impatience, tantrums, micromanaging, or force against her will because Christ never engages in these activities. Therefore, for a wife to submit to her husband in these selfish things is *not* to submit like the church to Christ—for *that type of submission never happens*! It is also not good for the husband's soul.

Likewise, the call to submit does not mean that she will never take primary initiative for leadership, protection, and provision in the home. The Bible commends women who exhort men and commends men who listen to the voice of their wives. The daughters of Zelophehad are right to speak with imperatives, telling Moses and the leaders of Israel to give them an inheritance (see Num 27). Even after marriage, they (and not their husbands) take the initiative to remind Joshua and Israel's leadership to give them their inheritance in the land (see Num 36; Josh 17). Naomi and then Ruth take the initiative to propose marriage to Boaz—and then he does what his future mother-in-law and wife tell him to do.

Christ tells his bride to speak to him in prayer—and teaches us to pray using imperatives: "Give us today our daily bread" (see Matt 6:9–13). Jesus commends prayer that looks like a widow pounding on a judge's door until he grants her request for relief (see Luke 18:1–8). On a wartime walkie-talkie, soldiers in the trenches tell commanding officers what to do. In this way, Christ is inclined to be persuaded by our appeals to him to do a certain thing. Thus, whatever submission means, it *does not* mean a passive wife who never exhorts, initiates, speaks, persuades, or leads. King Lemuel's mother taught him to seek a wife who uses her strength to take the initiative, going outside the home to protect and provide for the family (Prov 31:10–31). A woman who will not do these things is one whom she says can destroy kings (Prov 31:3). Thus, far from the wife being passive and only responsive, the flourishing of marriage depends in some way on her being strong and taking the initiative for protection and provision.

... RECIPROCAL BENEVOLENCE AND MUTUAL FLOURISHING ...

Love and benevolent care go both ways in the marriage covenant. They each are concerned for the flourishing of the other, for they are one flesh.

It would be ridiculous to assume that because the command to love is given to the husband, the wife is not called to love him. Of course, she is! We see this plainly in the relationship between Christ and the church: "We love because he first loved us" (1 John 4:19). As the love between Christ and the church is reciprocal, so it is between the husband and wife. And the call for her to love him is no different. A husband is called to sacrifice his own interests to pursue her flourishing. Likewise, a wife is to incline herself to set aside her interests to join him in flourishing (just as Jesus the man set aside his will for the Father's will—this is Christic). In a genuine way, the commands to the husband and the wife both require the very same thing.

> A husband is called to sacrifice his own interests to pursue her flourishing. Likewise, a wife is to incline herself to set aside her interests to join him in flourishing.

We see this regard for mutual flourishing in the relationship between Christ and the church. Christ is concerned for the flourishing of his bride: "I have come so that they may have life and have it in abundance" (John 10:10). Likewise, the church is concerned for Christ's flourishing in that it exists to see the word about Christ spread to the ends of the earth. If it does not cooperate in the pursuit of Christ's flourishing, it will wither and die. If Christ does not work for the church's flourishing, the church will not fulfill the Great Commission. God's purposes on earth are only accomplished insofar as Christ and his bride are devoted to mutual flourishing. The same is true for a marriage.

... AS THEY RECOGNIZE AND RESPECT ONE ANOTHER'S VALUE ...

Moses tells the Israelites, "God has chosen you to be a people for his treasured possession, out of all the peoples who are on the face of the earth" (Deut 7:6 ESV). God's people are his *treasured possession*—he values them more than anything on earth. Likewise, Christ loves and cherishes his church. Jesus never demeans, condemns, or shames his bride. Thus, a husband is called to value and cherish his wife more than anything on earth. He wants to be with her. He respects her.

Likewise, the church is called to recognize and respect the value of Christ. The church is never to demean, condemn, or shame Christ. So it is with a wife toward her husband. She is to recognize and respect him as a valuable person, made in the image of God and being transformed into the image of Christ. This too is Christic, for Christ always respected and cherished his Father as he lived on earth.

... AND PURSUE UNITY WITH ONE ANOTHER.

The culmination of the creation of the woman is the man pursuing perfect unity with her. Genesis 2 does not conclude, "Therefore the man shall leave his father and mother to rule over her and have her as his servant to do his bidding at a cost to herself." No, it concludes, "This is why a man leaves his father and mother and bonds with his wife, and they become one flesh. Both the man and his wife were naked, yet felt no shame" (Gen 2:24–25). He pursues unity—a bond with his wife—that is so perfect they can be described as one flesh, naked with no shame. That is a description of *perfect unity*. In this union, neither rules over the other. Instead, according to God's design, they will rule (see Gen 1:26) together.

That is what we see in the relationship between Christ and the church. The final picture we have of the new heavens and new earth is Christ reigning *with* his bride. Listen to the new song of the saints in heaven:

> You are worthy to take the scroll
> and to open its seals,
> because you were slaughtered,
> and you purchased people
> for God by your blood
> from every tribe and language
> and people and nation.
> You made them a kingdom
> and priests to our God,
> and they will reign on the earth. (Rev 5:9–10)

The Lamb that was slain and now reigns has done what with his people (his bride)? He has made them "a kingdom and priests to our God." And what will they do as a result? "And *they* will *reign* on the earth."

In Revelation, we later read, "Blessed and holy is the one who shares in the first resurrection! The second death has no power over them, but they will be priests of God and of Christ, and they will reign with him for a thousand years" (20:6). Note: they will reign *with him.* And note the last mention of "reign" in all the Bible: "and they will reign forever and ever" (22:5). "They" refers to his servants who worship him (22:3)—that is, those who submitted to his call and joined him in his purposes on earth. Christ's purpose for his bride is that he and she would reign together in unity. (Her reigning with him is also Christic—for Christ not only gives the kingdom to his Father, but the Father, Son, and Holy Spirit rule in perfect unity throughout eternity. To pursue such a union is Christlike of a wife.)

If such is the relationship between Christ and the church in the new covenant, what should it be between a husband and wife in the marriage covenant? They are to pursue a unity that allows them to *rule together* for the glory of God.

Whether you identify as complementarian or egalitarian or something else altogether, your understanding of marriage should be no less than Christic. For in a healthy, God-glorifying marriage, a husband and wife are both conformed to the image of Christ such that they are a covenantal display of Christ's glory, through which both husband and wife cooperate to display the gospel, imitating Christ in voluntary humility, reciprocal benevolence, and mutual flourishing as they recognize and respect one another's value and pursue unity with one another.

9

Parenting Boys and Girls Who Resemble Jesus Christ

Fathers, don't stir up anger in your children,
but bring them up in the training and
instruction of the Lord. —Ephesians 6:4

In the introduction, I (Elyse) traced my journey into a fuller understanding of the gospel. You'll remember that after I wrote *Because He Loves Me*, I wanted to push that grace-filled perspective out into every area of life, one of those areas being parenting. So, along with my daughter, Jessica Thompson, I wrote *Give Them Grace: Dazzling Your Kids with the Love of Jesus.*[1] In that book, we helped parents move past the rule-driven, fear-based, lockstep control seen in many parenting models. We wanted to help parents learn how to deeply connect the beauty of the gospel into the daily grind of getting kids to share their toys and sit still during church. Although we spoke in detail about the dos and don'ts of gospel-centered parenting, we didn't focus much on the kids themselves, what we were hoping to imprint on their lives, what our ultimate goals were. We'll do that now, but before we get started, here's a word about why that's so important.

THE EXVANGELICALS

During the last few years, we've heard many voices, especially from social media, of men and women identifying themselves as the "exvangelicals."[2] The story most of them tell is that they were raised in Christian homes, had originally acquiesced to their parents' religion, but now no longer believed.

Coming out from under a parents' influence is, of course, part of what it means to mature, to decide whether to make the faith one's own. On the other hand, many of the places where the exvangelicals now diverged seemed to be concerned with specific aspects of Christian culture and especially stereotypical parenting that really had nothing to do with what might be found in historic Christianity, like the doctrines listed in the Apostles' Creed. Many of them had been raised in "the purity culture"[3] or in ultra-conservative homes where the father was the unquestioned patriarch or where the world (and the people in it) were viewed as dangerous enemies. Daughters were taught that their primary reason for living was to get married, serve their husbands, and have children; that their highest value was as someone's wife or mother. Sons were taught that they needed to take initiative and embrace their role as leaders and expect women to submit to them. They were also taught that the struggle they had with sexual lust, (which is actually sin) would be cured by getting married and making their wife responsible for their sanctification in this area.[4]

However you may feel about any of the above, the truth is that it has nothing to do with the gospel. In Tara Westover's memoir, *Educated,*[5] we read about her family history and the religion that informed the way she and her siblings were raised. Honestly, as I heard Westover's story, I was sadly shocked by how similar it was to some of the ways we raised our kids. Of course, there were aspects of her history that I couldn't relate to at all, but way too much of it was sadly familiar. The family structure, especially the relationship between the males and females, was terribly toxic, abusive, and patriarchal. They would have said that they were Christian, but they lived that "faith" out in a Christless, gospel-free religion. They were Mormons.

Way too much of what passes for "Christian" parenting isn't Christian at all. If our philosophy, practice, and goals of parenting would seem appropriate in a Mormon or conservative atheistic family, it isn't Christian parenting. The only way we can be assured that we're following in the Bible's teaching on parenting is when we form it around these words that Paul used in Ephesians, *"of the Lord"* (Eph 6:4). We're convinced that some of those exvangelicals who are rejecting their parents' faith and training aren't rejecting actual Christianity. They're rejecting moralism, legalism, and stereotyping. And we don't blame them. We reject it, too.

"OF THE LORD"

Paul's words, *"of the Lord,"* have become so familiar that they don't shock or surprise us at all. They are part of the white noise that we assume in our Christianity. But to his early readers, this phrase would have been shocking. Greek fathers would have understood that they needed to discipline and instruct their children (primarily their sons). But the focus of their instruction would have been philosophers like Aristotle or Plato. Those fathers wanted to teach their sons how to live "the good life," how to be good, wise, successful citizens, and they went to Greek philosophy to do that.

The Jewish expatriates living in Ephesus would also have assumed that fathers should discipline and nurture their children. But the focus of their instruction would have been the Torah. They would have followed the teaching of Deuteronomy 6:1–2,

> This is the command—the statutes and ordinances—the LORD your God has commanded me to teach you, so that you may follow them in the land you are about to enter and possess. Do this so that you may fear the LORD your God all the days of your life by keeping all his statutes and commands I am giving you, your son, and your grandson, and so that you may have a long life.

Notice what the faithful Jewish father was supposed to do: teach his sons and grandsons how the statutes and ordinances would eventuate in a long life. The father was to repeat them to his children (Deut 6:7) and to recite the story of God's deliverance from slavery when his son asks him about the meaning of the "decrees, statutes, and ordinances that the LORD our God has commanded" (Deut 6:20).

Contrary to either the Greek or Jewish view, Paul commanded fathers to "bring [children] up in the training and instruction *of the Lord*" (Eph 6:4, emphasis added). This little phrase, "of the Lord," would have surprised his early readers. It is shorthand for all that we've been talking about in this book. It means that the most important truth parents can communicate to their children is the gospel.

What is training and instruction that is of the Lord? First of all, it's a gospel understanding of the purpose of rules: they can't make our children good, but they can help them see their need for the Savior.[6]

> Every way we try to make our kids good that isn't rooted in the good news of the life, death, resurrection, and ascension of Jesus Christ is damnable, crushing, despair-breeding, Pharisee-producing law. We'll either get shallow self-righteousness or blazing rebellion or both. ... We'll get moralistic kids who are cold and hypocritical and who look down on others, or you'll get teens who are rebellious and self-indulgent and who can't wait to get out of the house. ... We have to remember that in the life of our unregenerate children, the law is given for one reason only: to crush their self-confidence and drive them to Christ. The law also shows believing children what gospel-engendered gratitude looks like. But one thing is for sure. We aren't to give our children the law to make them good. It won't because it can't.[7]

Secondly, it's continually reminding them of the work of Jesus for lawbreakers: if they come to him by faith, he will forgive all their sins and grant to them his record of perfect obedience. They don't have to possess all the best toys or be the boss. They don't have to earn merit by being good girls and boys. Our children already have all they need by faith, whether they're winners or not: they have been loved, welcomed, adopted, and promised a future full of delight (see Matt 16:25; Luke 9:25; Rom 5:1, 8–9; 1 Pet 1:3–5).

And finally, our children are in the hands of the Lord. Their salvation and their perseverance in the faith is in God's hands (see Ps 68:20; Isa 12:2). So, as parents, we can relax and rest in God's good plans. We can be free to love them, to lovingly instruct and teach them about Jesus and how to love our neighbors and how to live lives to his glory. Imagine the joy of enjoying your children as fellow-heirs of God's love and not having to oversee their growth in presupposed gender roles.

> Our children already have all they need by faith, whether they're winners or not: they have been loved, welcomed, adopted, and promised a future full of delight.

OLD COVENANT DAUGHTERS AND SONS

Under the old covenant, the law declared a differentiation between the ways boys and girls were thought of, treated, and raised. From the eighth day of life, boys were marked with circumcision, a sign in the flesh (Gen 17:1–22) that declared that they were part of the covenant community. Girls, on the other hand, could only be assured of their membership in that community by their relationship to a circumcised father, husband, or son. As those who received the covenant sign, sons alone were raised to lead the way in Israel's relationship with the Lord. They were taught that the obligation, responsibility, and privilege of national representation belonged to them and not to their sisters. They alone bore the mark of their faith in their flesh. They alone would need to be trained to lead. Upon them alone was the burden to be Yahweh's representatives in the earth. This is demonstrated throughout the Old Testament as only sons are taught the obligations that came with their gender (see the book of Proverbs in particular). Of course, there are times, though comparatively few, where instructing children rather than sons is mentioned, but the preponderance is focused on the sons: they were to be groomed to be the head, they alone could be priests, they were God's representatives in the earth (see, e.g., Gen 12; Ps 127:3–4).

The life of a little girl under the old covenant was different. Although, unlike girls in the Greco-Roman world, who were frequently abandoned to die at birth, she was welcomed into the household faith, her value was always diminished. She didn't bear the sign. She could only be assured of her acceptance in the covenant community by her relationship with a man who did. While she was young, she was taught that her brothers had a privilege not available to her. Every time a boy viewed his genitalia, he knew, *I belong to God.* A little girl could know nothing like that. She would only be assured of her inclusion as her identity was tied to her father or brothers. Even as she matured and embraced the religion of her family, her identity would still be tied to her male relations, and then hopefully, if she was blessed, one day to a son of her own. Because of this, she needed to be taught from a young age how to care for a home because the home would be the place where those with the sign would reside and be raised.

As her father taught the family the Torah, she would learn that there was a differentiation between she and her brothers. When her mother birthed her, her mother would have been unclean for fourteen days. After her brothers were born, she was unclean for seven days. Once she began menstruating (a sign that she might be privileged to birth a son), she would be unclean for fourteen days (see Lev 12). On the other hand, if her brothers had a nocturnal emission, they would be unclean until evening (Deut 23:10).

Practically from day one of her life, she was taught to accept that there was something different about her. She only had value in a secondary way. Aside from the exception brought about by Zelophehad's daughters' request, she would not inherit anything from her father. She was completely dependent on her male relatives for life and especially for her identity as a godly woman. She could be given in marriage to anyone her father chose. Her attractiveness, homemaking skills, femininity, and piety (demonstrated primarily by her virginity and ultimately fertility) were all she had to rely on to interest a prospective husband and live a life of respectability, freed from destitution. She could not initiate a divorce if her husband didn't love her. Her entire value was tied to her reproductive system. She was even barred from the inner recesses of the synagogue in her village and the temple in Jerusalem. She was second class, and she knew it.

Because her brothers had different obligations and responsibilities, they needed to be trained in what passed for masculinity in that time. They would be called to mediate as priests in their home. They might be called to go to war to protect their family, so they needed to be trained in battle tactics. They were God's representatives to their family and to the watching world. Sons needed to be taught that they were the leaders. Daughters needed to be taught that they were the followers.

SONS AND DAUGHTERS ARE WELCOME HERE

But all of this—and we mean *all* of it—changed when the covenant sign of circumcision was replaced by the covenant sign of baptism. Whether you hold to paedo- or credobaptism, it doesn't matter for this discussion. What matters is that daughters are welcomed. The door has been thrown open. When the curtain in the temple was torn at Christ's death, it was torn for both girls and boys. The "keep out" sign was torn down. "All are welcome—even girls!" replaced it.

Girls could now bear the sign of inclusion in the new covenant family, the church. They were baptized. Like their brothers, girls were accorded the full rights of adoption, inheritance, instruction, and citizenship (see Rom 8:29; Gal 4:28; 1 Thess 1:4, 4:1; 5:27). Girls could approach the throne room of God (2 Thess 3:1; Heb 10:19) because they bore they mark of entrance into the community of believers: baptism. And, like their brothers, although they still needed a relationship with a circumcised, baptized male, they had it: they were brothers and sisters of Jesus Christ (Heb 2:17). They were part of his bride. They were sons and daughters of God, and they would equally

be called to faith and to follow him into the water (Matt 3:14f). And
when girls and boys would wonder, from time to time, whether they
were really his, they would remember their baptism. They had been
indelibly marked as his. Their gender would no longer exclude them
or give them special privilege.

Way too much of what is commonly pushed as "Christian" parenting for daughters and sons completely misses the realities these
changes brought in with the new cov-
enant sign. There simply are *no* commands about what to teach daughters
that differ in any way from what is
required from sons. Daughters are to
be taught to love and care for their
family. So are sons. Daughters are to
be taught to be pure and modest. So
are sons. Daughters are to be taught
to be devout. So are sons. Daughters
are to be taught to use their gifts for
the community of the faith. So are
sons. Way too much is drawn from
the old covenant about what it means
to raise masculine sons and feminine
daughters. Far too many girls have been made to feel that their only
option and entire worth as human beings is tied to finding a husband
and giving birth. Far too many boys have been pushed into "manly"
activities (whether they liked them or not). This really must stop.

> When girls and boys would wonder, from time to time, whether they were really his, they would remember their baptism. They had been indelibly marked as his. Their gender would no longer exclude them or give them special privilege.

The surprise we find in the New Testament are the many women
who had callings and ministries to the entire family of God. Jesus welcomed and utilized them. Paul honored and employed them. Churches
were founded in their homes. They had ministries of great importance
to the church. An unmarried European woman, Lydia, led the way for
all her sisters and brothers into the kingdom of God. Marriage, though
good if that is one's inclination or God's design, is just one option for
believing women.

CHRISTIC DAUGHTERS AND SONS

What does it look like to raise children who are Christic? In a nutshell, it looks like teaching them the many truths we've talked about in this book. There isn't a particular teaching for boys and a different one for girls. There's no place where parents are told to make sure their daughters are feminine and their boys know how to load a rifle. Since the New Testament is nearly silent about parenting (compare Eph 6:4; Col 3:21), we should be careful not to add to it. There's a reason that Paul didn't tell parents what to teach sons as opposed to what to teach their daughters. Sons and daughters are equally in need of hearing the good news. He only said teach them the gospel and don't exasperate them.

We must wonder whether at least a part of the pushback we're hearing from the exvangelicals is the outworking of the exasperation (Col 3:21) and stirring up of the anger (Eph 6:4) Paul warned about. If all that a child has heard about Christianity has to do with being nice, polite, voting a certain way, and following certain mid-century gender stereotypes, then we understand their angst. Way too many girls are reacting against stereotypical straightjacketing that plans out their whole life without reference to their inclinations, giftings, weaknesses, strengths, or even God's design. Far too many boys are responding to the toxic masculinity that demeans them if they're not manly enough (what is that?) or if they don't enjoy watching MMA fights.

The deadly dysfunction in Isaac's family is a perfect picture of two types of masculinity and what happens when parents favor one over the other.

> When the boys grew up, Esau became an expert hunter, an outdoorsman, but Jacob was a quiet man who stayed at home. Isaac loved Esau because he had a taste for wild game, but Rebekah loved Jacob. (Gen 25:27)

You likely know the end of the story: how their parents' favoritism eventuated in conflict and the rupturing of the family. The gospel teaches us that each of our children have been created in the image of

God and are being recreated in the image of the Son as unique individuals with unique gifts and inclinations. Perhaps one child's predisposition will align more closely with your own. Perhaps not. Let's just
be careful not to assume that the propensity that appeals to us means
that they're godlier. They're unique, and that's a wonderful thing.

Of course, we're not saying that one way of expressing gender
is better than another. We're not saying that staying home reading
books is better than being an out-
doorsman. Nor are we saying that a
woman who chooses a career in academia is better than one who stays
home and raises children. What we
are saying is that any stereotypical
straightjacketing of gender *in any
way* is harmful, exasperating, dis-
heartening, and completely unbiblical. Our children don't need to be
taught how to be masculine or feminine. This isn't Sparta or Athens.

> The gospel teaches
> us that each of our
> children have been
> created in the image
> of God and are being
> recreated in the image
> of the Son as unique
> individuals with unique
> gifts and inclinations.

This is the New Jerusalem, and our children need to be taught the
lifegiving, soul-nourishing freedom of justification through faith alone.

HEARTS SHAPED BY THE GOSPEL

You'll remember that in Chapters Six and Seven we examined what it
looked like to be Christic brothers and sisters. We said that it would
be seen in lives lived out in ways that could be observed in our relationships with one another. Let's consider how those characteristics
might be taught to and seen in the lives of the little Christic believers
in our homes.

- *Recognizing and respecting* others' value as made in God's
  image (Rom 12:10; Gen 1:27).
      Christic children must be taught the truth that their
  siblings and friends, whether male or female, have value

because they are made in God's image. What that means is that boys are taught they aren't better, godlier, or of greater value than girls simply because of their gender. Of course, the opposite is true also. Girls need to be taught that their brothers and male friends are God's precious creation and not to be denigrated simply because they're male. There is no place for misogynistic teachings about all girls needing to submit to all boys or girls only having value if boys like them. There is also no place for misandrist teachings that disrespect God's image in boys or assume that they're all selfish bullies or uncaring brutes.

- *Welcoming* one another into loving familial relationships because we are his sisters and brothers, members of one family (Rom 12:10; 1 Cor 11:33).

  Girls and boys need to be taught to welcome and love one another—not simply because they may be members of the same biological family, but because they are members of an eternal and more glorious one: the family of God. Sometimes that would mean that girls would welcome their little brothers into their play and vice versa, with never a whisper of "No Boys/Girls Allowed." Of course, sometimes children of the same gender love to play together, and we don't want to say that should never happen. It's just that neither one should learn that they're automatically excluded from "all the fun stuff" simply because of their gender.

- *Humbling* ourselves before one another, joyfully relinquishing the desire for authority and control (Phil 2:3; Gal 5:13).

  Like their older fellow believers, children need to be taught how to defer to one another in humility. Of all the things we need to both learn and teach ourselves; this may be the most difficult. No one likes to relinquish control. We certainly don't like to think that others are more important than ourselves. The only way to be free from our innate motivation to be the boss or make sure that everything goes the way we want is by soaking our soul in the humility and condescension of our elder brother, Jesus. He's the only one who can assure us that we'll be okay even if others get to guide the conversation, direction, or activity. Because he has not even spared "his own Son but gave him up for us all. How will he not also with him grant us everything" (Rom 8:32), and because he promised that he has richly provided us with all things to enjoy (1 Tim 6:17), we can learn to release control and, as the kids might say, "chillax."

> Like their older fellow believers, children need to be taught how to defer to one another in humility. Of all the things we need to both learn and teach ourselves; this may be the most difficult. No one likes to relinquish control.

Neither boys nor girls should be taught that they should always be in charge simply because of their gender. Boys should never be taught that their sisters should always acquiesce to their demands and serve them just because of their gender. Girls should never be taught that they have to do what boys tell them to, nor should they be taught to always try to be in charge because they are girls. Nor should they be taught that they are responsible for the sins of the boys around them. We all have enough of a burden to recognize and repent of our own sins—girls don't need to take on the responsibility of the sins their brothers struggle with. Both brothers *and* sisters need to learn to "put on the Lord Jesus Christ" and

not make plans "for the flesh to gratify its desires" (Rom
13:14). Humility of heart is not something any of us learns
easily or by nature. It is a function of continuous pursuit
of faith in Christlikeness.

- *Pursuing* unity with one another (Gal 3:28; Eph 4:3; Col
  3:14; Eph 2:14).

   Thinking too highly of ourselves is endemic (Rom
12:3), especially in this culture of belief in wholesale
self-esteem. Although it is a good to teach our children
to value their creation as *imago Dei,* they should also be
taught the dangers of thinking that they are better than
others. The result of this kind of unwarranted thinking is always conflict with others—the fight for preeminence, the fight to be boss, the fight to prove that one is
in the right. As Paul wrote, "Everyone should look out
not only for his own interests, but also for the interests of
others" (Phil 2:4). As we've said consistently throughout
this book, whenever the primary message is "who gets to
be in charge," unity will be rare. If all our children care
about are their own interests, there will never be unity
in the family. James asks, "What is the source of wars and
fights among you? Don't they come from your passions
that wage war within you? You desire and do not have.
You murder and covet and cannot obtain. You fight and
wage war" (Jas 4:1–3).

   The Greek word translated "passions" above is ἡδονή,
which is a "state or condition of experiencing pleasure for
any reason, pleasure, delight, enjoyment, pleasantness."[8]
The New Living Translation of this verse is, "What is
causing the quarrels and fights among you? Don't they
come from the evil desires at war within you?" The reason
children squabble and fight is that they have selfish

desires. They want to be boss. Brothers and sisters both want to enjoy the pleasure of overseeing what others do. This desire, as James says, is anything but godly.

Sadly, some boys are taught that it is their place, just by virtue of their gender, to be in authority. Since there is no passage in Scripture that teaches that all males at all times are to be in charge, and since the very desire to want things your way is evil, this teaching signifies there will be conflict in all relationships. Again, perhaps this is what we're seeing with the exvangelicals. Of course, it is also destructive to teach girls to *fight* for preeminence—though we don't see a lot of that in much Christian fare. There's a place in God's kingdom for Deborahs and for Abigails, for Esthers, Hannahs, Marys (all of them), and for St. Photine.

God will call some of our children into positions of leadership, and that is a good thing. It's good to train them to accept responsibility with humility and diligence. But it's especially good to teach them that leadership isn't certain just because they're one gender or the other.

- And finally, *devoting* ourselves to the flourishing of all (Rom 14:19; 1 Thess 5:11; 1 Cor 14:12).

If we're to be Christic moms and dads who train Christic girls and boys, we'll want them to learn what it means to be devoted to the building up and encouragement of others. We want them to experience the joy of watching others flourish. We might ask our son, "What could you do today to encourage your sister to remember she is loved by God?" We might ask our daughter, "How could you show your brother how important he is to the Lord today?" We might say, "You know there is real power in the words you say. You could help your brother/sister believe that they can follow the Lord. What do you see in them that shows you they have gifts God could use?" We know that might take a little convincing and probably more than a little training but think how worthwhile it would be for them to hear words of encouragement from one another.

CHRISTIC DAUGHTERS

It also looks like training girls to love and appreciate their bodies, that beauty, strength, and gifting is not the measure of their worth, and that though the Lord may indeed gift them with a husband and children, that's not their highest calling. They are free from any stereotype they may have heard about what girls are supposed to be like.

Since God has gendered them as female, they can ask the Lord to help them learn to love their body. If they feel jealous of boys and their strengths, they can ask for wisdom to see the goodness of being female. As they mature and they begin to change, they can see what is frequently a monthly painful difficulty as a way for the Lord to teach them what he knows about suffering and about how giving life to others always comes at a cost.

We understand how hard this might be for some. It appears that boys get to go through life more easily: They get to go out without their shirts on when it's hot. They don't have to wear bras or try to dress modestly all the time. They don't have to worry as much about attack when walking alone. They don't have to carry feminine products with them or try to figure out how to get to a toilet in time. They don't have to stay out of the pool or worry about an accident when they're menstruating. In addition, boys don't have to wear makeup or worry about how their hair looks or carry a purse with all the items above. And they seem to excel more easily at games or sports and are more frequently chosen to lead, whether they deserve it or not. Accepting their own worth while fighting envy of what seems to be an easier life is part of what it means to accept the identity of being a woman. Yes, in some ways, being a woman is a more difficult road. But knowing that the Lord is loving and good and has only good plans for us can help. One of the studies that might help is looking at the ways Jesus interacted with women.[9]

Because God values female bodies and sees them as beautiful for his purposes, woman can live that way with self-respect. Our daughters need to understand this: contrary to much teaching in what's known as the purity culture, virginity is not the most important thing about them.[10] Not by a longshot. The most important thing is believing that she belongs to our loving Savior and is walking with him in humility through all sins, follies, missteps, and faith. And when she questions whether the above is sufficient, she can remember that she bears the sign of his covenant on her body.

> Our daughters need to understand this: contrary to much teaching in what's known as the purity culture, virginity is not the most important thing about them. Not by a longshot. The most important thing is believing that she belongs to our loving Savior.

It's very difficult for girls to believe that they have value if they don't fit a certain mold. For instance, a daughter might struggle if she's not very pretty (by worldly standards) or if she's clumsy, uncoordinated, or "throws like a girl." Maybe she's happiest when she's got her nose stuck in a book or when she doesn't have to think about how she looks. Other girls really love working out or getting their makeup done and shopping for a new outfit. Whatever your daughters' giftings or inclinations, the way they dress or spend their interests does not make them valuable or feminine. They are valuable because God created them. They are feminine for the same reason. You can let them find their own way as girls, giving them gentle guidance when they might be tempted to obsess over their beauty or size. You can gently remind them that true beauty doesn't consist in "outward things like elaborate hairstyles or wearing gold jewelry or fine clothes, but rather what is inside the heart—the imperishable quality of a gentle and quiet spirit, which is of great worth in God's sight" (1 Pet 3:3–4).

By the way, having a "gentle and quiet spirit" is not the same thing as what is usually called femininity. It doesn't mean you never call out wrong or speak above a whisper. What it does mean is that you don't try to wrest control for situations or demand your own way. Rather, it means you trust in the Lord's goodness in all things.

Too many girls are taught, either in their home, in the church, or in the culture, that their worth is bestowed by the opinion of boys or men. They're taught that they don't have value unless they're in a relationship, and this only gets worse as they get older. Rather than teaching daughters that their worth comes from pleasing their father (as is found in some patriarchal homes)[11] or from their boyfriends (as is found in the culture), they are to be assured that they have value simply because they have been created in the image of God and are members of the household of faith.

It may or may not be God's plan for your daughter to produce children. If it is, that's good. If it isn't, that's also good. What is important is that she seeks to fulfill the Great Commission—making disciples and teaching them the gospel. Perhaps your daughter will want to play with baby dolls and loves holding little children. Perhaps not. Her pathway is her pathway, not ours to fashion. There are women who by inclination simply don't want to have children. There are others who want nothing more. Either or anything in between is perfectly acceptable.

The kingdom of God is open before believing daughters. None of the gifting passages from Romans or 1 Corinthians that we've already considered are gendered. None of the virtue passages are gendered. A woman might pursue a doctorate

> God's kingdom and his gifts, callings, and welcome are open to her now, and she is to spend her days seeking to fulfill the Great Commission by loving her neighbors.

degree in English literature, or she might spend her mornings reading *The Jesus Storybook Bible* to her babies. She might get up early to train with the men in her unit, or she might teach in a preschool. God's kingdom and his gifts, callings, and welcome are open to her now, and she is to spend her days seeking to fulfill the Great Commission by loving her neighbors.

CHRISTIC SONS

What does it look like in particular to train our sons to be like Christ? They are free from any stereotype they may have heard about what boys are supposed to be like: The world (and the church) places unrealistic expectations upon boys, standards that are not found in Scripture. To name a few, boys are expected to be particularly assertive, physically strong, competitive, and striving for athletic prowess—all these in ways that girls are not. It means that we can teach them to love and appreciate their bodies, and that strength and gifting are not the measure of their worth. They have been made male, and maleness is good.

Since the Bible commands that we are to care for our body,[12] we all should strive to find an exercise that fits with our needs. But being buff or being flabby are simply not the measure of a man's worth or his masculinity. Health is important, but as Paul says, it's of little value in comparison to godly character (1 Tim 4:8). That does not mean that all boys are excessively muscular or capable of amazing physical feats. As with women, physical strength varies from boy to boy—and that's okay! Living by faith in Christ with humility and gentleness is our aim. What ultimately counts is using their strength and gifting for the upbuilding of God's kingdom and for the good of those who do not have what they do.

In the same way that their sisters are not to be defined by relationships with boys, they are not defined by their relationship with girls. Men can prize women (no matter how they look outwardly) for their relationship with the Lord and their godly character. Relationships with girls are not their worth. As they struggle with sexual desires as they age, they can keep this in proper perspective, remembering that sex is designed by God to serve the other and not to please ourselves alone. Boys have value simply because they have been created in the image of God and are members of the household of faith, just like girls.

Having a family or the "right" career doesn't give them value either. Some boys will love color and fabric and want to be interior designers. Other boys won't notice if they're wearing two different socks when they roll out of bed and pick up their surveying tools. Some men love to work in finance while others delight in working in a classroom or social services. Others love to ride waves or horses or drive Formula 1 cars. It's all good.

Like girls, it's very difficult for boys to believe that they have value if they don't fit a certain mold. Boys are free to follow their gifts and inclinations in pursuit of the kingdom of God's goal of discipleship among the nations. Some will love to lead. Many will not. Boys don't have to lead according to tradition. They can example what it means to follow Jesus in humility and lead by pursuing unity with those around them.

> Boys don't have to lead according to tradition. They can example what it means to follow Jesus in humility and lead by pursuing unity with those around them.

As we close this chapter on raising Christic boys and girls, here's our bottom line: Aside from very specific instructions about biological functions, both genders are equally welcomed into God's family and are to be welcomed by one another without prejudice. There is no place in Christ's kingdom for either misogyny or misandry. We are to love our differently gendered neighbors as ourselves, all for the glory of the Son who was made human just like his brothers and sisters (Heb 2:17).

10

Siblings in the Household of God

But if I should be delayed, I have written so that you will know how people ought to conduct themselves in God's household, which is the church of the living God, the pillar and foundation of the truth. —*1 Timothy 3:15*

What is a church? When I (Eric) am asked that question, the same picture always comes to mind: the US Embassy in Riga, Latvia. The summer after my freshman year of college, I boarded a plane with a team of strangers to spend the summer ministering to college students in Riga. Shortly after we arrived in Latvia's capital city, we visited the US chancery to register our presence for the summer. As we approached, a familiar sight greeted us.

Inside the wrought iron fence stood a flagpole atop which flew the American flag. Entering the building felt like being back in the States (in a US government building, but the US nonetheless). The signage was in English first. The employees spoke our language without an accent. They treated us as though we belonged and were not merely visitors. It felt like home.

For the rest of summer, as we gathered each day near the Freedom Monument at the city center, I could look a few blocks away to see a glimpse of home. I would see Old Glory flying and know that, in that building, fellow citizens of my country were there to serve, help, and, if needed, protect me. There, in a foreign land where I was a temporary resident, was an outpost of home. So, when someone asks me what a church is, I tend to answer, "An embassy (or outpost) of the kingdom of Christ."

An embassy is "a group of people who work under an ambassador and represent their country in a foreign country."[1] That's precisely what a local church is: an embassy of Christ's kingdom. A local church is a group of citizens of the kingdom of Christ, representing that kingdom in a foreign land. The Father has "rescued us from the domain of darkness and transferred us into the kingdom of the Son he loves" (Col 1:13).

We're citizens of the kingdom of the Son, but his "kingdom is not of this world" (John 18:36). That means we are foreigners, living away from our true home (Heb 13:14). We are strangers and exiles (1 Pet 2:11)—but we are far more than just that.

Christians are ambassadors for Christ, representing the King's interests in this world (2 Cor 5:20). God has committed to us "the ministry of reconciliation" (2 Cor 5:18). God made us responsible for communicating the message of reconciliation to the world; he makes his appeal for reconciliation in Christ through us (2 Cor 5:19–20). Already we begin to see how this reflects the purpose of men and women.

The local church is an embassy—the headquarters for ambassadors living in a foreign land. Like the individual ambassadors, the embassy is not allowed to conduct itself in any fashion it chooses. It is given instructions for its order, purpose, and mission from the King. Kingdom representatives gather at the embassy for consultation, support, and instruction from their Chief Officer. If they are to accomplish his diplomatic mission, the representatives must share an understanding of their mission, instructions, and the necessity of working in unison to accomplish the King's Great Commission. Already, we can see how this might connect with the purpose of male and female: in Christ, believing men and women are to glorify God by cooperating for the advance of the gospel and imitating Christ in voluntary humiliation, reciprocal benevolence, and mutual flourishing.

In this chapter, we'll define a *Christic* church, looking particularly at how male and female Christians should conduct themselves in the embassy of Christ.

WHAT IS A CHRISTIC CHURCH?

As with some of the other chapters, we will offer a definition and then unpack it phrase by phrase.

A *Christic* church is a body of gospel-believing brothers and sisters who covenant together to glorify God by displaying Christ through ministry partnership, shared authority, respectful unity, voluntary humility, reciprocal benevolence, and mutual flourishing.

A *CHRISTIC* CHURCH IS ...

It is worth reemphasizing that our vision for all things—being male and female included—is shaped by how we see and receive God in the person and work of Jesus Christ. The church cannot be called the "body of Christ" unless it takes on the form and shape of Christ. If we begin with the questions of who has authority and who can do what, we've started in the wrong place. The church is first and foremost about God's glory in Christ, so the person and work of Christ must be both our beginning and our end.

> The church is first and foremost about God's glory in Christ, so the person and work of Christ must be both our beginning and our end.

... A BODY OF GOSPEL-BELIEVING ...

First and foremost, the church is an assembly of people who believe the gospel. To be an ambassador to this world for Christ, we must know Christ in a way the world does not (see 2 Cor 5:16). One must be made a new creation by receiving the grace of God brought to us in the message of reconciliation—"That is, in Christ, God was reconciling the world to himself, not counting their trespasses against them, and he has committed the message of reconciliation to us" (2 Cor 5:19).

When Paul writes to the church, he refers to the individuals in the church as *saints* (e.g., Rom 1:7; 1 Cor 1:2; 2 Cor 1:1; Eph 1:1; Phil 1:1; Col 1:2). A saint is a person who is sanctified, who has been made holy in Christ (see 1 Cor 1:30). Likewise, Peter addresses the church as "those who have received a faith equal to ours through the righteousness of our God and Savior Jesus Christ" (2 Pet 1:1). The church is a body composed of gospel-confessing individuals.

To approach being brothers and sisters in the church, it is essential to acknowledge that all church members are gospel-believing. First, this matters because we cannot be Christic apart from faith in Christ. Second, this reminds us that we do not enter the church based on gender; we enter the church based on faith in Christ alone.[2] Men and women do not become members of God's family differently. A woman does not enter the church under the headship of her husband or her father. Each person—man or woman, adult or child, Jew or gentile, rich or poor—enters the same way: by personal faith in Jesus Christ, crucified for sin and raised from the dead. The entrance gate to the church—the gospel—is thoroughly egalitarian, for every person must enter the church on the same grounds, immediately establishing the equality of every member.

> The entrance gate to the church—the gospel—is thoroughly egalitarian, for every person must enter the church on the same grounds, immediately establishing the equality of every member.

... BROTHERS AND SISTERS ...

Paul's favorite term for believers in the church is "brothers and sisters."[3] Men and women living together as siblings is a fulfillment of God's design for creation. Recall what the man exclaimed after God brought the woman to him: "This one, at last, is bone of my bone and flesh of my flesh" (Gen 2:23). When we hear these words, we generally think of marriage. But that is not the *only* relationship the Bible uses "flesh of flesh" to describe.

Leviticus 18 covers several old covenant sexual prohibitions against sexual relations with family members.[4] In verse 6, the Lord says, "None of you shall approach any one of his close relatives to uncover nakedness. I am the LORD" (ESV). The Hebrew behind "close relative" is literally "flesh of his flesh."[5] This makes sense, particularly when we consider that blood relatives share our "flesh and bone." The closest blood relation is biological brother and sister, for they take their DNA from the same sources. As the first woman was created from the man's flesh and bone, she would have shared his DNA almost exactly. They were like brother and sister, only more so.

In the law, this use of "flesh of flesh" "includes not only those whom we would call blood relatives (*e.g.*, a biological parent or sibling) but also blood relatives of those related by marriage (in-laws and step-relatives).[6] Thus the English translation "close relatives." So, what the man exclaims in Genesis 2:23 is more than a "She's the same stuff as me!" (though he certainly means that). The man is exclaiming, "She's family." And, of course, the entire human family will descend from this man and woman.[7]

"Flesh of flesh" is not first a description of marriage; it is a description of close family. And that is what happens in marriage—the man and the woman become close family, "flesh of flesh." Thus, the "one flesh" union of marriage goes well beyond sexual intercourse—it speaks of the closest family relationship. God intended for husbands and wives to understand "flesh of flesh" from the brother-sister relationship.[8]

God intended for all men and women to relate to one another as brother and sister. While marriage stands out as one important "flesh of flesh" relationship, the use of "flesh of flesh" elsewhere demonstrates God intended for it to go further than that covenant. "Flesh of flesh" was to extend in a real way to every relationship between God's people.

Unfortunately, the introduction of sin twisted and corrupted the "flesh of flesh" relationship between men and women. Instead of loving one another as "close relatives," the man would "rule over" the woman. One brother would kill the other; a wicked man threatens his wives with domestic abuse (Gen 4). The "close relative" relationship gives way to self-service and violence.

What the fall corrupts, Christ redeems. In the incarnation, Jesus became "flesh of our flesh." His life fulfills God's will for what it means for a human to live as a sibling. His interactions with men and women demonstrate how a sibling should treat his sisters and brothers. Jesus is the true and greater Brother. Having fulfilled this righteousness, Jesus receives the violent curse in his flesh for all the ways his people failed to be brothers and sisters. Then the God-Man rose from the dead to bring them into the true family, where they know God as Father (Gal 4:4–6). Believers have the same Father as Jesus. "That is why Jesus is not ashamed to call them brothers and sisters" (Heb 2:11).

What sin corrupts, Christ redeems. God is transforming his people into the image of Christ, who is the image of God (see 2 Cor 3:18; 4:4). This is God's aim in all our sufferings and groanings in the weakness of the flesh:

> We know that all things work together for the good of those who love God, who are called according to his purpose. For those he foreknew he also predestined to be conformed to the image of his Son, so that he would be the firstborn among many brothers and sisters. (Rom 8:28–29)

What a magnificent phrase, "the firstborn among many brothers and sisters." Jesus is the big Brother of the family of God. More than that, he is the model of what we all shall be—brothers and sisters who look, sound, and act like our big Brother. *That is to say, the relationship between men and women in the local church is Christic; Christ shapes it.*

This sibling imagery controls how we act in the church—"I have written so that you will know how people ought to conduct themselves in God's household, which is the church of the living God" (1 Tim 3:15).

Christians are to honor one another in age-appropriate ways—older believers as parents and younger believers as siblings (1 Tim 5:1–2).

Believers are to treat one another "with all purity." This means that, unless that believer is your "flesh of flesh" spouse, you're to treat them as "flesh of flesh" family—and all manner of sexual relations are off the table. How should believers view sexual immorality between professing Christians? The same way God viewed Israelites engaging in the behaviors forbidden in Leviticus 18. The Lord says they are detestable acts by which the land is defiled, "so I am punishing it for its iniquity, and the land will vomit out its inhabitants" (Lev 18:24–28).

If the church does not learn to love one another as brothers and sisters, Christ will vomit it out of his mouth (Rev 3:16). This means the local church must respond with great seriousness to sexual sin within its membership, as God instructed the Israelites to respond to incest within its people. The one who does these things is to be cut off from God's people (see Lev 18:28–30). This is precisely how Paul instructs the church to respond to the case of a man sleeping with his father's wife (see 1 Cor 5:1–7). Every church today would be scandalized to learn that a woman was sleeping with her son. But God says that sexual immorality between brothers and sisters in the church is no different. Christ demands that we treat it accordingly. The church is to discipline the erring member, putting them outside the church in the hopes that it may produce repentance.

Tolerance of such sin risks corrupting the whole family. When this happens, men and women in the church stop seeing one another as "brother and sister" and start seeing one another in sexual terms. Men and women see each other as either seducers or sexual conquests, hunters or prey. This should not be so. We must be taught to see one another as "flesh of flesh" siblings—and tolerate nothing less.

If a youth minister pursues or uses a youth for sexual pleasure, this is not a mistake or a bad decision. It is a detestable act by which he defiles himself.[9] If a woman seduces the choir leader, she is not merely "taking the relationship a bit too far." She is manipulating her brother into having sex with her—something the world doesn't tolerate! If a pastor preys upon a counselee, forcing her to perform sexual favors "as a ministry to him," he has not committed adultery, a minor "moral indiscretion," or merely been caught in a "morally inappropriate relationship." He is anathema—a father figure raping his daughter. None of this is how Christ treats his brothers and sisters. It is not Christic; it is anti-Christ. Each of these acts is a sibling sexually preying on a "close relative," a sibling, the flesh of their flesh. To protect the entire family, they must be cut off from the church until they demonstrate true repentance.[10]

On the positive side, the brother-sister paradigm should motivate love between men and women in the church. A man should be no more afraid of having a conversation (or friendship) with a woman in the church than he should be afraid of interacting with his beloved sister. A woman should offer counsel to a man in conversation the way a kind sister would advise her younger brother. As brother or sister, we view their children as nieces and nephews we want to see grow in healthy ways.

Church gatherings should resemble healthy family Christmas celebrations, where brothers and sisters, male and female cousins, and all manner of close family are thrilled to see one another. The gathering should be a weekly reunion with warm embraces, sincere interest in catching up, shared food and song, and the comfortable safety that allows you to fall asleep in grandma's living room without a bit of fear.

Family looks out for family. Brothers and sisters ought to drop everything to be there for one another. The church is a

> A man should be no more afraid of having a conversation (or friendship) with a woman in the church than he should be afraid of interacting with his beloved sister. A woman should offer counsel to a man in conversation the way a kind sister would advise her younger brother.

more genuine family and a longer-lasting blood relationship than any on earth. It is an eternal family, bought by the blood of our big Brother.

... WHO COVENANT TOGETHER ...

The local church is a covenant community. It consists of the people of the new covenant. A covenant is a solemn agreement between parties outlining the nature and expectations of the relationship. As we saw above, the local church members do not attend merely for some preaching and singing. They have a divinely appointed responsibility to encourage, admonish, instruct, rebuke, protect, and care for one another. No Scripture reference is needed to prove this point. Open your New Testament to any random passage—chances are you'll find teaching on the responsibility believers have toward one another. If your church does not expect and practice the familial commitment to one another depicted and expected in the New Testament, it might be time to find a new church. You might be enjoying a religious gathering, but that's not a church.

Jesus Christ is "the head of the body, the church" (Col 1:18). This means Jesus is the final authority over the church on earth. Apart from Christ, there is no other "head of the church," whether on earth or in heaven. Church officers have no headship over the church. The men in the church have no headship over the women. We all—male and female—together constitute the body over which Christ is head.

Jesus exercised his headship by reconciling everything to God, "making peace through his blood, shed on the cross" (Colossians 1:20). That means that any form of derived authority in the local church may only be exercised in a manner that looks like Christ. Christ pursued peace and unity with the church through voluntary humility and sacrificial service. Thus, wherever our various traditions and interpretations about church government land, no authority may be exercised in any manner other than that which resembles crucifixion for the sake of those you love.

In this age, Christ still persuades his church through his written word, loving it with patience, gentleness, joy, kindness, understanding,

and all such virtues. Even in discipline, any authority in the church
must address sin with patience, love,
and gentleness as long as possible.[11]
Even when Jesus threatens to vomit
a church out of his mouth, he follows
this by an invitation to receive his free
grace, an assurance of his love, and
the desire to enjoy true fellowship (see
Rev 3:14–20). In all ways, the covenant
body (and any authority therein) are
to be *Christic*—shaped and informed
by Christ, our head.

> Wherever our various traditions and interpretations about church government land, no authority may be exercised in any manner other than that which resembles crucifixion for the sake of those you love.

... TO GLORIFY GOD BY DISPLAYING CHRIST ...

Paul writes to inform Timothy "how people ought to conduct themselves in God's household, which is the church of the living God"
(1 Tim 3:15). The church is the house where God lives with his people.
He follows this with a substantial descriptor. He says that the church
is "the pillar and foundation of the truth" (3:15). That is an amazing statement about the purpose of the church—God's embassy in
this world.

The function of both a pillar and a foundation is to support a structure. God has appointed the church as the support structure of the
truth. What is the truth that Paul has in mind? He tells us in verse 16:

> He was manifested in the flesh,
> vindicated in the Spirit,
> seen by angels,
> preached among the nations,
> believed on in the world,
> taken up in glory.

Paul offers a poetic description of the incarnation, death, resurrection,
Great Commission, and ascension of Jesus Christ. In other words, the

truth is the gospel. The person and work of the incarnate Christ is the definitive revelation of God (see John 1:14, 18). The gospel is the supreme display of God's glory.

The church is a pillar and a foundation upon which sits the gospel message. It is the church's responsibility to both display and protect the message of Jesus Christ crucified for sins and raised from the dead. The church's purpose, given in the Great Commission, is to display Christ, who is the revelation of the glory of God.

That is why the Christic perspective on male and female matters. Not because all men represent Christ and all women represent the church; that idea is not found in Scripture. Jesus is the firstborn of many brothers and sisters, who are being conformed to his image (Rom 8:29). The church is where those brothers and sisters live. Their lives either confirm and reinforce the grace of Christ in the gospel or they distort and destroy the message. If men and women aren't *Christic*, the pillar crumbles and the foundation shakes—and what's on top of it comes down.

... THROUGH MINISTRY PARTNERSHIP ...

True ministry is a partnership between Christic men and women. The first ministry assignment given to God's people was a partnership between men and women (Gen 1:26–28). The Old Testament bears this out as courageous women of faith pepper the storyline to preserve the line of the Messiah and serve God's remnant.[12]

> The incarnate Lord Jesus certainly ministered alongside women, even as he did among men, assigning them important tasks like announcing the resurrection to the Eleven.

The incarnate Lord Jesus certainly ministered alongside women, even as he did among men, assigning them important tasks like announcing the resurrection to the Eleven.

Jesus, the bridegroom, commissioned his bride the church to take the gospel to all nations, assuring her that he would go with her (Matt 28:16–20). In the end, the church will reign on earth as the Lamb sits on the throne (Rev 22:3–5).

The Christic church is patterned after Christ's example in partnership. Though Paul has a vision of a Macedonian man pleading for help, he travels there only to meet a prominent woman who would be an essential partner in gospel ministry (Acts 16:9–15). Lydia, the first baptized convert in Europe, would host the apostles and a church in her home (Acts 16:15, 40).[13]

Paul describes Euodia and Syntyche as "women who have contended for the gospel at my side, ... coworkers whose names are in the book of life" (Phil 4:2–3). They did not minister under Paul as servants; they *fought for the gospel* at his side—not as subservient slaves but as *co-workers* who share in salvation.

Paul sent Phoebe, a deacon of the church in Cenchreae, to deliver his letter to the church in Rome. He commended her as one who should be welcomed "in the Lord in a manner worthy of the saints" (Rom 16:1–2). Since she had provided financial support for Paul and many other servants, the church in Rome should assist her in the same fashion.

Paul goes on to greet several women by name: Prisca, Mary, Junia, Tryphaena, Tryphosa, Persis, Rufus' mother, Julia, and Nereus' sister (Rom 16:3–16). Prisca, along with her husband, is described as a co-worker who risked her neck for his life. Junia is noteworthy (16:7). Tryphaena and Tryphosa "worked very hard in the Lord" (16:12). Paul says that Rufus's mother is also his (16:13), alluding to his affection for her (and possibly the influence she had on him). Her husband may have been the man who carried Christ's cross (Mark 15:21). All these, along with the men mentioned, are saints who are to "greet one another with a holy kiss," even as "all the churches of Christ" send them greetings (Rom 16:15–16). Although it isn't common for men and women in our culture to kiss in greeting, it might be more so if we actually viewed one another as siblings, brothers and sisters.

Space is not adequate to cover all such women mentioned in the New Testament.[14] Suffice it to say that New Testament ministry was a partnership between men and women in Christ.

Today's church should carefully consider the long-term effects of continually separating men and women in discipleship and ministry work. Men's and women's ministries can play an essential role in strengthening same-gender friendships in the church. They provide a place for discussion and discipleship that may be uncomfortable for some in a mixed-gender environment. But if this is the sole means by which men and women are discipled, they will not learn to grow together or partner with one another. The friendships and trust necessary for partnership will not be there. Likewise, if men's and women's ministries are the only avenues through which outreach and ministry happen, men and women will never even think about linking arms in gospel combat.

... SHARED AUTHORITY ...

God intended for men and women to rule together with shared authority. We see this in God's words in Genesis 1, "*they* will rule" (Gen 1:26, emphasis added); "God said to *them* ... 'Rule'" (Gen 1:28, emphasis added). In Genesis 2, Moses highlights this shared authority as he focuses on the creation of the man and then the woman. First, God creates the man and places him in his garden sanctuary, giving him authority and responsibility for priestly service. But the Lord declares that the man alone is insufficient for this task. So, he creates the woman from the man's flesh and bone—his equal—to join him. The man was to pass along the *very same instructions* that he received to the woman. (This is why the woman uses the plural "*We* may eat" in Gen 3:2, even though God delivered the instructions in the singular, "*You* are free to eat," in Gen 2:16). This creation order emphasizes that they share the same authorization and task. Together, they will work and watch the garden of Eden; together, they will reign on earth.

This unity in the same task, as authorized by God, is demonstrated in an unlikely passage. First Corinthians 11 is undoubtedly a confusing and challenging passage. Christians debate how to handle the nature and applications of head coverings for a woman praying and prophesying in the assembled local church. Nevertheless, the unity of the man and the woman is apparent.

Paul opens with a general truth: "But I want you to know that Christ is the head of every man, and the man is the head of the woman, and God is the head of Christ" (1 Cor 11:3). At the very start, "Paul issued a principle for application in corporate worship—the principle of voluntary submission to authority."[15] Christ (the incarnate Lord), who is equal in nature and authority with God, voluntarily submits to God to accomplish his purpose on earth. Likewise, then, for every man and woman. (It seems likely that by "man" and "woman," Paul means "husband" and "wife," given these words are interchangeable. He uses similar language in Eph 5:22–23; Col 3:18–19). The husband voluntarily submits himself to Christ, thus to God's purpose in Christ (even as Christ voluntarily submits to God). The wife (as seen in Chapter Eight) voluntarily submits herself to the husband (who voluntarily submits to Christ, who voluntarily submits to God). Through this presentation, Paul establishes that *all* (Christ, man, woman) voluntarily submit to the *same authority and purpose.*

Paul goes on to highlight this order in 1 Corinthians 11:7–9:

> A man should not cover his head, because he is the image and glory of God. So too, woman is the glory of man. For man did not come from woman, but woman came from man. Neither was man created for the sake of woman, but woman for the sake of man.

At first blush, this passage appears to make the woman subservient to the man. Nothing could be further from the truth. When Paul writes that woman was created "for the sake of man," he does not indicate that a wife is to be the maidservant to a wedded master. The husband is not free to order his wife to do whatever he pleases. For the husband is not free to do as he pleases.

The man was created for the sake of God (to display his glory), but he was insufficient to fulfill "the sake of God"—that is, to display God's glory. Therefore, the woman was created "for the sake of man," *which is "the sake of God."* She was not made to do whatever she pleases, choosing her own purpose. She was made to join the man in his purpose, which is the purpose of God. *The woman is the final (and most important) point in displaying God's glory, even as the (re)creation of Christ's bride is the final step in displaying God's glory on the earth.* The man is incapable of being the "glory of God" without the woman, who is "the glory of man."[16] Without her, the display of God's glory is aborted.

Both the man and woman are devoted to the same purpose—displaying the glory of God as his united representative rulers. Paul gives this instruction in the context of the local church. Unless men and women are voluntarily submitted to displaying the glory of God in Christ, the local church is incapable of fulfilling its purpose.

Paul's wording, so seemingly offensive to modern ears, is actually a strong statement of the equality and shared responsibility of men and women in the church (and the home). Both the man and the woman are created for the very same purpose, tasked with the same role, authorized by the same God. They are both *Christic*—imitating the incarnate Lord Jesus Christ in voluntary submission to God, displaying his glory on the earth. Neither the man nor the woman can fulfill their purpose without the other. This is why Paul is quick to add a strong statement of mutuality: "In the Lord, however, woman is not independent of man, and man is not independent of woman. For just as woman came from man, so man comes through woman, and all things come from God" (1 Cor 11:11–12). Man and woman are incapable of functioning rightly and fulfilling their joint purpose unless they depend on one another, even as they depend on the Lord. Again, Paul gives this instruction in the context of the local church. *Unless believing men and women depend on one another, the local church is incapable of fulfilling its purpose in Christ.*

Already we can see that God's creation purpose—men and women ruling together in submission to God's purposes—is being restored "in the Lord," in Christ's church. This is what Christ came to do, to redeem a people who would reign *together* on earth (Rev 5:10; 22:5). Christ's inclusion of his people in his reign set a model for male-female relationships in the church:

> No one has greater love than this: to lay down his life for his friends. You are my friends if you do what I command you. I do not call you servants anymore, because a servant doesn't know what his master is doing. I have called you friends, because I have made known to you everything I have heard from my Father. (John 15:13–15)

Jesus does not view his relationship with his people as a "master-slave" relationship. Rather, his people are his *friends* because he makes them know what he is doing in accord with his Father's purpose. Men and women in the church are not masters and slaves. They are *friends*, jointly submitted to and authorized for the same purpose.

> Unless believing men and women depend on one another, the local church is incapable of fulfilling its purpose in Christ.

We see this joint authority in the letters of the New Testament. These letters are sent by apostles—those commissioned directly by the risen Christ to speak with his authority in the establishing of the New Testament church. The apostles write with the authority of Christ to instruct the church, often addressing a local congregation. These letters often address some error (in doctrine or practice), offering correction and instruction on how the congregation is to believe and behave. Given the focus on doctrine and practice in the local church, we might expect the letters to be addressed to the congregation's elders, but they aren't. They are consistently sent to "all the saints" (Rom 1:7; 1 Cor 1:2; 2 Cor 1:1; Eph 1:1; Phil 1:1; Col 1:2), "the church" (1 Cor 1:2; 2 Cor 1:1; Gal 1:2; 1 Thess 1:1; 2 Thess 1:1), "faithful brothers and sisters" (Col 1:2), or some other phrasing to indicate local assemblies of believers (Jas 1:1–2; 1 Pet 1:1–2; 2 Pet 1:1; 1 John 2:1; 2 John 1; Jude 1; Rev 1:4).

In each of these instances, the recipient is the local church. There are only five occasions on which a New Testament letter is sent to an individual. Titus, along with 1 and 2 Timothy, are written by Paul to apostolic representatives left by him to put local churches in order. Paul writes to Philemon to deal with the matter of a returned slave. Third John is likely written to a pastor to warn him about a false teacher.

This is amazing: when writing to correct or encourage the doctrine and practice of the local church, the apostles *always* write to the congregation, all the saints, the laity, the corporate body. They do not write to the officers of the church.[17] This communicates something of the authority of the assembled church—they are able to understand Paul's letter and responsible for seeing it carried out. The apostles do not see the average Christian as below them. Paul and James call them "brothers and sisters" (Col 1:2; Jas 1:1–2). Peter addresses these everyday Christians as "those who have received a faith *equal* to ours" (2 Pet 1:1, emphasis added).

How much authority does the assembled congregation of a local church have? They are expected to recognize false doctrine and condemn such teachers (Gal 1:6–9). The entire church (not merely the elders) is accountable for what leaders they select (2 Tim 4:3–4). The church (not the elders) is charged with judging its members and excommunicating unrepentant members (1 Cor 5:4–5, 9–13; Matt 18:15–17). This discipline is decided by the majority of the congregation (2 Cor 2:6). Even the apostles bring in the "whole company of the disciples" to resolve disputes and authorize representatives to serve on their behalf (Acts 6:1–6; 11:22; 15:2–4).

The final authority for discipline, disputes, doctrine, membership, and selection of its leaders and representatives is given to the local church congregation. This is a restoration of creation purposes and the sanctuary in Eden—men and women, ruling together.

Some may object to this because the author of Hebrews exhorts the church to "obey your leaders and submit to them" (Heb 13:17).

Again, the word "obey" means "be persuaded by"; the submission of the church entails a disposition inclined to be persuaded by its leaders (presumably its elders). Hebrews 13:7 informs us of how these leaders persuade: "Remember your leaders who have spoken God's word to you." The means by which elders lead a church is through speaking the word of God to the congregation. The elders have no authority in and of themselves, whether as individuals or as a collective body. Their authority is found solely in the word of God, which they are called to "command and teach," giving their attention to the "public reading, exhortation, and teaching" of God's word (1 Tim 4:11–13).

> The final authority for discipline, disputes, doctrine, membership, and selection of its leaders and representatives is given to the local church congregation. This is a restoration of creation purposes and the sanctuary in Eden—men and women, ruling together.

Notice Paul's instruction to Timothy on honoring elders: "The elders who are good leaders are to be considered worthy of double honor, especially those who work hard at preaching and teaching" (1 Tim 5:17). The second half of that sentence defines the first. To be a "good leader" as an elder is to "work hard at preaching and teaching." The central role of elders—and the means by which they lead—is by explaining God's word and publicly exhorting the congregation to obey it. They "rule" only by firm persuasion from Scripture. It is worth noting that the office of elder is a carryover from the elders of the Jewish synagogue. Elders are not the New Testament equivalent of, nor do they connect to, the priestly class of Israel. The old covenant priesthood finds its fulfillment in the priestly status of every believer through the high priest Jesus Christ. The centrality of teaching to the role of the elders is seen in their qualifications: an overseer (a synonym for "elder") must be able to teach (1 Tim 3:2).

When we compare the qualifications for elders with those for deacons, we find only two differences. First, there is no requirement that deacons be able to teach. They function to serve the congregation through practical means to address tangible needs (such as caring for those in need) and not to lead through persuasion. Second, women may serve as deacons. In 1 Timothy 3:11 Paul goes out of his way to emphasize and highlight that the church may ordain women to the office of deacon by inserting a verse devoted entirely to the topic: "Women, likewise."[18]

In the local church, men and women are ordained to serve side by side for the gospel.

... RESPECTFUL UNITY, VOLUNTARY HUMILITY, RECIPROCAL BENEVOLENCE, AND MUTUAL FLOURISHING.

Our definition of a Christic church ends with the qualities of unity, humility, benevolence, and flourishing—each concern shown by one gender toward the other. These qualities and their mutuality should be evident in what we discussed above and in other chapters. Suffice it to say, the concern that men and women have for one another in a Christic church is nothing less than the love of Christ, extended to them in the life, death, and resurrection of the Messiah.

Beginning in Chapter One, we've said that if your first question is "Who gets to be boss?" then you've missed the implications of the incarnation. In church discussions, that often boils down to the questions, "Who gets to be an elder? Is the office of elder open to men and women?" We know that it might be disappointing to some of our readers, but we're not going to answer that question for you. While we agree that it is an important issue, we don't think it is the starting point in the discussion about how the incarnation informs the relationship between men and women in the church. And, besides, we've already said that, under the lordship of Christ, the gathered church has ultimate authority. The authority of elders is limited to persuading the flock regarding the word of God.

This is what we're willing to say, however: No matter what we believe about who can be an elder in your local context, we need to understand that all of us are called to relinquish our rights for the sake of mutual flourishing, even as Christ did. Jesus existed in the form of God but did not "consider equality with God as something to be exploited. Instead he emptied himself by assuming the form of a servant ... becoming obedient to the point of death" (Phil 2:6–8). That is the attitude God calls us to adopt.

The most important answer to all our questions always needs to come back to this: It's all about Jesus. It's about his incarnation: his life, death, resurrection, ascension, reign, and return. And it's about loving our siblings, our flesh-of-flesh brothers and sisters, with whom we share a common calling: to preach this good news to the world.

To be an embassy of the kingdom of Christ, the headquarters of Christ's ambassadors in this world, men and women must lay aside their will, wishes, and desires as Christ did in the garden of Gethsemane. They must fix their eyes firmly on the glory of the gospel and make its display their unified aim. This means we see one another as Christ sees his people—as brothers and sisters of whom we are not ashamed, friends with whom we share a common purpose. It is this sort of "household of God" that protects and displays the beauty of Jesus:

> The most important answer to all our questions always needs to come back to this: It's all about Jesus. It's about his incarnation: his life, death, resurrection, ascension, reign, and return.

> He was manifested in the flesh,
> vindicated in the Spirit,
> seen by angels,
> preached among the nations,
> believed on in the world,
> taken up in glory. (1 Tim 3:16)

11

Voices into
the Culture

And it will be in the last days, says God, that I will pour
out my Spirit on all people; then your sons and your
daughters will prophesy, your young men will see visions,
and your old men will dream dreams. I will even pour
out my Spirit on my servants in those days, both men
and women and they will prophesy. —Acts 2:17–18

We hope you've gained a vision for women and men co-laboring together as respected and beloved equals, each with his or her own gifting—each with his or her own "haunting," each with his or her own dream of laying down their one life for the one excruciatingly glorious call of death to self and resurrected life for all.

We hope you've had a heart transplant. We hope you've been given the heartbeat of our Lord, a precious heartbeat that pulses with humility, surrendered authority, and love, and that your former heart's question of, "Who gets to be in charge?" has been replaced with, "How can I give away whatever power I believe I have for the sake of those without it?"

We've purposely chosen to avoid conversation about the culture wars: we simply don't believe that we've been called to try to foist either conservative or liberal ideologies upon anyone. But we have been called to give them the gospel story: the incarnation, sinless life, substitutionary death, bodily resurrection, ascension, reign, and return of the One who gave it all away ... for us. And because of that, we can offer forgiveness and freedom from all the ways we thought we had to justify ourselves. We've purposed to step away from labels and easily codified litmus tests and instead call us all, wherever we land on any question of so-called gender roles, to seek to encourage, equip, and raise up our brothers and sisters for the glory of the Incarnate One.

What would Christic ministries led by brothers and sisters be like? They would sound like a beautiful symphony of male and female choruses blending their differing gifts, inclinations, desires, and ministries, collaborating together in one song of praise to their incarnate King and the whole world. They would sound like the bride in heaven calling out with the Spirit, "'Come!' Let the one who is thirsty come. Let the one who desires to take the water of life freely" come! Even now there are a myriad of voices speaking into this broken world, offering the water of life, pointing to a better path. These people aren't waiting for permission to follow their gifting. They are impelled by the Spirit. They are redeemed by the blood of the humble Lamb.

Like you, they're walking with Peter and the apostles as they awaited the gifting of the Spirit in the upper room. They joined hands in prayer with Mary, our Lord's mother, and with those who had walked and loved her Son, their Savior (Acts 1:14). Soon, they would be joined by many new believers, both men and women (Acts 5:14; 8:12). Some would stand in awe and gratitude as a servant, Dorcas, was raised from the dead (Acts 9:36–42). Some would meet together with Mary (John Mark's mother) to pray for their brother Peter (Acts 12:12). They'll join with Eunice and Lois, with Thessalonian and Athenian women and men who joyfully found forgiveness and freedom (2 Tim 1:5; Acts 17).

They have joined with Paul, who partnered with Lydia and Phoebe, Onesimus and Philemon, Euodia and Syntyche and Clement, Priscilla and Aquila, Neurus' sister and Olympas, Nympha and the church in her home, Andronicus and Junias, Tryphaena and Tryphosa, Rufus and his beloved mother, Philogus and Julia, Nereus and his sister, and

Olympas. They're part of the company that welcomed Mary of Rome (Rom 16:6), who had worked very hard for the church there. Look again at that list above. Brothers and sisters united in one call: working hard to imitate Jesus as they lived out their gender. That's the vision we have for a Christic perspective today.

We're not proposing anything new here. We're only hoping that the church may recover a sense of the glorious blending together of the work that Christ has called us to today. The culture doesn't need us to stand for or against conservative or liberal ideologies. The world around us is in desperate need of a Christian witness that says that all people, women and men, who have been created in God's image can find true personhood and redemption through the blood of the humble incarnate Christ who loved his brothers and sisters and called them to lives of self-sacrifice and deep relationship and meaning.

What follows now is a compilation of short testimonies from sisters and brothers who have chosen the road of self-sacrifice and ministry. Many of their stories were born out of deep pain, rejection, and sorrow. Some have been encouraged by their local congregations, others have had to fight their way in, and still others have had to strike out on their own, finding a place for the call that would not let them go. Some of them are married, some are not. Some have been ordained by a church body, some have international ministries without any ecclesiastical sponsorship. Some have sought higher education and work in academia. Others have more quiet ministries, working in their local churches or neighborhoods. One thing is certain though: they're walking in the footsteps of the women and men who walked with Jesus, Peter, and Paul, and did not love their lives to the death.

MEET YOUR SIBLINGS

Aimee Byrd: Author and Speaker ... Your Sister[1]

I kind of stumbled into becoming an author. I began as a reader and a thinker in the church, wanting to learn more about how theology impacts our discipleship. I noticed there wasn't much out there to encourage women to take theology seriously—so I wrote about it myself. From there, I was invited into many opportunities to speak. This made me explore the reasons why women's resources are so troubling, how we view women's ministry, and how it affects the whole church. In my writing, I have labored to bridge the gap between laywomen and church officers, encouraging leaders to invest in women as disciples—necessary allies in the church, their homes, and society.

Writing about and discussing this revealed another issue: how men and women view one another in God's household. We have a serious problem with our Christian message if men and women can't even relate in meaningful, dynamic, and pure ways. As I began writing and speaking on this issue of sacred siblingship, I pressed further into the question of what the communion of the saints actually looks like. But I quickly realized as a woman writing about discipleship that more questions needed to be tackled: *Does a female lay disciple have the same agency as a male lay disciple in communicating God's word, communing in it, and passing it down to the next generation? What's distinctly meaningful about male and female disciples? What is our aim?* Sadly, these questions and topics have generated a lot of controversy. I think that is revealing.

> We have a serious problem with our Christian message if men and women can't even relate in meaningful, dynamic, and pure ways.

Our theology really does impact our discipleship. Now, I am writing about the meaningfulness behind our sexes, wanting to restore the dignity and personhood of both men and women. The triune God wants to reveal himself to us, and he delights in his people. Our bodies are theological, signifying the gift that the Father gave to the Son in eternity and the spousal love of God for his people. We are created for eternal communion with the triune God and one another. And once you see the beauty of Christ's love for his people, you can't unsee it. And you want to call others to it.

Eric Chappell: Stay-at-Home Dad,
Ordained Pastor ... Your Brother

The dream began with daycare drop-offs. After our first was born, we decided it was in our family's best interest to remain a dual income household. We enrolled our infant son in an amazing daycare with qualified and caring staff. Though we loved the interaction he was receiving from other adults and kids, I still felt like I was missing so much. I'd regularly be in tears after dropping off my kids. Childhood is short, and I didn't want to miss a moment of it. But stay-at-home parent seemed like an unrealistic path in Southern California. And stay-at-home papa? There were literally no guys I knew pursuing that calling, and certainly none with graduate theological training.

After seven years of vocational ministry in the church, I'm a stay-at-home papa of three kids (ages six, four, and one). And loving it. Though still called to word and sacrament, my primary calling as husband and father needed to take precedence for a season. There's a ton I miss about being a full-time pastor, but now my ministry involves PB&J sandwiches, story time, folding laundry, Costco runs, and diapers. My only complaint is there's not a lot of yoga pants for men. In this dad's opinion, the church is not doing enough to equip men to think creatively about a domestic calling and provide them with the support they'll need to faithfully fulfill it. As Warren Farrell and John Gray say in their book *The Boy Crisis* (2018), in research, "dad deprivation surfaced as the leading cause of more than twenty-five social, psychological, academic, and physical health problems" in the lives of children. Maybe society and the church could use a few more full-time fathers. In Genesis 1, God the Father builds the house, makes the bed, does the chores, and sets the table for his

> Maybe society and the church could use a few more full-time fathers. In Genesis 1, God the Father builds the house, makes the bed, does the chores, and sets the table for his children Adam and Eve.

children Adam and Eve. It's a humbling challenge and profound joy to serve our Father and my neighbor by imaging God in all things domestic.

Dr. Pamela MacRae: Author, Professor in Applied
Theology and Church Ministry ... Your Sister

When I was a junior in high school, my teacher's wife invited me to a conference for women at her church. I don't know why she invited me. None of my friends were invited. But I know God wanted me there. That event gave me a picture of ministry I had not even known how to imagine. I especially could never have imagined that someday I would do the very same thing.

I had Sunday school and high school Bible teachers who were women, but I had never seen a woman stand behind a pulpit, exegeting Scripture to women tightly packed into church pews. At that time, I was not conscious of how that was shaping my thinking. Yet years later, I connected the dots when it was I who was teaching women God's word.

Now I equip women to do the same. Since 2005, I have led the Ministry to Women major at Moody Bible Institute, which was in the Pastoral Studies Department. I worked closely with a terrific group of male colleagues who were supportive and wonderfully collaborative. Later, I also started the Ministry to Victims of Sexual Exploitation major.

Yet one of my favorite courses to teach came out of a departmental discussion where the issues we were discussing led us to agree that we needed a required course for our male pastoral students on how to effectively pastor women. Thus, I created and continue to teach a course called Pastoral Care of Women.

I believe the importance and influence of a male pastor on a woman cannot be overstated. Women ministering to women will always be essential, but godly male pastoral care for women is extremely vital. Men also need women ministering to them. Sadly, the assumed risks associated with ministering to women, and often a sense of one's own lack of personal competency, can discourage male pastors from pastoral care to women. This is a great loss for everyone. My hope is for women in the church to be well cared for by both their brothers and sisters.

Like most people, where I find myself now as a grandparent is not where I imagined I would be when I was in high school. The path our Lord marked out for me has been to care for women in the church—by both direct ministry and by strengthening and equipping male pastors for ministry to women.

Raleigh Sadler: Author, Human Trafficking
Advocate ... Your Brother[2]

I felt it in my gut at a conference in Atlanta on human trafficking in 2012. After hearing about human trafficking globally and the demand that each of us creates for it, I *had* to respond. The only problem was that I had questions. Did I need to change my vocation? Do I have to become a lawyer? A police officer? I studied to be a pastor, not to kick down doors of brothels. These questions sent me on a journey far from my life's purpose. In short, I ran until I ran out of options. There was nothing left for me but this sense of calling for which I felt uniquely unqualified.

However, something miraculous happened. As I became aware of my limitations, I began to see the needs of others more clearly. I came to believe that God motivated vulnerable people like me to love other vulnerable people by becoming vulnerable for us. Without knowing how it would pan out, I took a step of faith in 2012 into the unknown. I moved to NYC.

> I came to believe that God motivated vulnerable people like me to love other vulnerable people by becoming vulnerable for us.

Since then, I've started Let My People Go (LMPG), a ministry that exists to empower the local church to fight human trafficking by loving those most vulnerable. LMPG works with churches to equip them to recognize and respond to those most vulnerable in their communities,

giving them the tools to care for those most often targeted by traf-
fickers. By caring for those in the margins, your church is doing the
work of prevention, intervention, and aftercare all in one fell swoop.

Carolyn McCulley: Filmmaker, Author, Speaker,
Podcast Producer ... Your Sister[3]

I discovered the power of storytelling in kindergarten during show and
tell, and I've been a storyteller ever since. When I became a Christian
nearly ten years into my career, I saw how memorably Jesus told stories and how his narratives inspired or rebuked his listeners—which,
as the Logos of the world, his narratives should. But often the stories
we tell in churches can create a limited, one-size-fits-all concept for
what godliness looks like for both men and women. So I see my calling as telling the stories of people at the margins, whose lives aren't
predictable but whose faith is memorable.

I also feel that, as a single woman, I exist to remind the church at
large not to fumble the siblinghood of Christ. For the last thirty years
or so, the church has elevated the nuclear family but done so often
at the expense of the church family. Instead of cultivating a brother-
and-sister dynamic across churchwide relationships, some churches
have cast a suspicious side-eye at single adults as potential stumbling
blocks to solid marriages or ignored them as though they are in the
waiting room of adulthood. But this is not the organic and gifted body
of Christ described in the New Testament. Also, as I've gotten older, I
have seen there are precious few resources that consider the full arc
of a woman's life and envision women for fruitfulness in the second
half of life—even while they are still young. So my ministry writing
and speaking has primarily focused on challenging the lopsided narratives told about both singleness and womanhood.

Finally, whenever I'm entrusted with telling the story of someone
else's most challenging or tender moments, I want to push the established pace of Christian testimonies. I want to make sure that in the
desire to glorify God, we don't rush the storyline and skip over the
hard parts where faith was built and tested. No listener is truly edified

by the truncated testimonies that gloss over the dark night of the soul. The most powerful testimonies are not the ones that end in worldly success and dreams achieved. Rather, the stories of trusting God when he doesn't make sense, when failure looms, or when the prayers seem to go unanswered are the stories that make faith shine brightest.

Wendy Alsup: Author, College Math Teacher, Church Servant … Your Sister[4]

I'm a mom of two teenage boys and a math teacher at my local community college. I have written several books about practical theology, biblical womanhood, and Scripture. I have long been burdened that women understand the deep things of the word of God. As a math teacher, I work at breaking complex concepts into understandable smaller steps. Some folks are put off by theology similar to math, and I have found that some tools I employ to make math understandable transfer to theological concepts as well. I hate when theologians assign big words to simple concepts in Scripture, and I have worked to write deep but accessible studies geared toward women.

Though some might first label me a Christian author, the most important ministry I do is in my own local community. I am also a part of a church plant in my racially segregated hometown of South Carolina. Our little church community is beautiful. We have a racially and economically diverse core team, and everyone pitches in. Some Sundays I give the prayer of thanksgiving after our offering. Some Sundays I pray with folks who come up after the service. Some Sundays I clean up after Communion. Most Sundays, I at least water plants.

I also help lead our women's mini-retreats, where we gather at my farm on a Saturday, sit under my old live oak tree, eat, and review the last Sunday sermon series. My pastor often asks for my input on his sermons, and I regularly teach youth on Sunday nights. In a church plant, everyone pitches in where they are needed. I do a lot of things that fit my gifting. But sometimes, I have to step out of my comfort zone to help make sure balls aren't dropped. I love the men and women on mission together in our church. Stepping out of my comfort zone is easy when we do it in Jesus' name with people we love.

Brian Croft: Pastor Emeritus, Ministry Executive
Director, Husband, Father ... Your Brother[5]

I've been a pastor for twenty-five years. I invested heavily in men, preparing them for pastoral ministry. If you would have accused me of being neglectful to women in my ministry, I would have sternly pushed back. I felt I had cared well for women as a pastor and had encouraged service by them in the local church. However, about ten years into my first senior pastor role, I had a couple of strong, gifted women in my church ask to meet with me. They understood and affirmed the New Testament teaching and conviction of our church that only men could serve as pastors. And yet, they asked a piercing question I was not prepared to answer.

> So, I understand why women cannot serve as pastors, but why can't women serve in other public ways, such as praying and reading Scripture in the public gathering?

This question should not have stumped me, but it did. I had an answer to this question, but it dawned on me in this moment it was not a good one. See, I had been so focused on training men to be pastors that I had neglected to think about all the ways women could still serve our local church in public ways. I had wrongfully affiliated public leading with pastoral calling. As a result, I had sadly held back some very gifted women in our church who possessed public gifts to lead.

I felt convicted and realized a change was necessary. And you can imagine this was not easy, especially in a church where this conviction was taught—under my leadership! For the next seven years until my transition as pastor, I chose to fight these battles I had created for myself to encourage and empower women to serve and lead in roles of public leadership historically seen as pastoral and reserved only for men.

By the time my seventeen years as pastor of our church had come to a close, our Sunday morning service had women praying, reading Scripture, and visibly leading in several ways. Our worship leader who planned most of our services, prepared the music teams, and led our congregational singing was a very gifted woman. Additionally, half of my paid staff and lay leaders were women. The battles were worth fighting, and God brought a unique blessing to our church as these ladies began to lead.

> I chose to fight these battles I had created for myself to encourage and empower women to serve and lead in roles of public leadership historically seen as pastoral and reserved only for men.

Hannah Anderson: Writer, Public Speaker, Wife, Mom ... Your Sister

I started publicly speaking and writing about theology about the same time that I realized that my six-year-old daughter would grow up to be a woman. At the time, it was a startling, if not predictable, realization. I had somehow found a way to deny that she, as my oldest child, would grow up and imagined her as a young girl forever. But then one day, I looked her in the face and saw that she'd aged. I don't know what it was in particular, whether it was a certain tilt of her head or her hands on hip mimicking of me, but I suddenly knew something else: this young girl would grow up to be her mother.

Then a second thought hit me: The biggest influence in my daughter's life would not be a church discipleship program or celebrity influencer. It would not be a book or famous Christian speaker. The biggest influence in my daughter's life was me; and whatever I wanted her to learn about being a disciple of Christ, I had to first learn myself. More than anything, I wanted my daughter to become a woman who loved Jesus and obeyed his voice when he called—even when he called her to step into unexpected callings. Especially then.

It's been over a decade since that day, and my daughter has grown, as has my ministry as a theological writer and teacher. Most of my work emerges from questions that I'm wrestling with in my own spiritual walk, and I assume that if I'm working through them, other women probably are too. Writing gives me a space to clarify my thoughts and serve others in the process. I do not want my life or spiritual process to replace the work readers have to do for themselves, but I do want to lay a pathway that will help them recognize and voice their struggles—all while leading them back to the One who called us in the first place.

It's a sobering thing to realize that you're responsible for another person's development, but God used that moment of awareness to cultivate a larger awareness in me. We cannot lead where we have not first walked. So, insofar as he calls me, I hope to continue to develop my gifts as a speaker and writer—not simply for my own self-fulfillment, but out of a deeper sense of stewardship and responsibility. For the sake of all God's children.

Lore Wilbert: Author, Speaker, Wife ... Your Sister

Growing up, "theology" seemed like too big of a word for someone like me. Even into my teens and twenties, ideas about God and God himself seemed too complex, too unreachable, and too inaccessible for me. I couldn't make the God I heard about on Sunday mornings relate to the grief, doubt, sadness, and pain of my life. This led to an eventual faith crisis where I had to confess that all my doubts about God were actually rooted in this belief: that he was too wondrous for someone like me to know. This, coupled with a seeming gift for the written word, became my aim in life: to make God knowable or "sayable," to use the poet Rilke's term.

My desire is to make what is true about God accessible to normal people, to not leave theology to the theologians but to make theologians of all of us. After all, we all already believe things about God; we're all living some kind of theology. My interest is in helping people remember that the stuff of life—the laundry, the politics, the

miscarriages, the careers, the joy, the hopes, the failures, all of it—
reflects something of the God who made us and loves us and is very
much in the process of redeeming us and the world in which we live
right now. I think of it like putting pants on the gospel: everybody
needs them, they're made of earthy matter, and we all put them on
one leg at a time.

Tom Maxham: Elder, Counselor, Writer,
Retired Fire Captain ... Your Brother

The complexities of counseling in the local church led me to seek all
the training I could get; I obtained both a national certification and
graduate degree in biblical counseling. After years of applying what I
had been taught in counseling marriages, I realized my training did
not provide an awareness of the abuse taking place within the church.
I came to see that not all marriage problems require marriage counseling, but some require abuse counseling.

As a pastor, I began to see that the church admirably protected
marriage but often missed protecting vulnerable victims of abuse. The
perilous spiritual state of the abuser was also not given adequate consideration (Heb 3:13; Jude 22–23). The culture of the church allowed
abuse to go on under the radar, in some cases for decades. There
was an ignorance, including the misuse of Scripture, and a shameful
missing of the obvious destructive
effects of non-physical abuse on
image-bearers. There was wisdom
needed for both "let no man separate" and "let no man oppress."

With a new awareness of abuse,
Scripture became clearer as to God's
heart for protecting the oppressed
(Ps 10:17–18; Mal 2:14). As abusive
spouses were held accountable (and
some disciplined by the church),
there was strong pushback from

> The culture of the
> church allowed abuse
> to go on under the
> radar, in some cases for
> decades. There was an
> ignorance, including the
> misuse of Scripture, and
> a shameful missing of
> the obvious destructive
> effects of non-physical
> abuse on image-bearers.

multiple sources. Their desired emphasis on headship was vehemently defended, and lording-over behavior was justified. As a result, much effort was put into proactively training the church in gospel-centered marriages (no longer emphasizing role-centered marriages) and abuse in the church.

All of this required the elders of the church to study and agree on these things and, most importantly, to take responsibility for our part in the past harm done to abuse victims under our watch. A full year was spent reconciling the elders with multiple victims, and the lack of proper care for these victims was publicly acknowledged to the church. All this can be avoided.

It is easiest in the short run to manage a marriage with the extreme of overstressing authority (or even removing all authority). It is a long, hard-fought path of sanctification to instead change a marriage and a church culture to embrace humble leadership as defined at the cross (Phil 2:8).

Dianna Huston: Counselor, Ministry Leader ... Your Sister

After my husband was diagnosed with a terminal illness and I found myself experiencing panic attacks in my sleep, I knew I needed help. I sought out Christian counsel, and although it was helpful, I found it lacking the depth my heart was longing for. I wanted to hear fresh the words of Christ and be comforted by Scripture. About that time, a local seminary was offering courses in biblical counseling, and a friend encouraged me to attend. I heard, for the first time, gospel principals being applied to real-life issues. I was able to find help and relief for my weary and discouraged heart. I went from those classes to earn a master's and a certification on biblical counseling.

I wanted to bring the hope of Christ to the family of God at my local church. My pastors and my husband encouraged me to begin working with other women who were facing challenges in their lives. I was so grateful to be able to use the experiences that God had brought me through and to connect with these women the hope of Christ! He came to earth to take care of our largest issue, sin, but also being fully

God and fully man, he understands our weakness and struggles. He has faced all of our problems. He came to give us life, to give us hope, and to stand with us in the midst of our struggles. He is a God who is close.

Over my many years of counseling, working with men and women, teens and children, I have been blessed to follow the call I believe God has given me. It took an adversity to bring me to a place to hear the call of the Lord, but I praise him for it. Out of a place of darkness, he has brought me to a place of light. It is my honor to bring that light of the gospel to others.

Karen Swallow Prior: Author and Research Professor of
English and Christianity and Culture ... Your Sister[6]

I grew up in the church and grew up reading books. In the church, I was told that if I really loved God, I needed to be willing to be called to serve in the mission field in some far away land.

I was not willing, so I just continued reading books and figured I didn't really love God enough to serve him.

It wasn't until I was nearly finished with my PhD in English that I realized that I could serve God and the church through my love of literature.

When I finished my doctorate, I took a position at a Christian university where I taught for many years, and I now teach at a college attached to a seminary. For more than two decades, I have been teaching students (and myself) how to find God's truth in the pages of good books, how to better love our neighbors by learning about them through the stories they tell, and how to glorify our Creator through our own creativity.

I love that God is using the thing I love to help others love him more.

No, all literature isn't good or God-honoring. No, human words are not God's word. But learning to weigh, discern, and sift the words that form human stories helps us to understand the words of God's story even more. Expanding the limitations of our own experiences and perspectives by exposing ourselves to the experiences of others enlarges our minds and our hearts. Measuring the shifting values and views reflected in the literature of thousands of years of human experience against the unchanging truths of God's words and ways is discipleship.

God took the thing I loved and, in his goodness, grace, and great irony, has allowed me to use this passion—put in me by his divine providence—for the church, and nothing gives me greater joy.

As it turns out, I really do love God.

Quina Aragon: Spoken Word Poet, Writer ... Your Sister[7]

When the Lord was drawing me to himself at age sixteen, I was struck by the Bible's poetry, filled with every color of emotion. I'm glad I recognized this about God's word because my life, in so many ways, fell apart shortly after I first trusted in Christ. In the midst of the chaos and trauma of my last two years of high school, and as I began to grow in my walk with Christ, I wrote poetry in my journal. Somehow one of my English teachers found out, so as she put together a poetry slam, she encouraged me to participate. I performed spoken word pieces about my newfound joy in Christ, about addiction, and about suffering in light of hope. Afterward, my peers approached me with tears in their eyes. That's when I realized God had given me a gift, and I wanted to use my writing and performing for his glory.

My life's path didn't become clear or easy through my four years at the University of South Florida. I had quit club volleyball my senior year in high school because I was overwhelmed with the multiple traumas happening at home and because my high school coach maliciously told me I had reached my peak and would never improve. I tragically believed that lie and ruined my chances at getting recruited. That huge aspect of my life was gone throughout college, and it left an ache I still feel today. Still, I continued writing and performing poetry, and I spent much of my time evangelizing and teaching Bible studies in my dorm room.

Although I did well academically, my college years were confusing. What did it mean for me to live a fruitful life for Christ? Some of my spiritual leaders seemed to think it was best for women to become homeschooling moms, so I was discouraged from getting my master's in English education even though I had already been admitted into the program. I focused on studying the Bible as much as possible, and that, of course, was beneficial. But I never developed much of a sense of calling or vocation. Still, I continued writing poems and performing them when I could.

It wasn't until I met my now-husband and a new community of Christians that I was really pushed to create spoken word videos and to write for various publications. Now, with much credit to his (and their) constant encouragement and support, I'm an author and spoken word poet. I write children's books and books for grown-ups, too. I create spoken word videos and performances for various organizations and projects. And I edit part time. After hearing for the last sixteen years, "Your poem (or book, or article) really helped me put words to what I'm experiencing," I believe a big part of my calling is to offer words that bring clarity to the inner life and to the Spirit's interaction with us throughout our life journeys.

Todd Bordow: Ordained Pastor, Podcaster ... Your Brother

I am the pastor of Cornerstone Orthodox Presbyterian Church in Houston, TX. It was not too long after I was ordained to the ministry twenty-three years ago that I began hearing stories from wives who had been abused by their husbands who were caught up in the modern patriarchy movement. Though every person is unique, there was a common thread woven into each story: an insistence by the husband that he was the authoritative head of the home and that his wife must submit to his desires. This idea was supported by the same literature from the same sources and resulted in these women asking to meet with my wife and me, pouring out in tears excruciating stories of years of abuse. Because of these experiences I began to study

I began to study both this movement and what the Bible actually says about marriage, divorce, headship. I found that the Bible did not teach what this movement was suggesting.

both this movement and what the Bible actually says about marriage, divorce, headship, etc. I found that the Bible did not teach what this movement was suggesting, and I actually wrote my dissertation for my DMin on divorce in the church.[8] Since then I continue to teach the proper, biblical, and cross-centered view of true leadership and mutual submission that is to characterize all God's redeemed people.

Chris Caine: International Ministry Leader, Writer, Speaker ... Your Sister[9]

I was left in a hospital unnamed and unwanted when I was born and adopted by Greek parents who had fled to Australia from Alexandria, Egypt after the 1952 revolution. We experienced extreme marginalization because of a strong anti-Greek sentiment that existed, and I was also the victim of childhood sexual abuse. I was a young woman filled with shame, guilt, anger, and condemnation. When I became a follower of Jesus and was exposed to the Word of God, I began to experience freedom and healing and was radically transformed. I could not stop talking about what Jesus had done in my life, and I was desperate for everyone to know that freedom is possible in Christ. I was living proof that Jesus Christ truly transforms lives and is no respecter of persons. Perhaps because not many people were talking about abuse back then, especially women, I began to be invited to different gatherings to share my story. First locally, then regionally, then nationally, and within a few short years internationally. I had a passion to see people experience freedom in Christ in the same way I had, and doors to speak kept opening across most streams of the church, all over the world. I was speaking several times a week in community, government, and corporate events, and virtually every single weekend in a church. Each time I spoke in a church, people would always surrender their lives to Christ when I gave the invitation. I actually didn't know that was not normal because it was my normal.

> I was living proof that Jesus Christ truly transforms lives and is no respecter of persons.

In 2007, I went to speak at a women's conference in Thessaloniki, Greece. While waiting for my bags to arrive, I noticed a poster in the airport that highlighted the faces of dozens of women and children who were missing—the suspected victims of human trafficking. I did not even know that this crime still existed in 2008, let alone the fact that it was the fastest growing crime in the world. At that moment, the seed of what has now become A21, a global human trafficking organization, was planted in my heart. I wanted to see slavery abolished everywhere forever, and so we became engaged in the fight to end human trafficking. In 2014, I founded Propel Women to help women internalize a leadership identity and to create pathways and pipelines for women of all generations to outwork their God-given purpose in every sphere of life. Propel has chapters operating on the ground in over 100 nations because the message of freedom in Christ is a message for all people in every nation.

Rachel Joy Welcher: Author, Speaker,
Magazine Editor ... Your Sister[10]

As a high school English teacher, I spent years talking with my students about strong verbs and *Lord of the Flies*, but I also got the chance to learn about their lives: what they cared about, worried about, and the questions they felt timid to ask. I noticed that so many of them carried burdens of sexual shame and confusion. Having grown up in the church as a pastor's daughter, I read all the books on purity and dating that were popular at the time, books like *I Kissed Dating Goodbye* and *Romance God's Way*. I followed the rules in those books and taught others the same basic principles I had internalized. Five years into my first marriage, my personal life fell apart when my husband left the Christian faith and divorced me. Between the burdens I saw in my students and my own reality of a broken marriage, I decided it was time to dig into this movement that influenced so many Christians in the late 1990s and early 2000s, to figure out which messages were biblical and which weren't. I decided to make researching American evangelical purity culture the topic of my master's thesis. By the time

I graduated with my master's degree in divinity from The University of St. Andrews, multiple books critiquing purity culture were on the market. I noticed that most of the critiques were from a perspective that had not only rejected purity culture teachings, but also a traditional, biblical sexual ethic. I wanted to address the damage purity culture has caused while maintaining an orthodox view of sexuality. After much prayer, I decided to write *Talking Back to Purity Culture: Rediscovering Faithful Christian Sexuality*. My hope was—and still is—that God would use this book to bring healing, the comfort of the gospel, and needed conversations to the forefront of our churches and communities.

Justin Holcomb: Episcopal Priest, Seminary Professor, Speaker, Author ... Your Brother; Lindsey Holcomb: Speaker, Advocate for Victims of Sexual Assault, Author ... Your Sister[11]

A large part of our calling as a couple is to offer accessible, Christ-centered hope, help, and healing to survivors of various types of abuse. We work to advocate for survivors and to empower parents and Christian communities to prevent, recognize, and respond to abuse.

For many years we have ministered to survivors of sexual assault, intimate partner abuse, child abuse, and spiritual abuse. These people want and need a clear explanation of how the gospel applies to their experience of abuse and its effects in their lives. Our goals are to provide survivors with compassionate and hopeful resources to help them move toward healing and to provide parents and Christian communities with wisdom to prevent and recognize abuse but also to respond and care for survivors in ways that are compassionate, practical, and informed.

Tragically, many churches and Christians are woefully unprepared to help those who have been abused. Worse still, many Christian leaders and parents are ignorant of this epidemic because ashamed survivors are reluctant to simply disclose the disgraceful things that have been done to them, and parents and untrained leaders do not recognize the signs of abuse or know how to lovingly ask questions. So many parents, spouses, ministers, and friends are looking for solid, gospel-based information that would be helpful in serving survivors. Informed supporters are very important for the healing process for survivors.

Our experience in the area of abuse, both personally, professionally, and pastorally, led us to minister in these ways. Lindsey has worked as a case manager advocating for survivors at a sexual assault crisis center and a domestic abuse shelter. She provided crisis intervention to survivors and conducted a variety of training seminars to service providers. Lindsey earned a master in public health, focusing on violence against women. Currently she works for Samaritan Village, which is a safe home and therapeutic program for adult survivors of sex trafficking.

When Justin was twelve he was sexually assaulted by a distant family member. He knows personally what survivors are experiencing. Justin has taught at numerous seminaries since 2000, but in the past few years he has also started teaching Abuse and the Church at these seminaries. Lindsey has served as a guest lecturer for some of these courses. Justin has served on the board of G.R.A.C.E (Godly Response to Abuse in Christian Environments) for more than a decade. He is also an ordained minister and has provided pastoral care for survivors and their families.

We have quite a family, haven't we? We are proud of them and thank God for them. But none of them would say that there's anything radically unique about them. They loved God and heard a call. And they're following it.

12

Jesus and His Christic Brothers and Sisters

*He is also the head of the body, the church; he is the
beginning, the first born from the dead, so that he might
come to have first place in everything. —Colossians 1:18*

We began our study together stating that a *key* aspect of our faith,
as it relates to gender, has been commonly overlooked, and
by now you know what that aspect is: the incarnation. Through the
previous chapters, we've shared a new way to approach the topic of
gender roles and relations, focusing on the life, death, and resurrection
of Jesus Christ. We hope we've also shown how to build relationships
for the glory of God through voluntary humiliation, reciprocal benevolence, and mutual flourishing. When brothers and sisters are focused
on living out these three Christic attitudes in every sphere of their lives,
the world will be convinced of our faith, the gospel will go forth, and
God will be glorified. Rather than fighting over who gets to be boss,
men and women who have been transformed by the condescension
of the Son of God into our Kinsman-Redeemer will willingly turn
from their thirst for power and authority and will instead follow in
his humble footsteps.

We haven't spent a lot of time calling out what is in error on either side of the gender debate. That's because we wanted to use our time to paint a new vision for the future—a vision mirroring Christ's gentle and lowly heart. There are dear brothers and sisters on both sides of this debate, and we're thankful for them. In addition, we know some of our readers would have liked us to choose sides so they can be assured of our mutual orthodoxy. We've purposely chosen not to because we want to encourage our readers to lay down their swords and pick up the towel and basin. We refuse to get drawn into the discussion on ordination or male headship because we want everyone to seek to appreciate Jesus ... then sort those particulars out on your own. Our goal is to bring glory and praise to the One who humbled himself, took on the form of a servant, and became obedient unto death so he might bring life to women and men. There's nothing more important than the work he's done. Absolutely *nothing*.

We've spent a great deal of time unpacking the self-humbling message Philippians 2:5–8 teaches: Don't exploit power and position, empty yourself and become a servant, humble yourself and sacrifice everything for the sake of raising others to holiness and love. Bending ourselves to "adopt the same attitude as that of Christ Jesus" (Phil 2:5)—this is where we should be focused ... and that's not an easy thing to do. But it isn't anything new since Christ had led the way.

In fact, the call to Christic partnering between brothers and sisters originated in the garden of Eden. It was the way man and woman were to fulfill God's command to rule the earth together as unified, though different, co-regents representing their King. Moses's surprising command to husbands to leave the security of their home and lay down their lives for their wife should have set the tone for every relationship to come. But it took the example of the Incarnate One to demonstrate what real love looked like ... and we're still learning from him.

We consider the family as fundamental to who we are as human beings, and in particular we considered how we're to relate to one another as brothers and sisters. Remember this was particularly important because wrong teaching about differing natures between men and women destroys the unity our shared *imago Dei* builds. We are one family with one Father and one Brother. What all this ultimately means is: in the kingdom of God, the many things we share as women and men are far more important than the aspects of our lives that are different. Sisters and brothers are all being fashioned into the image of Christ, "For those he foreknew he also predestined to be conformed to the image of his Son, so that he would be the firstborn among many brothers and sisters" (Rom 8:29).

Since the incarnation, the original plan to make God-glorifying image-bearers through marriage and childbirth has been transformed to the spiritual calling of the Great Commission.

Now brothers and sisters are to partner together in evangelism and disciple-making, in the sure knowledge that their ascended, incarnate Lord is ruling over all the earth and is with them.

One of the reasons God created male *and* female was so they would image his nature as a Trinity: three distinct persons in glorious creative union. Brothers and sisters in God's kingdom are now called to duplicate the Trinity's creative activity and joyfully work in harmony to nurture and protect those remade into Christ's image. We would not experience the joy of life-giving partnership had we not been made in the image of our triune God to delight in our differences and unity while we seek to grow together in godliness. At its very core, our relationship with one another as women and men has just one overarching tenet. It isn't authority and submission, it's not gender roles, femininity or masculinity. No, it is love.

As Christic brothers and sisters, we love one another by being devoted to mutual flourishing. This devotion to others' flourishing means we make it our life's goal to see others grow in their faith and appreciation of God's gifts in their lives. To fail to seek the development of one another's calling and gifts is to break the commandment to love.

When believers fully grasp the story of the incarnation, they can give away their life for the good of the other. For this reason, the gospel, and in particular the life of Jesus—not gender roles—must be the central teaching of our churches.

When a brother and sister enter into a marriage covenant, every principle of Christic relationship becomes even more important. The model of voluntary humiliation, reciprocal benevolence, and mutual flourishing especially impacts the way two people become one. Together they are to follow in their Savior's footsteps, partnering together in the Great Commission for the glory of God. Both the husband and the wife have been given a Christic calling—their ultimate aim is to look and act like Jesus.

Once we understand our calling as brother and sister, husband and wife is to incarnate Jesus to the world, the pathway forward with children won't be unexpected. Rather than striving to teach roles of "masculinity" or "femininity," parents are to teach children to be Christic: what it looks like to voluntarily lay down their rights, seek the good and growth of their siblings, parents, and the culture, and work to help each other learn what it means to flourish because of the great gifts given by Jesus.

Christic brothers and sisters are also called to partner together in a covenant community, the church. In this community they are called to glorify God by displaying Christ through ministry partnership, shared authority, respectful unity, voluntary humility, reciprocal benevolence, and mutual flourishing.

The church is the body of Christ on earth and should resemble the Incarnate One. It does that by working together in voluntary submission to the elders of the church as the elders endeavor to follow Christ and resemble him. The church is first and foremost about God's glory in Christ, so the person and work of Christ must be both our beginning and our end. Jesus is the sole head of the church. Yes, he uses appointed leaders as means, but those leaders only have authority when they are following him and when those in the church have freely chosen to follow them. The church's ultimate purpose, given in the Great Commission, is to reflect Christ, who lives to reveal the glory of God. Unless men and women are voluntarily submitted to displaying the glory of God in Christ, the local church is incapable of fulfilling its purpose. Questions about male or female ordination are to be decided in local church contexts where members freely choose to follow Christ as their conscience and the light of Scripture is made known to them.

Finally, we shared the testimonies of brothers and sisters who have been called to particular ministries. We've included this chapter here because we want to illustrate how Christic men and women are living out their individual callings for the benefit of the church and the world. This kind of partnership isn't anything new … it's been going on for millennia as Jesus, the head of the church, his body, is filling the world with Christ-loving, Christ-following reflections of his Father.

As the authors, a spiritual brother and sister, have partnered together to present this Christic model of male and female relationships, we earnestly pray you've come away with one predominant thought: Jesus Christ is magnificent. He's the one who gave up everything for our sake. He led the way in humility, benevolence, and flourishing, and now we can walk in his way because "God highly exalted him and gave him the name that is above every name" (Phil 2:9). He is the Lord. He is Lord of his church, he is Lord over all creation, throughout all time. And he will bless and bring flourishing to every one of his brothers and sisters who seek to walk in this Christic way. Join us, won't you?

Study Guide

Whether you're coming to this study alone or in a group, the book and study you are about to begin may be different from others you have done in the past. Sure, it's a Bible study, but it also tackles some very deep topics. With the Bible as our foundation, we have answered basic identity questions, like *What does it mean to be created in God's image? What does it mean to be a man or a woman? What should our relationships look like?* We believe that an accurate understanding of these topics is key to living the abundant life that Jesus spoke of in John 10:10. So, we're hoping that you'll begin now to bathe your study in prayer, as your authors have.

Our goal in writing this book and study has been that, in partnership with the work of the Holy Spirit, you would find understanding, wisdom, deep comfort, and transformation. We're also praying that whether you end up agreeing with us or not, you would walk away from this study with a surer belief in Jesus' great love and condescension in becoming one of us. There's nothing more important than the work he's done. Remember that.

The topic we're examining has the potential to be controversial. In light of that, it would be wise to approach it in prayerful humility, especially if you're working through this study with a group. We recognize that some of our readers may have already formed firm opinions, and they're coming to this study to have them confirmed—or to judge where we've erred. We hope that these dear readers will pray for open minds, as some of this content may challenge them. The individual and group discussion questions that follow are meant to press the truths of each chapter deeper into your understanding. Ask yourself: *Is there a possibility that I need to learn something new here?*

We also recognize that some of our readers come to this study with broken hearts. Some prevailing paradigms have denigrated and straightjacketed both men and women; and some readers have even experienced differing forms of abuse under the guise of certain teachings. These brothers and sisters should feel welcome to participate only as they feel comfortable. We're all on a journey of healing—especially when some of the wounds we've received have come from our very own brothers and sisters, those who should have loved and protected us. Please pray that you'll experience the comfort of the incarnate Christ and loving family members as you work together through this study. The study guide that follows is meant to gently push you to ask Jesus to free you from your past hurts and to help you experience the consolation of the One who gave up his rightful authority for you. Ask yourself: *What have I missed about the love of Jesus, my brother?*

And still others are coming to this study in confusion and perhaps even wondering if Christianity is true after all. We know that many believers, especially younger ones, are questioning whether all the talk about "gender roles" and all the stereotypes that don't seem to fit the way they feel might mean that the Bible really isn't all that they've been told. We understand those questions, and we hope that you'll find some solid answers in the book and the study. Too much time has been spent confusing cultural Christianity and the incarnation, life, death, and resurrection of the Son of God. We're with you if what you want to do is question (and throw off?) everything that isn't the real deal. Jesus is the real deal. The rest of it can go. Ask yourself: *Where have I confused the truth of the gospel with the stereotypes of American Christianity?*

CHAPTER ONE:
SISTERS, BROTHERS, AND THE GOSPEL

In Paul's first letter to the Corinthians he confronted the prevailing attitudes of his audience: the religious elite who sought power and the pagan philosophers who fancied themselves wise. He said, "God's foolishness is wiser than human wisdom, and God's weakness is stronger than human strength" (1 Cor 1:25). He described those whom God chose in this way,

> Not many were wise from a human perspective, not many powerful, not many of noble birth. Instead, God has chosen what is foolish in the world to shame the wise, and God has chosen what is weak in the world to shame the strong. God has chosen what is insignificant and despised in the world—what is viewed as nothing—to bring to nothing what is viewed as something. (1 Cor 1:26–28)

We started off Chapter One remembering a childish refrain we've all heard, "You're not the boss of me!" In doing so, we set the direction of our study: this book will not be about who gets to be boss. In fact, we stated that merely asking the "who gets to be in charge?" question proves that we haven't yet taken to heart the lessons that Jesus sought to teach. We've failed to understand the self-humbling message that Philippians 2:5–8 teaches: don't exploit power and position, empty yourself and become a servant, humble yourself and sacrifice everything for the sake of raising others to holiness and love. "Adopt the same attitude as that of Christ Jesus."

A biblical understanding of gender must grow out of, and be anchored in, the person and work of Jesus Christ. If we fail to take him into account, we'll find ourselves bogged down in the ongoing war of the sexes and the desire for power. It shouldn't be like that among us—no matter which side of the war we've chosen. Rather, we should embrace the humble life of our Savior and through that life receive all that God has provided for us.

> So let no one boast in human leaders, for everything is yours— whether Paul or Apollos or Cephas or the world or life or death or things present or things to come—everything is yours, and you belong to Christ, and Christ belongs to God. (1 Cor 3:21–23)

Personal Study Questions

1. What are you hoping for in reading this book? For instance, you might be new to this discussion, and you don't know the right questions to ask. Or, you might have already studied this topic and are looking to reaffirm your beliefs. On the other hand, you might have begun questioning whether what you've believed in the past is right. What are you hoping for?

2. How many books have you read on the topic of manhood and womanhood? What have you thought about them? If you haven't read a lot yet, that's fine. Do you have any ideas grounded in the work of other authors? Which books/authors have had the most impact on you?

3. When we started out by saying that this book would be different, what did you think? Do you think it's possible to come into a conversation in a fresh way—even if you're already familiar with the topic?

4. Would you consider yourself complementarian or egalitarian? Why? If you're not familiar with these words, that's fine. Basically, complementarians believe that only males can be ordained and husbands are called to lead in the home. Egalitarians don't. In between those two very basic definitions is a panorama of nuance and implication. Where do you think you land on this question? Are you open to any discussion from the other side?

5. What do you think of Paul's admission that he is powerless to fulfill the law? How does this encourage or discourage you? Why is the law's weakness salient to this discussion?

6. How much have you thought about the implications of the gospel in your consideration of what it means to be a man or woman?

7. Summarize what you've read in four or five sentences. We've found this exercise particularly helpful when trying to remember the contents of a book.

Group Discussion Questions

1. How familiar are you with the various perspectives and popular teachings about gender? In *one sentence*, define what you believe the Bible teaches. Don't worry about trying to build a case one way or the other. Just be prepared to share your beginning perspective with the group. *I believe the Bible teaches:* _____

2. What does the term "incarnation" mean? Why would it be important to remember Jesus' life, death, and resurrection in this discussion about who we are as men and women? Have you ever considered the gospel when you've thought about this topic before?

3. Read Philippians 2:5–8 aloud as a group. Choose one facet of Jesus' humiliation that you find most pertinent to our discussion and be prepared to share it.

4. The authors make some bold statements in this first chapter. For instance, they say that if you want to be in control, you've missed one of the primary teachings of Jesus. What do you think of that statement?

5. Have you ever heard the term "Christic" before? Share your understanding of the term and why you do or don't think it's a good term to use in this discussion.

6. Name several ways Jesus used his authority. What does
   that teach you? How important is the topic of authority
   in your life?

Prayer Time and Dismissal

Depending on time constraints, two or three people might volunteer
to pray that the Holy Spirit would illumine the hearts of all who are
studying, especially that they would find the incarnation more and
more meaningful.

CHAPTER TWO:
WHEN WE FORGET

In the previous chapter we introduced you to a particular way of thinking about the roles and relationships between men and women, a way
that is rooted in the incarnation of the Second Person of the Trinity,
Jesus Christ. We called this way of considering our place in God's
world "Christic" manhood and womanhood, a depiction that finds
its genesis in Jesus, God's Son.

   This way of thinking about godly relationships between the sexes
might seem new to some of you. Surely, calling what we're doing
Christic does. But the truth is that the nature of the relationship we're
envisioning is not new at all. In fact, it was established in Eden, before
the fall of Adam and Eve. It was the way that the man and woman
were to relate to each other and fulfill God's command to rule the
earth together as unified, though different, co-regents representing
their King.

> This is why a man leaves his father and mother and bonds with
> his wife, and they become one flesh. Both the man and his wife
> were naked, yet felt no shame. (Gen 2:24–25)

The blessed design of women and men partnering together in
humble unity, without shame, is the original intention of their Creator.
So, when we speak of this kind of relationship between the sexes,

we're not talking about anything new. This is the original design, but because of sin, we're barely aware of it. From the very beginning the man was to sacrifice for his wife, and she was to receive his love and partner with him for God's glory.

This chapter might be somewhat difficult for some of our readers. It's hard to consider the wonderful intentions the Lord had in creation, and then to look at what we've become. In this chapter, we will consider the many ways that this blessed perspective has been twisted, shattered, and destroyed by sin. Our goal in highlighting these evils is not to discourage or confuse. Rather, our goal is to demonstrate that when we drift away from the Christic message, terrible things happen. But Christ is powerful to redeem.

As you work through the questions below, remember to do so prayerfully, asking the Lord to help you understand the ways in which he will mend what's broken and make all sadness come untrue.

Personal Study Questions

1. Spend time considering Genesis 2:24–25. What is the primary goal of marriage? How does that goal line up with what you've thought, been taught, or experienced?

2. Although the passage is very familiar to many of us, we must look at it from the perspective of the culture in which it was written. What surprising action does the husband take? Why is this significant? What would this action have meant to a bride?

3. Sin has corrupted the marriage and family relationship, relationships between women and men in the church, and our testimony in the world. What examples did the authors give in the chapter? What examples have you personally experienced?

4. The authors wrote that Cain was the first person to use an act of worship to glorify himself. Can you think

of any ways in which this sin has been seen in more recent times?

5. Biblically speaking, Christlikeness is not defined in either masculine or feminine terms. What do you think about that statement? Do you agree/disagree? Why is this an important point?

6. Summarize what you've learned in this chapter in four or five sentences.

Group Discussion Questions

1. Read Genesis 2:24–25 aloud in the group. If there are different translations available, read those as well. The authors state that this passage and its implications are nothing new but may seem so. Did you learn anything new from your reading regarding it?

2. The Genesis 2:24–25 passage lays out the original intention for the relationship between the man and wife. What do you see there? Did you learn anything new?

3. How does the incarnation demonstrate that original intention? In other words, what does the Son becoming one of us teach us about that original command to the husband?

4. Which one of the examples of how this Christic paradigm has been corrupted spoke most deeply to you? Share what you're comfortable with in the group.

5. How do we see anti-Christic attitudes played out in the home, church, and society today? What did you think of the *D-Day Girls* story? Are there any other stories like this one that you're aware of?

6. The authors admit that we are called to a battle ... not
   against one another, but rather together against our
   common enemy. Can you think of any steps you might
   take to begin to embrace a more Christic perspective
   in your own life? Share them with the group if you
   are comfortable.

Prayer Time and Dismissal

Depending on time constraints, two or three people might volunteer
to pray that the Holy Spirit would illumine the hearts of all who are
studying, especially that they would find hope that the original design
of Christic relationships between the sexes would be seen in our day.

CHAPTER THREE:
BROTHERS, SISTERS, BRIDES, AND SONS

In Chapter Three we considered the family as fundamental to who
we are as human beings. Even though we come from different biological families, as Christians we are part of a vast spiritual family.
Surprisingly, Scripture portrays this family as being made up of brothers *and* sisters, female *and* male sons, and male *and* female brides!
Although this may be old news for some of us, its significance is frequently overlooked. The fact that we're all one family, sharing the
same nature with Jesus, is important for several reasons.

First, and most importantly, it means that we share a common
human nature with Jesus, the incarnate Son. "Therefore, he had to
be like his brothers and sisters in every way, so that he could become
a merciful and faithful high priest in matters pertaining to God, to
make atonement for the sins of the people" (Heb 2:17). There isn't a
distinctly "female" nature that is ontologically (in its essence) different from a male nature. Otherwise, how could Jesus have taken on
both in his incarnation?

That Jesus shared the one human nature in his incarnation means
that it is possible for women to be saved. Simply put, if Jesus didn't

take both a woman's *and* man's nature in his incarnation, his record of perfect law-keeping, substitutionary death, and bodily resurrection in our place wouldn't be sufficient to save women. Everyone, men and women, need his substitutionary life.

Also, in his creation of the woman from the body and nature of the man, God was giving a good and flawless gift. If a woman is somehow deficient *by nature*, then God wasn't giving Adam a good helper, and Adam has a right to complain about "the woman you gave me." If, as some say, a woman's ability to discern and stand for truth is intrinsically flawed, then God isn't good.

As the correct translation of the Greek word *adelphoi* signifies, many of the commands in the New Testament are addressed to both brothers *and* sisters. We are not wholly other, like something from a different planet, but rather we are beloved siblings who share a common ancestry, nature, and ultimate inheritance. Because of this, we are to deeply love and care for one another.

What all this discussion about nature and gender ultimately means is that in the kingdom of God, the many things we share are far more important than the aspects of our lives that are different. Sisters and brothers, men, and women, are all being fashioned into the image of Christ, "for those he foreknew he also predestined to be conformed to the image of his Son, so that he would be the firstborn among many brothers and sisters" (Rom 8:29).

Personal Study Questions

1. When you read the word "family," what do you think of? Have there been any fictional families that you've really enjoyed? Despised? Do you have any siblings? How important are they to your understanding of your personal identity?

2. In this chapter we've talked about how women and men don't have differing natures, as proven by the fact that

Jesus was like both his brothers *and* his sisters. In Chapter Five we will talk about the unique purpose that God had in creating male and female, but for the time being, what do you think about the fact that Jesus has our shared nature? Does it make any difference to you as you think about yourself and your relationships with others? Why?

3. If you don't have a Christian Standard Bible, look up the verses on pages 64–66. How does the translation of *adelphoi* encourage or discourage you?

4. Hebrews 2:11 says that Jesus is not ashamed to call us brothers and sisters. Respond.

5. Have you seen examples of discrimination against women in your church experience? How would acknowledging our shared nature and family have changed the way some women are treated?

6. Summarize what you've learned in this chapter in four or five sentences.

Group Discussion Questions

1. Take a few moments to allow two or three people to share about their family—particularly about their relationship with their siblings. Much of our identity comes from our understanding of our place in family groups. Allow some sharing on this topic.

2. The Christian Standard Bible has chosen to translate the Greek word *adelphoi* as "brothers and sisters." Why is this important? How does it influence how a particular passage is understood or experienced by women in the group? (For instance, see Rom 8:29; 15:14; 1 Cor 14:26; 15:58; Gal 6:1–2; Phil 3:17; 4:1.)

3. Why is understanding the shared nature of both men and women important? How does it impact our salvation, our relationships, our understanding, our identities, our future?

4. The authors write that all teachings that denigrate a woman's nature are attacks against God's goodness. Do you agree or disagree? Why?

5. They say that this teaching always ends up attacking the goodness of God, the efficacy of the atonement, and ultimately our shared creation in the image of God. In addition, many who propose that women are intellectually, emotionally, and spiritually weaker than men use physiological differences between female and male bodies to bolster their presuppositions about gender roles.

    Have you heard teaching like this? Have you heard this kind of teaching particularly from those who talk about "gender roles"? Respond.

Prayer Time and Dismissal

As your meeting draws to a close, pray that the Holy Spirit, who is instrumental in the creation of male and female in God's image, the conception of Jesus in Mary's womb, and our recreation into the image of Christ, would illumine and expand the group's understanding of the familial relationships between brothers and sisters in the group. Pray that those who are struggling to understand or who have been harmed by false teaching will be comforted and encouraged.

CHAPTER FOUR:
ONE FAMILY, ONE CALLING

Chapter Four opens with a discussion about the concerning rise of suicide—a rise that is indicative of the rise of meaninglessness, purposelessness, and general disunity and conflict rife in our time. While the statistics about suicide are heartbreaking, it's important to

realize that God has made a way for women and men to find meaning and purpose in the common goal of bringing God glory. This
shared meaning and purpose were first delineated at the creation
of mankind.

In the beginning, Adam and Eve were each given the Creation
Mandate:

> Be fruitful, multiply, fill the earth, and subdue it. Rule the fish
> of the sea, the birds of the sky, and every creature that crawls
> on earth. (Gen 1:28)

The man and the woman were to cooperate to make more God-
worshipers who would fill the earth and subdue it. They were called
to rule over the earth together as co-equals made in God's image. And
they were called to reign as vice-regents, collaborating in their shared
vocation as God's representatives on earth. Because "aloneness" wasn't
God's good plan for either of them, he made the woman to stand with
the man united in calling: neither one ruling over the other, neither
one more important, neither one striving for preeminence.

You know what happened next. They failed to cooperate, they
sought their own glory, and their fellowship was infected with isolation,
pain, and death. In the new covenant, the plan to make God-glorifying
image-bearers has been transformed from the former mandate of
physical procreation to the spiritual calling of the Great Commission:

> Go, therefore, and make disciples of all nations, baptizing them
> in the name of the Father and of the Son and of the Holy Spirit,
> teaching them to observe everything I have commanded you.
> And remember, I am with you always, to the end of the age.
> (Matt 28:19–20)

Now brothers and sisters are to partner together in evangelism and
disciple-making, in the sure knowledge that their ascended, incarnate
Lord is ruling over all the earth (see Matt 28:18). The truth that being
alone is still "not good" is proven by the fact that Jesus has promised that he will not leave them alone. Can you see how this Great

Commission is the ultimate fulfillment of the Creation Mandate and that sisters and brothers are called to the same mission: to rule as men and women together as God's representatives? As the authors wrote, "Our shared purpose is to reign with Christ as his image-bearing body and bride, both now and forever." Christians are still called to fill the earth and rule it for God's glory.

How are they to do that? They do it by displaying God's character and showing others what Jesus is like. In the way that they live, in the relationships they maintain, in the truths that they hold dear, they are either demonstrating what Jesus is like, or they are demonstrating how the fall has broken them. The authors wrote,

> In Christ, believing men and women are to glorify God by cooperating for the advance of the gospel and imitating Christ in voluntary humiliation, reciprocal benevolence, and mutual flourishing.

Many of the important questions that you may have about how believing women and men are to relate to one another can be summed up in those three phrases: voluntary humiliation, reciprocal benevolence, and mutual flourishing—as they follow in the footsteps of their incarnate Lord.

Personal Study Questions

1. The authors began this chapter with a discussion about meaninglessness, purposelessness, and personal value. How much have you thought about your identity, your meaning, purpose, and value as a man or woman in Christ? How have you sought to answer those questions?

2. Read Genesis 1:28. What do you learn from that account about the "why" of your creation?

3. Read Matthew 28:19-20. What do you learn from there about the New Testament "whys" of your faith in Christ?

4. How are these two commands different? How are they the same? Do you see anything in either of them that demonstrates a difference between a male and female's calling? If so, what?

5. The authors propose that our shared purpose as brothers and sisters is, "In Christ, believing men and women are to glorify God by cooperating for the advance of the gospel and imitating Christ in voluntary humiliation, reciprocal benevolence, and mutual flourishing." Do you think this definition is satisfactory to give you a purpose and value? How have you seen this worked out in your experience? How has it failed to be worked out?

6. Summarize what you've learned in this chapter in four or five sentences.

Group Discussion Questions

1. Read Genesis 1:28 and Matthew 28:19–20 aloud. How are these commands the same? How do they differ?

2. Take time for a few members to talk about how they have seen brothers and sisters fulfill these commands together.

3. The authors wrote, "Our shared purpose is to reign with Christ as his image-bearing body and bride, both now and forever." Spend time discussing what it might look like for men and women to learn to rule together now for the advance of the gospel. What might that look like in your local church context? What might stop your local church from pursuing that kind of partnership?

4. Read and discuss Philippians 2:3–4. How should this passage inform and impact relationships between brothers and sisters?

5. The authors wrote, "Jesus is exalted above all others because he humbled himself by becoming a servant below all others," a statement that functions as a definition of the Christic life. Perhaps a few people could speak to what that kind of life would look like in their local context.

6. What would it be like to be in a community shaped by love, filled with reciprocal benevolence? What steps would members of the group want to take to pursue this kind of community?

Prayer Time and Dismissal

As time permits, a few members of the group could ask that the Holy Spirit would enable them to look for opportunities to grow in voluntary humiliation, reciprocal benevolence, and mutual flourishing for the good of the community and the glory of God.

CHAPTER FIVE:
SISTERS AND BROTHERS IN GOD'S IMAGE

Have you ever wondered why God, in his wisdom, chose to make men *and* women? Is there a way to understand his sovereign purposes? The authors believe so, and their answer to this question begins at the beginning, when the creational refrain of "Good, good, good" becomes, "Not good." The Lord considered that the aloneness of Adam was positively bad and so he created another Adam for him ... but this Adam was called Eve and had a unique form and purpose.

> God created a being, "man," in his image and divided that being, "man," into male and female image-bearers.

The woman was created in the image of God in the same way the man was. In essence, she was a duplicate of him, but with a distinct purpose. Why didn't God just make another man? He didn't make another man because two identical persons wouldn't be able to image God, who is three. The Christian God is a Trinity: three distinct persons yet in completely unified diversity.

What it means to be created in the image of God is to know the joy of partnering together with another in creative exuberant love. God desired for his image-bearers to share in the same joy he knew when the "us" of Genesis 1:26 partnered together to make others who are like them, yet different. Humanity would be called to duplicate this creative activity over and over in thousands of instances as men and women (who are different but unified) work in harmony to nurture and protect life made in God's image.

This doesn't mean at all that the only reason God created woman was to have babies. No. In fact, the New Testament teaches that the life-giving partnership between men and women reaches far beyond the stereotypical roles seen in the Old Testament narrative. Masculinity and femininity are not defined by marriage roles alone, though marriage is good if that is God's plan for one's life. Women and men are called to fulfill the Great Commission, something they must partner together to do.

Remembering that the fruit of the Spirit encompasses traits that are generally considered "feminine" (such as gentleness) is also helpful. Jesus himself fulfilled the role of the life-giving mother who nurtures her beloved through his own body and blood. He is also the valiant warrior who fights to protect his beloved. Godliness is not gendered. "Christic men and women nurture life and use their strengths for others."

Personal Study Questions

1. Have you ever thought about what it means to be created in the image of God? What do you think of the perspective that God's image in humanity is primarily seen in our desire to love and to create?

2. Why did God create two different genders? Remember that biological procreation can't be the only answer

because God could have populated the world with millions of people if he had chosen to.

3. You have been created as a two-part being: body and soul. How has your gendered body shaped and informed your non-gendered soul? How important is it for men and women to recognize both our similarities and our differences?

4. In the Apostles' Creed we confess that we believe in the "communion of saints." Why would this fellowship between believers exist? Why didn't God simply populate the planet with brothers who all worked together and got along famously?

5. Why is diversity and unity together so important for us to grasp?

6. Summarize what you've learned in this chapter in four or five sentences.

Group Discussion Questions

1. God judged that Adam's aloneness was "not good." Why is that? What is it about pursuing isolation and individuality that might be considered wrong?

2. The Trinity, the Divine "Us," partnered together to create a human being and then split that human being into two distinct, yet very similar, forms. Share any thoughts you might have on why the Lord would do that. In what ways do you see that as a good? In what ways do you see that as difficult?

3. The authors propose that one aspect of being created in the image of God is the delight of partnering together to create new image-bearers. Share an instance when

you've had delight in partnering with another to create something new.

4. The nature/nurture discussion never seems to get resolved. Discuss which you think is more important. The authors pointed out that both perspectives have the propensity to end in difficulties. Is there a better way to think about our identities?

5. The authors strongly resist the idea that there is only one way to express masculinity or femininity. Discuss this as a group. What are the problems with that on either side?

6. Read aloud Colossians 3:12–14; Ephesians 4:32, 5:2; and Matthew 5:1–11. What do these verses say about the stereotypical expressions of gender?

Prayer Time and Dismissal

As time would permit, two or three people might pray that the Holy Spirit would help the group see the joys attendant to creative partnering together with those who are different and yet the same. Pray that understanding of the uniqueness of the male/female experience would be both understood and appreciated as part of what it means to image God.

CHAPTER SIX:
SIBLINGS SERVING TOGETHER

Although Jesus' command to love one another is known and accepted by most Christians, the living out of that command seems to be sorely lacking in our day. It seems that some of us, admittedly the authors included, find it's easier to love specific doctrines or expressions of faith than others with whom we disagree. But Jesus taught that the veracity of our faith is proven before a watching world by the way we love one another (John 13:35), not our agreement on specific points of doctrine. What testimony do we have before a watching world? Have they watched us love each other? Or have they simply seen us fight for power and preeminence just like everyone else? When we hear the command to love and automatically put parameters around it like, *I can't love someone who believes …* or *I love my neighbor, but just don't think it's appropriate to spend time with him or her*, or, *I know that not all women/men act this way, but …* or, finally, *Sure, that person is qualified for the job, but I think I'd better hire this less-qualified one instead because …* we are failing to love.

The command to love reaches across gender barriers. Rules that cause women to experience being ignored or objectified are in fact failures to love. Rules that cause men to be misjudged or excluded are failures to love. Jokes that denigrate either sex because they are male or female are sinful and transgress Jesus' command to love. These failures may take the form of sexism, favoritism, or partiality, sins that the New Testament warns us about. Jesus loved men and women, and he demonstrated it by the bold relationships he had with them.

"At its very core, our relationship with one another as women and men has just one overarching tenet. It isn't authority and submission, it's not gender roles, femininity or masculinity. No, it is love." When the relationship between women and men is primarily concerned with defining who gets to be in charge, unity will be difficult to achieve. That's not to say that freely choosing to be in a subordinate position in any particular setting will automatically destroy unity. It's that the de facto insisting that one person is above another not based on free agency but on supposed "roles" will cause strife and disunity. Jesus wasn't intent on describing who got to be in charge. He was intent on fulfilling his mission to love into life his brothers and sisters. We must do nothing less.

Personal Study Questions

1. Christic men and women are known by the way we act. Respond.

2. Here are the five aspects of Christic love we mentioned in the chapter. Jot down a note or two about each one and then consider how you may or may not be walking in them.

   a. Recognizing and respecting one another
   b. Welcoming each other
   c. Humbling ourselves before one another
   d. Pursuing unity with one another
   e. Devotion to the flourishing of others.

3. Which one of the above is most difficult for you? Why?

4. Although we all know that love for one's neighbor is commanded, we frequently fall into patterns of sexism, favoritism, partiality, and even hatred. Respond.

5. The Heidelberg Catechism Q and A 55 states: "What do you understand by *the communion of saints*? First, that believers, all and every one, as members of Christ, are partakers of Him and of all His treasures and gifts; second, that every one must know himself bound to employ his gifts readily and cheerfully for the advantage and salvation of other members." Since we are in communion with one another, how are you working for the flourishing of others in your sphere of influence?

6. Summarize what you learned in this chapter in four or five sentences.

Group Discussion Questions

1. The primary calling on the church, and indeed its ability to prove the truth of its faith, is to love its neighbor. In what ways have you experienced that love? In what ways have you longed to experience it?

2. The authors suggested five ways to demonstrate love for one another. What are they? How could you pursue them in your community?

3. Read Romans 12:10; 1 Corinthians 11:33; Philippians 2:3; Galatians 5:13; Ephesians 4:3; Colossians 3:14; and 1 Thessalonians 5:11 aloud in the group. How might these passages inform the ways that the genders relate to one another?

4. Failure to see our shared nature, being created in the image of God, creates problems of love and acceptance. When we view the opposite gender as strangers or wholly different than ourselves, we'll automatically put up barriers. In what ways are we the same? How will this help us love?

5. On his way to Calvary, Jesus prayed that we might all be in unity, one as he and his Father were (John 17:21–23). What can we do to be part of the answer to his prayer? What might we have to sacrifice? What might we need to believe about others?

6. In this chapter, we've defined three aspects of the failure to love that are commonly seen in gender relationships: sexism, favoritism, and partiality. These failures have real world consequences. Discuss ways that you've seen both successes and failures to love in your experience. What do you think about the authors' proposition that these failures to love are actually hatred?

7. Martin Luther perceptively said that the "communion of saints" is a truth that can only be believed by faith, since it was as lacking in his day as it is in ours. Can you think of any ways you and your community might more fully demonstrate the love that you're called to?

Prayer Time and Dismissal

Because this chapter may have been particularly hard for some readers, spend time praying that the Holy Spirit will work powerfully to help everyone learn to love one another, no matter whether they agreed with all the propositions or not. Remembering that we are called to love and not necessarily to agree, ask the Spirit to illumine each heart and open each understanding to what love looks like in your community.

CHAPTER SEVEN:
THE PURSUIT OF MUTUAL FLOURISHING

In the previous chapter the authors wrote that one of the ways we can love our neighbor is by being devoted to their flourishing. This devotion to the flourishing of others means making it a life-goal to see others grow in their faith and their use and understanding of God's gifts in their lives. To fail in this commitment to others' development and joy is to fail to love, to sin against Jesus' great commandment. While most of us would not purposely set out to thwart others' use of their gifts, to be apathetic or disinterested in how others are growing is the same thing.

The apostle Paul was dedicated to the flourishing of others, especially those in Ephesus. Over and over in his epistle to the Ephesians, he reminded them about the great love and supply that is embodied in the gospel message. Indeed, flourishing begins in the believer's understanding and belief in the gospel message. The gospel tells you that you are already beloved, forgiven, adopted, counted holy, and are part of Jesus' family of brothers and sisters. It tells you that you don't need to spend your life seeking preeminence, reputation, or revenge. It tells you that you've been given everything in Christ (1 Cor 3:21–23). When believers fully grasp this beautiful message, they can give away their life.

Sometimes, people who have been grievously sinned against might feel like they'll never be able to flourish or be devoted to the flourishing of others. As the stories of St. Photine and Joseph demonstrate, it is possible, through the ministry of the Holy Spirit and the incarnate Christ, to grow past the pain others have inflicted upon you. In saying that, the authors aren't saying, "Just get over it." Not at all. We recognize that for some, the process of healing may take decades. But we're also saying that the good news of the love of Jesus combined with the ministry of others devoted to your flourishing may bring you hope. For this reason, the gospel and in particular the life of Jesus, not gender roles, must be the central teaching of our churches. In the same way that Jesus was devoted to the mutual flourishing of all his brothers and sisters, we should be as well.

Paul believed that every member of the community, men and women alike, had gifts given by the Spirit that would benefit the body. Part of what it means to love, to be devoted to the flourishing of one another, is to help each member discover and utilize their individual gifts. In each church context, particularities will look different. Wherever your community has landed on the topic of gender-specific ministries is immaterial to this discussion. Both men and women have been given gifts by the Holy Spirit for the building up of Jesus' bride. To ignore or thwart the use of these gifts is to sin against love. Let each of us seek to fulfill Romans 12:4–6:

> Now as we have many parts in one body, and all the parts do not have the same function, in the same way we who are many are one body in Christ and individually members of one another. According to the grace given to us, we have different gifts.

Part of what it means to be devoted to the flourishing of your sister and brother is to seek to discover and then make a way for these gifts to be utilized, all to the glory of God.

Personal Study Questions

1. How devoted to the flourishing of others are you? What does that look like in your context?

2. Consider again the stories of St. Photine and Joseph. What do you learn from their suffering and their flourishing? How does that encourage you?

3. Sometimes our gifting or calling presents itself like a niggling, a feeling of disturbance, an itch that needs to be scratched. Do you sense something like that in your own heart? Can you identify what that might be?

4. Being devoted to the flourishing of another means you help them find and fulfill their call. What would stop you from doing that?

5. The only people who are free enough to devote their lives to the flourishing of others are those who have themselves drunk deeply of Christ's love and devotion. Respond.

6. Summarize what you've learned in this chapter in four or five sentences.

Group Discussion Questions

Leader note: It may be that someone in the group will be triggered by the stories of the abuse of St. Photine or Joseph discussed in this chapter. Please reassure your group members that the authors are not suggesting that they "just get over it" or that a deeper understanding of the gospel message will magically make their pain disappear. Please be sensitive to their concerns and allow them to speak or be silent according to their comfort level.

1. Spend time defining what being devoted means. Next, discuss what the word "flourishing" means. In light of these definitions, some members could share what they are devoted to and how they would know.

2. Invite group members to share what it would mean to be devoted to others or what it would look like to be

devoted to the flourishing of your brothers and sisters. They might also try to understand what might prevent them from this kind of life of love.

3. Invite a few members of the group to reflect on how they have experienced the love of others when they knew that the men and women around them were committed to their flourishing.

4. Invite group members to share how devotion to the flourishing of others has been part of what they've tried to do. Is there anyone in their life for whom that is their goal? For instance, when they think about their circle of friends, is there anyone about whom they would say, "I pray and work toward _____'s thriving"? Is there anyone about whom they would say with John that it's their greatest joy that they walk in truth?

5. It's easy to fall into a trap of being too devoted to the flourishing of others, like parents who cheat so that their children can get ahead. Discuss the ease of falling into this form of faux love and what real love would look like.

6. Ask some members to share what they have learned about their own gifting and a time when they were encouraged in their gifting by others. The authors wrote that sometimes our calling can only be understood "in the rearview mirror." If that's the experience of any in the group, share it.

Prayer Time and Dismissal

Pray that the members of the group would live in grace toward one another, that they would long for the flourishing of all those they know and that the Lord would grant them wisdom to know the difference between loving others for their good and the faux love that is actually self-focused. Pray also for any who may have known abuse, that they would experience the comfort of encouragement of the Holy Spirit as they heal.

CHAPTER EIGHT:
HUSBANDS, WIVES, AND THE GOSPEL

Throughout this study, the authors have crafted a model of relationships between women and men that is consistently cruciform: rooted in, shaped, and informed by the incarnate Christ. Every relationship should resemble what is seen in the life, death, and resurrection of Jesus Christ ... even—especially—the relationship between a husband and wife in marriage. But teaching on this relationship is frequently devoid of this Christic model, as obsolete Greco-Roman and Old Testament understandings about power dynamics, authority, and subordination take center stage. We propose that in this, the most intimate and life-shaping relationship there is, a consistent proclamation of the gospel message is imperative. Marriage is,

> a covenantal display of Christ's glory, through which both husband and wife cooperate to display the gospel, imitating Christ in voluntary humility, reciprocal benevolence, and mutual flourishing as they recognize and respect one another's value and pursue unity with one another.

Drawing a line from the Genesis command to pursue oneness for shared rule all the way to the book of Revelation, marriage has one purpose: to reflect the relationship between the incarnate Christ and his bride, the church, as they partner together to establish God's kingdom on earth.

Marriage is a voluntary covenant, a living parable of the covenant relationship Christ has with the church. This covenant is unique to marriage, and its obligations shouldn't be foisted upon any other relationship, especially not other relationships between all men and women. Both the husband and the wife have been given a Christic calling—their ultimate aim is to look and act like Jesus.

The husband is to look and act like Jesus, never demanding obedience or subordination of the wife. He is not told to *be* the head; he is simply told that he *is* the head. Nor is he told he is to lead. It is an extrabiblical extrapolation of the wife's call to submit to say that the husband is to be the leader and to insist on submission. The Christic husband is to die to himself for the sake of the marriage. He is to die to his dreams, ambitions, reputation, and potential and live for his wife's flourishing and their unity. They are to cooperate to display the gospel as brothers and sisters.

The wife is to look and act like Jesus in humility, benevolence, and living for the mutual flourishing of her husband. Although the wife is called to submission, as Christ's bride, she always retains free agency to choose to partner together with her husband. As he persuades her that he is following the Lord, she is free to join him as an ally in the purpose of marriage. As Genesis 3:16 declares, she should rightly desire to partner with her husband, fulfilling what God has called them both to do, whenever his direction is wise and consistent with the Lord's mission. But she always maintains free agency and isn't obligated to submit to anything that would contradict Scripture and plain reason. The wife's Christic subordination comes from a place of strength and free agency and is never averse to her personal flourishing.

Again, both are equally called to voluntary humility, reciprocal benevolence, and the mutual flourishing of one another. Both the husband and wife are to pursue unity, never ruling one over the other.

Personal Study Questions

1. This chapter proposes a perspective on marriage that may be different from one you have heard in the past. How is it different? How is it the same?

2. In Ephesians 5:32, Paul writes that the marriage relationship is primarily a picture of the relationship between Christ and the church. In what ways is it similar? In what ways is it different?

3. The Bible begins and ends with a marriage ceremony. In addition, the primary paradigm in the New Testament is not the personal marriage of man and wife, but rather the marriage between Jesus and his bride the church. What does this tell you about the importance of marriage?

4. The authors emphasized that the primary calling of the husband is not to "lead" or insist on the wife's obedience or submission. Respond. What is his primary calling?

5. The authors emphasized that the primary calling of the wife is a calling of free agency where, because she is free in Christ, she can choose to partner together with her husband in their shared call. She is free to rule, to initiate, to submit, to speak, to persuade, and to lead. Respond.

6. Both husband and wife are to recognize and respect one another's value. What is that calling? How might husbands or wives fail to value one another?

Group Discussion Questions

1. The authors have proposed that Christic marriage is a "covenantal display of Christ's glory, through which both husband and wife cooperate to display the gospel, imitating Christ in voluntary humility, reciprocal benevolence, and mutual flourishing as they recognize and respect one another's value and pursue unity with one another." Spend time discussing each phrase in that definition:

   a. What does it mean for the marriage to be covenantal? How would that make the parameters of marriage different than any other relationship between men and women? (Hint: Extrapolating that all women should submit to all men is unbiblical.)

b. How does marriage display Christ's glory—especially through his covenant with his bride, the church?

c. How does marriage display the gospel?

d. How might a husband or wife imitate Christ in
   i. Voluntary humiliation
   ii. Reciprocal benevolence
   iii. Mutual flourishing

e. What are some ways that a husband or wife might recognize or respect one another's value?

f. How can they pursue unity with one another?

2. In the time remaining, discuss how extrabiblical stereotypes of "gender roles" can harm a marriage.

3. If there are any singles in the group (and we hope there are!), how would observing a Christic marriage encourage you as you think about your relationship with the Lord?

Prayer Time and Dismissal

Take time now to pray that the Holy Spirit would bring freedom and healing to each member of the group. Ask him for help in growth, learning to partner together in pursuing the roles of co-regents in Christ's kingdom.

CHAPTER NINE:
PARENTING BOYS AND GIRLS WHO
RESEMBLE JESUS CHRIST

In this chapter the authors have developed a model of parenting that reflects life after the incarnation and in the new covenant. Under the old covenant, the primary message was that merit could be earned by keeping the law. In the new covenant, the primary message is that a perfect law-keeper has come and fulfilled the law in our place, granting complete righteousness to all who believe, both daughters and sons.

In addition, girls and boys would have been raised differently under the old covenant because different expectations were placed upon them. Girls would be valued for their beauty, purity, and ability to birth children, particularly sons. A girl's highest aspiration was to find her identity as a member of the community in her relationship with males who bore the sign of circumcision. On the other hand, as those who bore the sign of the covenant, boys would be valued as they represented the covenant community through strength, leadership, faithfulness, and diligence. But once the gender-specific sign of the covenant was replaced by the gender-inclusive sign of baptism, everything changed. Under the new covenant, women would no longer be assured of their inclusion in the family of faith through husbands, fathers, or sons. Their primary assurance was their faith in the One who was circumcised and baptized in their place, the incarnate Son. Because of this, the training and expectations now placed on sons and daughters would be very similar.

Way too much of what is commonly pushed as "Christian" parenting for daughters and sons completely misses the realities these changes brought in with the New Covenant sign. There simply are *no* commands about what to teach daughters that differ in any way from what is required from sons. Daughters are to be taught to love and care for their family. So are sons. Daughters are to be taught to be pure and modest. So are sons. Daughters are to be taught to be devout. So are sons. Daughters are to be taught to use their gifts for the community of the faith. So are sons. Way too much is drawn from the old covenant about what it means to raise masculine sons and feminine daughters. Far too many girls have been made to feel that their only option and entire worth as human beings is tied to finding a husband and giving birth. Far too many boys have been pushed into "manly" activities (whether they liked them or not). This really must stop. There's a reason that Paul didn't tell parents what to teach sons as opposed to what to teach daughters. Sons and daughters are equally in need of hearing the good news. He only said teach them the gospel and don't exasperate them.

Personal Study Questions

1. What have you heard about the exvangelicals? What do
    you think about how they're speaking out and respond-
    ing? Do you think that there is a possibility that they're
    reacting to gender straightjacketing they were taught in
    the church?

2. How much thought have you given to the impact of the
    gospel on your responsibilities as a parent? How would
    your parenting model change if you focused more on the
    work of Jesus Christ?

3. Hebrew boys were differentiated from their sisters by
    circumcision. That mark has been changed now to be
    gender inclusive. What difference should this change
    make in the way that sons and daughters are raised?

4. What teachings are you aware of that assume certain ste-
    reotypical gender roles for boys and girls? What is your
    opinion of them? Were you raised with them?

5. Summarize what you've learned in this chapter in four
    or five sentences.

Group Discussion Questions

1. The most important message for parents to communicate
    to their children is the gospel: that through faith in the
    work of the incarnate Son, they can receive full forgiveness
    of sins, be counted completely obedient, and be assured
    of their adoption and inclusion in God's family. Discuss
    whether parents in the group communicate this message
    to their children and what stops them from doing so.

2. Women in the Old Testament were frequently described
    by their beauty, purity, and desirability as wives or

mothers. But in the New Testament, aside from Mary and Elizabeth, women are not described by their beauty or by their children. What does this change speak to?

3. Whether your church practices paedo- or credobaptism, this sign of covenant inclusion in the family of God is offered to both girls and boys. Discuss the importance of this change and what it might mean for parents as they raise their children.

4. The New Testament offers very few parenting commands. Why might this be?

5. The New Testament doesn't delineate one way to raise daughters and a different way to raise sons. Why might this be? Why do you think Scripture doesn't refer to "masculinity" or "femininity"?

6. Can you see any connection between extrabiblical gender stereotypes and the exvangelical movement we're experiencing today?

Prayer Time and Dismissal

In light of the fact that there may be parents in the group whose children have left the faith or identified as exvangelical or older parents who might feel guilty about the way they parented their children, spend time asking the Holy Spirit to comfort and assure each heart. Remembering that God loves our children more than we do and that we are forgiven for sin will be a helpful reminder to all.

CHAPTER TEN:
SIBLINGS IN THE HOUSEHOLD OF GOD

In this chapter the authors have sought, once again, to build a paradigm for relationship between sisters and brothers that is consistently

Christic. In this chapter they're considering the church, which they define as

> a body of gospel-believing brothers and sisters who covenant together to glorify God by displaying Christ through minis-try partnership, shared authority, respectful unity, voluntary humility, reciprocal benevolence, and mutual flourishing.

One of the primary ways the church is described in the New Testament is as the body of Christ. It follows then that it cannot be called his body unless it takes on the form and shape of Christ—unless it resembles him. If we begin with the questions of who has authority and who can do what, we've started in the wrong place. The church is first and foremost about God's glory in Christ, so the person and work of Christ must be both our beginning and our end.

Paul's favorite term for believers in the church is "brothers and sisters." This shouldn't be surprising because men and women living together as siblings is a fulfillment of God's original design. Brothers and sisters are "flesh of flesh." Even married couples who are in "one flesh" union are also brothers and sisters. Recognizing and living into our one-flesh-ness as brothers and sisters is Christic because that's exactly what Jesus did when he became the "firstborn among many brothers and sisters" (Rom 8:29).

Further, Jesus Christ is "the head of the body, the church" (Col 1:18). This means Jesus is the final authority over the church on earth. Apart from Christ, there is no other "head of the church," whether on earth or in heaven. Church officers have no headship over the church. The men in the church have no headship over the women. We all—male and female—together constitute the body over which Christ is head. And the church's ultimate purpose, given in the Great Commission, is to reflect Christ, who lives to reveal the glory of God.

The church is to be filled with Christic ministry that supports the truth about who Jesus is and what he came to do. Christic ministry is a partnership between Christic men and Christic women who are continuing the partnership originated in the garden of Eden. Thus,

both men and women are to be devoted to the same purpose: displaying the glory of God as his united representative rulers. Paul gives this
instruction in the context of the local church. Unless men and women
are voluntarily submitted to displaying the glory of God in Christ, the
local church is incapable of fulfilling its purpose.

Ordained elders in the local congregation only have authority
as the members of the church choose to voluntarily submit to their
leadership and as they proclaim the truth about the Christ. Every
member has free agency to choose to follow those the congregation
has appointed to lead them and only as the leaders follow Christ.
Questions about male or female ordination are to be decided in local
church contexts where members freely choose to follow Christ as
their conscience and the light of Scripture is made known to them.

Personal Study Questions

1. In what ways is the church like an embassy? Have
   you ever needed help from an embassy? What was
   your experience?

2. Men and women in the church are to think of themselves
   as family, "flesh of flesh." If you have siblings, how does
   your experience inform that perspective?

3. Why is it important to know that we are brothers and
   sisters, "flesh of flesh"? How would believing that transform the way you think of and treat people around you?

4. Leaders in the church only have authority as they speak
   the word. Respond.

   a. In what ways do you believe this is true?
   b. What has your experience been in churches? (i.e.,
      some leaders try to impose traditions or rules that
      are not clearly rooted in the word, or particularly in
      the gospel.)

5. As you've considered the implications of the incarnation, what have you decided about ordination? If you believe in male-only ordination, how did you arrive there from the incarnation? If you believe otherwise, how did you get there?

6. Although questions of ordination are important, we don't believe that they should be the dividing line between the orthodox and the heterodox. Respond.

7. Summarize what you've learned in this chapter in four or five sentences.

Group Discussion Questions

1. The authors wrote,

> Jesus Christ is "the head of the body, the church" (Col 1:18). This means Jesus is the final authority over the church on earth. Apart from Christ, there is no other "head of the church," whether on earth or in heaven. Church officers have no headship over the church. The men in the church have no headship over the women. We all—male and female—together constitute the body over which Christ is head.

Take time to discuss this statement in the group.

2. How does the fact that Christ, who is equal in nature and authority with God, voluntarily submitted to God to accomplish his purpose on earth impact our understanding of what it means to submit to leaders in a local church?

3. First Corinthians 11 is a difficult passage to understand. No matter what one might think about head coverings or headship, one point is obvious: in the same way that

the incarnate Son submitted himself to his Father's plan, brothers and sisters in the church are to submit themselves to Christ's purpose in bringing glory to God. All members are to submit themselves to the same authority and purpose. What is that authority, and what is this overarching purpose?

4. The authors write, "Men and women in the church are not masters and slaves. They are *friends*, jointly submitted to and authorized for the same purpose." Discuss what this friendship, this siblinghood, would look like in a church that seeks to be Christic.

5. What implications can we draw from the fact that the apostles usually addressed their letters to correct or encourage the doctrine and practice to the members of the church rather than their leaders? What does this communicate about the authority of the assembled church?

6. In 1 Corinthians 11, Paul adds a strong statement of mutuality in the Lord. He writes, "Woman is not independent of man, and man is not independent of woman. For just as woman came from man, so man comes through woman, and all things come from God" (1 Cor 11:11). Why do you think Paul included this caveat?

7. The authors conclude, "Unless believing men and women depend on one another, the local church is incapable of fulfilling its purpose in Christ." Respond.

Prayer Time and Dismissal

As you spend time in prayer now, ask the Holy Spirit to enable you to understand and believe that the church is God's pillar of the truth about the gospel. Some of the members of the group may have very fixed opinions about male or female leadership. Ask the Spirit to help each one respect and pursue unity with others who may disagree. Wherever your group may land on that question, the desire to function together as "flesh of flesh" brothers and sisters must be paramount.

CHAPTER ELEVEN:
VOICES INTO THE CULTURE

In this chapter, testimonies of women and men who are called to differing vocations are given. Each of these sisters and brothers have shared their testimony because they believe that the Lord has called them to particular ministries and because they want to encourage our readers to discern and pursue God's calling in their own lives. These friends come from different faith traditions. But they are each one faithful believers in the gospel who have given their lives in service of the one call to partner with others and fulfill the Great Commission.

Personal Study Questions

1. Do you think that there is something particularly differ-ent about these brothers and sisters? What do you appre-ciate the most about them? Is there one particular story that spoke to you?

2. None of these sisters or brothers really fit the stereotypes. That should be encouraging to you. Respond.

3. After briefly answering the other study questions, take time now to write out your personal testimony of how the Lord has called you to himself and is using you.

4. Summarize what you've learned in this chapter in four or five sentences.

Group Discussion Questions

1. Perhaps some of the members of the group are not accus-tomed to hearing from people from other Christian

faith traditions about God's call in their life. Spend time unpacking any presuppositions that members may have.

2. How are members of the group blessed by reading how God is using others in surprising ways? What do they learn from them?

3. After taking a few moments to discuss whichever testimonies the group would like, ask as many as would be willing to to share the testimonies they wrote.

Prayer Time and Dismissal

Spend time in prayer thanking the Holy Spirit for calling so many wonderful men and women to himself. It would be important to appreciate these testimonies as the power of God to use ordinary people. But it might also be a temptation to envy or discouragement. Pray that the Spirit would encourage each member that the Lord will use them in his own time and way.

CHAPTER TWELVE:
JESUS AND HIS CHRISTIC
BROTHERS AND SISTERS

In this chapter, we've furnished a summary of the book. We've seen how the primary message of the Bible is the building of God's kingdom through the unimaginable condescension of the second Person of the Trinity. Brothers and sisters who have been created in God's image and are being recreated in the image of their elder brother, Jesus, are to partner together in whatever way God has gifted them, to the building of the Lord's kingdom here on earth. To emphasize any other way of considering gender is to fail to grasp the centrality of Jesus' life, death, and resurrection and will never achieve the unity spoken of throughout the Bible and particularly in Genesis 2:24. It is not Christian.

Personal Study Questions

1. As you review the chapter, highlight areas where you were challenged, encouraged, or still have questions. Write them out and be prepared to share them with the group.

2. The authors are seeking to move past the arguments about who gets to be in charge to develop an incarnational culture of humility, mutual growth, and flourishing. How do you see that happening in your life? In your ministry?

3. How might brothers and sisters relate to one another in a more Christic way in your local community? What needs to change? What can you do?

Group Discussion Questions

1. Spend time considering the content of the book. You may do so by reading over the summary sentence you wrote at the end of each chapter.

2. What areas of the book did the participants find most

    a. Challenging
    b. Encouraging

3. What areas of the book did the participants still have questions about?

4. What do you believe about the authors' vision for the future? How might you or your community be involved in that?

5. Do you have hope that the church can become more Christic? Why or why not?

Prayer Time and Dismissal

After thanking God for the time the group has had together, ask the Holy Spirit to help you delight in the good news of the gospel: Jesus Christ voluntarily left heaven, didn't think that equality with God was something to be grasped, and humbled himself to take on the form of a human servant—one who could die. This is what it looks like to live Christic lives. Ask the Lord to enable you to walk in forgiveness and humility and to live for the mutual flourishing of one another.

Notes for Group Leaders

Whether you're going to use this study in a mixed gender small group or in a men's or women's study, it is important to keep in mind the shared purpose of the group. Groups are intended as a support to those who are exploring new ways of thinking about and living with God. Here are a few bits of advice to keep in mind as you lead the group.

- Advertise the formation of the group in your church bulletin including the title of the book and the dates/times/ locations of the study. It's best to meet at a consistent time and place so that members can form habits of gathering together.

- Choose a regular day/time to meet. You could meet weekly or biweekly to discuss each chapter. You'll need to develop a calendar with dates and chapter numbers to distribute at the first meeting for those who might fall behind. Note: Considering the length of the chapters, it might be easier for some to meet every other week, but either way is fine.

- Assure the participants that they should attend the meeting even if they weren't able to complete all the work. The discussions and the video will be helpful, even if they can't get to every question. Remind them that many of the questions are subjective in nature: there aren't right or wrong answers. The authors simply want to prepare a platform to spur discussion and growth.

- Suggestions for group courtesy: Because this topic may be new, controversial, difficult to understand, or triggering for some members, encouragement to treat one another with respect and kindness may need to be reinforced weekly. It is possible that some attendees will have already formed firm opinions on the topic, and they will need to be reminded to treat with patience and gentleness those who disagree or are just learning. Help group members to remember that the most important aspect of the study is not what one ultimately believes about "gender roles," but rather the great love, patience, condescension, and holiness of our elder Brother, Jesus Christ. In addition, prayer requests and any concerns shared in the group should be kept in confidence.

THE STRUCTURE OF THE MEETINGS

In the first meeting *only*: The members of the group will assemble, open in prayer, introduce themselves, answer questions about why they're interested in the topic, and receive the schedule of meeting dates and chapters, a list of members for weekly contact, and a copy of the book. They will then watch the video, which will introduce the material and the first chapter. After watching the video, they can review the plan for the following weeks and what will be expected. The meeting can be dismissed with prayer and prayer requests, time permitting.

During subsequent meetings: The members will assemble, open in prayer, read the short introduction to the questions aloud, and discuss the "Group Discussion" questions below (1–30 minutes). The answers to the "Personal Study Questions" don't need to be discussed unless someone has a concern they'd like to discuss. Watch the video (15–20 minutes). Close with prayer requests and prayer (10–15 minutes).

For the final meeting: After gathering for prayer and discussion of the group questions, watch the conclusion video, and then spend time asking what members have learned. Using the summary sentences at the end of each individual study question section will be helpful to stimulate conversation. The questions for the final chapter reflect this suggestion.

Notes

Introduction

1. Specific areas that I thought needed a gospel witness: Counseling—*Counsel from the Cross* (Crossway, 2009); Parenting—*Give Them Grace: Dazzling Your Kids with the Love of Jesus* (Crossway, 2011); Our oneness with Christ—*Found in Him: The Joy of the Incarnation and Our Union with Christ* (Crossway, 2013); Eternity—*Home: How Heaven and the New Earth Satisfy Our Deepest Longings* (Bethany House, 2016).

Chapter One: Sisters, Brothers, and the Gospel

1. Rachel Green Miller, *Beyond Authority and Submission: Women and Men in Marriage, Church, and Society* (Phillipsburg, NJ: P&R Publishing, 2019), 198.

2. Eric Schumacher, "21 Places Women Emerge Front and Center in Scripture's Storyline," https://www.thegospelcoalition.org/article/21-places-women-emerge-front-and-center-in-scriptures-storyline; and Elyse Fitzpatrick and Eric Schumacher, *Worthy: Celebrating the Value of Women* (Minneapolis, MN: Bethany House Publishers, 2020), 251–55.

3. Some people have pushed back against this stereotype. See, for instance, Nate Pyle, "Why Christ wouldn't aspire to 'Christic Manhood,'" RNS, February 21, 2020, https://religionnews.com/2020/02/21/why-christ-doesnt-fit-in-christic-manhood/.

Chapter Two: When We Forget

1. For more on the Genesis narrative in relation to gender, see Fitzpatrick and Schumacher, *Worthy*.

2. J. A. Brooks, *Mark*, vol. 23 (Nashville: Broadman & Holman, 1991), 202.

3. J. R. Edwards, *The Gospel According to Mark* (Grand Rapids, MI: Eerdmans, 2002), 379.

4. Tim Evans, Joe Guillen, Gina Kaufman, Marisa Kwiatkowski, Matt Mencarini, and Mark Alesia, "How Larry Nassar abused hundreds of gymnasts and eluded justice for decades," *IndyStar*, last modified April 4, 2018, https://www.indystar.com/story/news/2018/03/08/larry-nassar-sexually-abused-gymnasts-michigan-state-university-usa-gymnastics/339051002/.

5. For an excellent first-hand account by a Nassar abuse survivor, see Rachael Denhollander, *What Is a Girl Worth?* (Carol Stream, IL: Tyndale House, 2019).

6. Tim Evans, Mark Alesia, and Marisa Kwiatkowski, "A 20-year toll: 368 gymnasts allege sexual exploitation," *IndyStar*, last modified February 8, 2018, https://www.indystar.com/story/news/2016/12/15/20-year-toll-368-gymnasts-allege-sexual-exploitation/95198724/.

7. Sarah Rose, *D-Day Girls: The Spies Who Armed the Resistance, Sabotaged the Nazis, and Helped Win World War II* (New York: Crown, 2019), 15–16.

8. Rose, *D-Day Girls*, 16.

9. Rose, *D-Day Girls*, 18.

10. Rose, *D-Day Girls*, 18.

11. Rose, *D-Day Girls*, 276–77.

Chapter Three: Brothers, Sisters, Brides, and Sons

1. The Greek word *adelphois,* traditionally translated "brothers," is best translated "brothers and sisters" as in "fellow believers," which would include both male and female. See Johannes P. Louw and Eugene Albert Nida, *Greek-English Lexicon of the New Testament: Based on Semantic Domains* (New York: United Bible Societies, 1996), 124. For discussion of the CSB's rendering of *adelphois* as "brothers and sisters," see Mark L. Strauss, "A Review of the Christian Standard Bible," *Themelios* 44, no. 2 (August 2019): https://www.thegospelcoalition.org/themelios/article/a-review-of-the-christian-standard-bible/.

2. Aristotle believed that the deformity in women was evident not only at conception, but also during each stage of growth: "For while still within the mother, the female takes longer to develop than the male does; though once birth has taken place everything reaches its perfection sooner in females than in males—e.g., puberty, maturity, old age—because females are weaker and colder in their nature; and we should look upon the female state as being as it were a deformity, though one which occurs in the ordinary course of nature." Prudence Allen, *The Concept of Woman, vol. 1: The Aristotelian Revolution* (Grand Rapids, MI: Eerdmans, 1997), 97.

3. In the words of C. J. Neal, "Women, Psychology of," ed. David G. Benner and Peter C. Hill, *Baker Encyclopedia of Psychology & Counseling*, Baker Reference Library (Grand Rapids, MI: Baker Books, 1999), 1261: "Traditional beliefs about women significantly affected the lens by which scientists examined women's growth and experience (if they chose to examine her experiences at all). Woman as intellectually and morally inferior was the prevailing theme surrounding the discussions. Western views of woman as inferior originate in Judeo-Christian traditions and teaching. Common interpretations of the early biblical story casting woman as evil and responsible for introducing sin into the world include (quotes cited from Gundry, 1986, 21):

> "Augustine: 'The woman herself alone is not the image of God: whereas the man alone is the image of God as fully and completely as when the woman is joined with him.'

> "Aquinas: 'As regards the individual nature, woman is defective and misbegotten, for the active force in the male seed tends to the production of a perfect likeness in the masculine sex, while the production of women comes from a defect in the active force or from some material indisposition, or even from some external

influence, such as that of a south wind.'

"Tertullian: 'God's sentence hangs still over all your sex and his punishment weighs down upon you. You are the devil's gateway; you are she who first violated the forbidden tree and broke the law of God. It was you who coaxed your way around him whom the devil had not the force to attack. With what ease you shattered that image of God: Man! Because of the death you merited, the Son of God had to die.'

"These were authoritative words that have had profound impact on the views of women throughout history."

4. Thomas Aquinas, *Summa Theologica,* Part 1, Question 92, Reply to Objection 2, as quoted in Andrew Bartlett, *Men and Women in Christ: Fresh Light from the Biblical Texts* (London: IVP, 2019), 6.

5. Wayne Grudem, *Evangelical Feminism & Biblical Truth: An Analysis of More than One Hundred Disputed Questions* (Wheaton, IL: Crossway, 2012), 72. He further writes, "God gave men, in general, a *disposition that is better suited to teaching and governing in the church, a disposition that inclines more to rational, logical analysis of doctrine and a desire to protect the doctrinal purity of the church, and God gave women, in general, a disposition that inclines more toward a relational, nurturing emphasis that places a higher value on unity and community in the church* (v. 14). ... Paul understands the kinder, gentler, more relational nature of women as something that made Eve *less inclined to oppose the deceptive serpent and more inclined to accept his words as something helpful and true.*"

6. Joseph A. Pipa Jr., "Leading in Worship," in *Equipping Preachers, Pastors & Churchmen: Selected Articles by the Faculty of Greenville Presbyterian Theological Seminary,* ed. Zachary Geoff (Taylors, SC: Presbyterian Press, 2017), 97, emphasis added. Pipa continues, "If [a woman] is more susceptible to deception, then, when she teaches other women and children in the church, she should use materials approved by the elders." While we agree that ordained leadership should oversee the content of the teaching in the church, it should not be because women are more susceptible to deception than men. In fact, if Eve's deception and fall is the reason for Paul's injunction against women teachers, why would the sons of Adam be given authority since their sin was out and out rebellion and not deception? Pipa continues, "[a woman] is not to speak, except corporately along with the rest of the congregation, *nor may she attempt to get around this injunction by using a question to get across her view or to instruct*" (94), for fear that she might inadvertently teach a man something deceptive.

7. Raymond C. Ortlund Jr., "Male and Female Equality and Male Headship: Genesis 1–3," in *Recovering Biblical Manhood and Womanhood: A Response to Evangelical Feminism,* ed. John Piper and Wayne Grudem (Wheaton, IL: Crossway, 1991), 102.

8. Wayne Grudem, *Evangelical Feminism and Biblical Truth: An Analysis of More than One Hundred Disputed Questions* (Wheaton, IL: Crossway, 2012), 72, emphasis added.

9. This is why the Westminster Confession of Faith states that "God alone is Lord of the conscience, and hath left it free from the doctrines and commandments of men, which are, in anything, contrary to His Word, or beside it, in matters of faith or worship."

It goes on to state that requiring adherance to extrabiblical commands is to "destroy liberty of conscience, and reason also." Thus, to require adherance to models of manhood and womanhood not contained in God's word but discerned from nature alone is not permissible in the church. See also The Baptist Faith and Message (2000), article XVII.

10. That's not to say that we can't learn anything from looking at nature and observing it. But we have to remember that what we see is fallen and not the way it was originally.

11. See chapters 8–10 in Fitzpatrick and Schumacher, *Worthy.*

Chapter Four: One Family, One Calling

1. Clay Routledge, "A crisis of meaninglessness is to blame for the rise in suicides," *The Dallas Morning News*, last modified June 25, 2018, https://www.dallasnews.com/opinion/commentary/2018/06/25/a-crisis-of-meaninglessness-is-to-blame-for-the-rise-in-suicides/.

2. See Elyse Fitzpatrick, *Finding the Love of Jesus from Genesis to Revelation* (Grand Rapids, MI: Bethany House, 2018).

3. D. A. Carson, *The Gospel according to John*, The Pillar New Testament Commentary (Grand Rapids, MI: Eerdmans, 1991), 569.

Chapter Five: Sisters and Brothers in God's Image

1. Dr. Iain Duguid, unpublished course notes, quoted in Elyse Fitzpatrick, *Helper by Design* (Chicago, IL: Moody Publishers, 2003), 34.

2. Compare Calvin's comments on Acts 17:28: "No one can look upon himself without immediately turning his thoughts to the contemplation of God, in whom he 'lives and moves.' " *Calvin: Institutes of the Christian Religion*, ed. John T. McNeill, Library of Christian Classics (Philadelphia, PA: The Westminster Press, 1960), 35.

3. Michael Reeves, *Delighting in the Trinity: An Introduction to the Christian Faith* (Downers Grove, IL: IVP Academic, 2012), 26.

4. Reeves, *Delighting in the Trinity,* 31, emphasis added.

5. G. I. Williamson, *The Shorter Catechism: A Study Guide* (Phillipsburg, NJ: P&R Publishing, 1970), 35.

6. Calvin, *Institutes of the Christian Religion*, 189.

7. Michael Horton, *The Christian Faith: A Systematic Theology for Pilgrims on the Way* (Grand Rapids, MI: Zondervan, 2011), 397–404.

8. E.g., see Karl Barth, Geoffrey William Bromiley, and Thomas F. Torrance (*Church Dogmatics: The Doctrine of Creation*, part 1, vol. 3 [London: T&T Clark, 2004], 198) write, "But what is the original in which, or the prototype according to which, man was created? ... it is the relationship and differentiation between the I and the Thou in God Himself. Man is created by God in correspondence with this relationship and differentiation in God Himself: created as a Thou that can be addressed by God but also as an I responsible to God; in the relationship of man and woman in which man is a Thou to his fellow and therefore himself an I in responsibility to this claim."

9. Reeves, *Delighting in the Trinity,* 61.

10. Reeves, *Delighting in the Trinity*, 55.

11. Carolyn Custis James, *Lost Women of the Bible: Finding Strength and Significance Through Their Stories* (Grand Rapids, MI: Zondervan, 2005), 37, emphasis original.

12. The Hebrew word used is דָּבַק (*dābaq*), meaning "cleave, cling, stick to, stick with, follow closely, catch, keep close to, join to, overtake (Earl S. Kalland, "398 דָּבַק," *Theological Wordbook of the Old Testament*, ed. R. Laird Harris, Gleason L. Archer Jr., and Bruce K. Waltke [Chicago: Moody Press, 1999], 177). The Hebrew term also carries the sense of clinging to someone in affection and loyalty (178).

13. The term *ʿāzar* "generally indicates military assistance" (Carl Schultz, "1598 עָזַר," *Theological Wordbook of the Old Testament*, 660. James includes this explanation of *ezer*: "*Ezer* is a military term ... twice referring to the woman, three times for military powers Israel turned to for help (Isaiah 30:5; Ezekiel 12:14; Daniel 11:34); the remaining sixteen occurrences refer to God as Israel's helper, each time with military imagery (Exodus 18:4; Deuteronomy 33:7, 26, 29; Psalm 20:2; 33:20; 70:5; 89:19; 115:9, 10, 11; 121:1–2; 124:8; 146:5; and Hosea 13:9)" (see James, *Lost Women,* 233n5).

14. *Easton's Bible Dictionary* offers defines *ezer kenegdo* as "a help as his counterpart" or "a help suitable to him." M. G. Easton, *Easton's Bible Dictionary* (New York: Harper & Brothers, 1893).

15. Dr. Saul McLeod, "Behaviorist Approach," Simply Psychology, updated 2020, https://www.simplypsychology.org/behaviorism.html.

16. Cited in John Stott, *The Cross of Christ, Centennial Edition* (Downers Grove, IL: IVP, 2021), 96.

17. Dr. Gary Welton, professor of psychology at Grove City College, writes, "the current obsession with the idea of being transgender has become the latest adolescent hurdle, but it is based on a faulty sense of what it means to be male or female ... The problem is not the inconsistency between our gender and our sex. The problem is that we have bought into an excessively narrow view of gender. The notion of what it means to be female, or what it means to be male, is extremely broad." "My Human Identity Transcends Gender," The Institute for Faith and Freedom, July 20, 2017, https://www.faithandfreedom.com/my-human-identity-transcends-gender/.

18. Prudence Allen, *The Concept of Woman, vol. III: The Search for Communion of Persons 1500–2015* (Grand Rapids, MI: Eerdmans, 2016), 17–18.

19. Until recent times, death in childbirth was the most common source of fatality among women. This was particularly true in ancient times when very young women (age 13+) were given in marriage to older men and were expected to have multiple children. See Cohick, Lynn H., *Women in the World of the Earliest Christians: Illuminating Ancient Ways of Life,* (Grand Rapids, MI: Baker Academic, 2009), p. 135–137.

20. Allen, *The Concept of Woman, vol. III*, 477.

21. Tia Ghose, "Women in Combat: Physical Differences May Mean Uphill Battle," *Live Science*, December 7, 2015, https://www.livescience.com/52998-women-combat-gender-differences.html.

22. Allen, *The Concept of Woman, vol. III,* 478.

23. Eowyn Stoddard, "Musings on Gender Archetypes, Types and Stereotypes," *The Eowiggle* (blog), February 25, 2019, https://theeowiggle.blogspot.com/2019/02/some-musings-on-archetypes-types-and.html.

24. Dane Ortlund, *Gentle and Lowly: The Heart of Christ for Sinners and Sufferers* (Wheaton, IL: Crossway, 2020).

25. The poisonous fruit of male dominance, bolstered by erroneous gender stereotypes, has brought ruination to many ministries and disillusioned many women and men who were part of them. Given the toxic masculinity rife throughout much of our church culture, it's no wonder that numbers of high visibility celebrity pastors have resigned in recent years because they've been accused of bullying, something that Paul warns about in 1 Timothy 3:3 and Titus 1:7. See, for example, Julie Roys, "Top 10 Stories of 2020," The Roys Report, January 11, 2021, https://julieroys.com/top-10-stories-2020/; Carey Lodge, "Mark Driscoll and the culture of bullying: is it a one man stand?" Christian Today, April 16, 2014, https://www.christiantoday.com/article/mark.driscoll.and.the.culture.of.bullying.is.it.a.one.man.stand/36839.htm; Justin Taylor, C.J. Mahaney: 'Why I'm Taking a Leave of Absence,' " The Gospel Coalition, July 7, 2011, https://www.thegospelcoalition.org/blogs/justin-taylor/c-j-mahaney-why-im-taking-a-leave-of-absence/; Emily McFarlan Miller, "Willow Creek confirms abuse allegations against Hybels' mentor Gilbert Bilezikian," January 28, 2020, https://religionnews.com/2020/01/28/willow-creek-confirms-abuse-allegations-against-hybels-mentor-gilbert-bilezikian/; Rob Speight, "Powerful Personal Video Testimony by Victims of Bill Hybels and Willow Creek," *Rob Speight's Blog*, December 14, 2019, https://robsp82.com/2019/12/14/powerful-personal-video-testimony-by-victims-of-bill-hybels-and-willow-creek/; Brandon Ambrosino, "'Someone's Gotta Tell the Freakin' Truth': Jerry Falwell's Aides Break Their Silence," *PoliticoMagazine,* September 9, 2019, https://www.politico.com/magazine/story/2019/09/09/jerry-falwell-liberty-university-loans-227914; Michelle Boorstein and Sarah Pulliam Bailey, "Southern Baptist leader Paige Patterson fired over handling of sex abuse allegation," *The Washington Post,* May 30, 2018, https://www.washingtonpost.com/news/acts-of-faith/wp/2018/05/30/southern-baptist-seminary-fires-paige-patterson-over-handling-of-sex-abuse-case/.

Chapter Six: Siblings Serving Together

1. Michelle Lee-Barnewall, *Neither Complementarian nor Egalitarian: A Kingdom Corrective to the Evangelical Gender Debate* (Grand Rapids, MI: Baker Academic, 2016), 141–42.

2. Lee-Barnewall, *Neither,* 143.

3. Louw and Nida, *Greek-English Lexicon,* 662.

4. From Greek word περισσεύω, meaning "to be or exist in abundance, with the implication of being considerably more than what would be expected—'to abound, to

be in abundance, to be a lot of, to exist in a large quantity, to be left over' " (Louw and Nida, *Greek-English Lexicon*, 599).

5. Daniel L. Akin, *1, 2, 3 John*, The New American Commentary 38 (Nashville: Broadman & Holman, 2001), 157.

6. *Britannica Online*, s.v. "Sexism," by Gina Masequesmay, accessed August 8, 2021, https://www.britannica.com/topic/sexism.

7. *Lexico*, s.v. "Favoritism," accessed August 8, 2021, https://www.lexico.com/en/definition/favoritism.

8. Louw and Nida, *Greek-English Lexicon*, 767.

9. "Apostles' Creed," Translation © 1988, Faith Alive Christian Resources, Christian Reformed Church in North America.

10. Daniel G. Reid et al., *Dictionary of Christianity in America* (Downers Grove, IL: InterVarsity Press, 1990).

11. Online Etymology Dictionary, s.v. "Communion," accessed August 8, 2021, https://www.etymonline.com/word/communion.

12. Louw and Nida, *Greek-English Lexicon*, 445.

13. Donald G. Bloesch, *The Last Things: Resurrection, Judgment, Glory* (Downers Grove, IL: InterVarsity Press, 2004), 155.

Chapter Seven: The Pursuit of Mutual Flourishing

1. *Lexico*, s.v. "Flourish," accessed August 8, 2021, https://www.lexico.com/synonyms/flourish.

2. Barclay M. Newman Jr., *A Concise Greek-English Dictionary of the New Testament* (Stuttgart, Germany: Deutsche Bibelgesellschaft; United Bible Societies, 1993), 187.

3. *Operation Varsity Blues* ends with the statement that Stanford University received $770,000 from Singer. The university claims to have donated the money to other needy students.

4. See Erin Moon's Lenten devotional *Memento Mori*. See "Our Shared Purpose in Christ," available at https://1drv.ms/w/s!AkhkqHXrxLl6iz2gK-KHRHgmlGGE.

5. The underlying Greek terms are φιλόστοργος and φιλαδελφία (Robert L. Thomas, *New American Standard Hebrew-Aramaic and Greek Dictionaries: Updated Edition* [Anaheim: Foundation Publications, 1998]).

Chapter Eight: Husbands, Wives, and the Gospel

1. Other examples include God's covenants with Adam, Noah, Abraham, David, and his new covenant people in Christ.

2. Terry L. Wilder, "1 Peter," in *CSB Study Bible: Notes*, ed. Edwin A. Blum and Trevin Wax (Nashville, TN: Holman Bible Publishers, 2017), 1978.

3. The meaning of "disobey the word" in 1 Peter 3:1 is to not believe the word of the gospel.

Chapter Nine: Parenting Boys and Girls Who Resemble Jesus Christ

1. Elyse M. Fitzpatrick and Jessica Thompson, *Give Them Grace: Dazzling Your Kids with the Love of Jesus* (Wheaton, IL: Crossway, 2011).

2. Josiah Hesse, "'Evangelicals': why more religious people are rejecting the evangelical label," *The Guardian,* November 3, 2017, https://www.theguardian.com/world/2017/nov/03/evangelical-christians-religion-politics-trump; Bradley Onishi, "The Rise of #Exvangelical," Religion & Politics, April 9, 2019, https://religionandpolitics.org/2019/04/09/the-rise-of-exvangelical/.

3. See Rachel Joy Welcher, *Talking Back to the Purity Culture: Rediscovering Faithful Christian Sexuality* (Downers Grove: IVP, 2020).

4. For more on this topic, see Sheila Gregoire, *The Great Sex Rescue: The Lies You've Been Taught and How to Recover What God Intended* (Grand Rapids, MI: Baker Books, 2021).

5. Tara Westover, *Educated: A Memoir* (New York: Random House, 2018).

6. The law as means to earn merit only brings death and condemnation (see 2 Cor 3:7–9).

7. Fitzpatrick and Thompson, *Give Them Grace,* 36–37.

8. William Arndt et al., *A Greek-English Lexicon of the New Testament and Other Early Christian Literature* (Chicago: University of Chicago Press, 2000), 434.

9. See chapters 8–10 of Fitzpatrick and Schumacher, *Worthy.*

10. See Welcher, *Talking Back to the Purity Culture.* In Eric Ludy and Leslie Ludy's *When God Writes Your Love Story* (Colorado Springs, CO: Multnomah, 2009), we read about a young woman who "had made the mistake of giving [her boyfriend] her most precious gift—her virginity" (237).

11. See Coleen Sharp, "Spiritual Abuse Q&A with Adia Barkley," *Theology Gals*, podcast, http://theologygals.com/2021/04/spiritual-abuse-qa-with-adia-barkley/. Adia Barkley talks about her experiences growing up in a Family Integrated Church where her father/step-father acted as her mediator and decided whether she was worthy to receive communion; See also Scot Mcknight, "Patriarchy By Any Other Name Is Still Patriarchy," *Christianity Today,* August 4, 2020, https://www.christianitytoday.com/scot-mcknight/2020/august/patriarchy-by-any-other-name-is-still-patriarchy.html.

12. The commandment against murder includes proper care for our own bodies: "The duties required in the Sixth Commandment are, all careful studies, and lawful endeavors, to preserve the life of ourselves and others ... " *Westminster Larger Catechism*, Answer 135.

Chapter Ten: Siblings in the Household of God

1. LearnersDictionary.com, s.v. "Embassy," accessed April 20, 2021, https://www.learnersdictionary.com/definition/embassy.

2. Paul makes this argument succinctly in Galatians 3:25–26.

v. 26: "Through faith you are all sons of God in Christ Jesus." When people ("you ... all") believe the gospel ("through faith"), they are heirs of salvation ("sons of God") by virtue of their status "in Christ."

v. 27: "For those of you who were baptized into Christ have been clothed with Christ." Paul is restating his previous phrase in a different way to emphasize his point. At their baptism, they were united with Christ ("baptized into Christ") and "clothed with Christ"—the old person is put off, and Christ covers them now. Paul uses baptism as a synonym for faith because baptism is a whole-body appeal to God for salvation (see 1 Pet 3:21–22).

v. 28: "There is no Jew or Greek, slave or free, male and female; since you are all one in Christ Jesus." Under the old covenant made with Israel at Sinai, the law stipulated that inheritance typically went to free, Jewish, males. But these standards do not apply in the new covenant in Christ. Since every believer has the same status ("in Christ Jesus") through faith, this means that any individual believer is equal to any other believer ("you are all one"). That implies that no believer has a higher or lower status in the local church than any other believer.

v. 29: "And if you belong to Christ, then you are Abraham's seed, heirs according to the promise." Being an heir to the promise made to Abraham is not a matter of being a physical Israelite. Now, every *believer* inherits the promised inheritance the same way—by union with Christ through faith. Thus, the only way to enter God's people (the church) is by confession of faith in Jesus Christ.

3. See discussion of *adelphos* in Chapter Three and notes.

4. The practice of incest is also forbidden in the new covenant (see 1 Cor 5:1).

5. Kenneth A. Matthews, "Leviticus," in *CSB Study Bible: Notes*, ed. Edwin A. Blum and Trevin Wax (Nashville, TN: Holman Bible Publishers, 2017), 184.

6. Christopher J. H. Wright, "Leviticus," in *New Bible Commentary: 21st Century Edition*, ed. D. A. Carson et al., 4th ed. (Downers Grove, IL: InterVarsity Press, 1994), 146.

7. We must assume that Adam and Eve's sons and daughters married one another and that such marriages were common until the population grew large enough for the practice to cease. The prohibition of marriage to a "close relative" was not codified until the Mosaic law, though such marriages were likely already forbidden. Mark F. Rooker notes, "Laws against incest exist in almost every culture" (*Leviticus*, The New American Commentary 3A [Nashville: Broadman & Holman Publishers, 2000], 242). Rooker notes that incest prohibitions needed to be strictly codified in Israel because they were forbidden from marrying foreigners and had to marry within their clan, drastically reducing the number of eligible mates.

8. Consider the marriage romance we find in the Song of Solomon. The man exclaims, "You have captured my heart, my sister, my bride" (4:9). And the woman later laments, "If only I could treat you like my brother, one who nursed at my mother's breasts, I would find you in public and kiss you, and no one would scorn me" (8:1). The woman is lamenting her inability to show public affection. While she had other options of acceptable public affection to use in the analogy, notably, she chose the brother-sister relationship.

9. We use the word "defiled" strictly to describe the perpetrator of abuse. Abuse victims are not defiled. Sin has been committed *against them*; they have not sinned.

They should feel no shame or guilt. They have done nothing wrong. All the defilement is on the perpetrator alone.

10. It is also a crime that church leaders must report to law enforcement and the appropriate child services.

11. This does not mean ignoring crimes or allowing a person access to others through which harm may occur. It must always be clear that sin is sin and unacceptable—anything less is not grace.

12. E.g., Tamar, Rahab, Deborah, Ruth, Bathsheba, and Huldah the prophetess, to name only a few of these women of whom the world is not worthy.

13. For more about Lydia and the church in her home, see Fitzpatrick and Schumacher, *Worthy*, 196ff.

14. For more on women in the New Testament church, see chapter 11 in Fitzpatrick and Schumacher, *Worthy*.

15. Daniel L. Akin, "The Bible and Sexuality," in *CSB Study Bible: Notes*, ed. Edwin A. Blum and Trevin Wax (Nashville, TN: Holman Bible Publishers, 2017), 1827.

16. "Glory" is a display of value and worth. "Pagan practice, which viewed human creation as an ignoble creation of warring and vain gods," taught that men should cover their heads (Akin, "The Bible and Sexuality," 1827). Paul forbids it since man is not an "ignoble creation." As God's image, he is the display of God's excellence! That the woman should cover her head does not indicate that she is not made in God's image. Instead, Paul says that she is "the glory of man"—she displays what is excellent about the man, which is the glory of God. So, in the end, both are a united display of God's excellence. In the Corinthian context, the wife covering her head as she ministered in church demonstrated that she was not independent of her husband. Instead, she was voluntarily submitting to and joining him in the purpose for which God created them—male and female—as his ruling image-bearers.

17. Only the introduction in Phil 1:1 mentions church officers, and that is in reference to a subset of the congregation.

18. The Greek word used here may be translated as either "women" or "wives." The context determines the meaning. If Paul intended "wives," this sentence would make more sense following his instructions on the family in verse 12. As it stands, it suggests that these women are part of the diaconate. The NASB, a translation known for efforts to be literal, translates verse 11 as "Women must likewise." Unfortunately, the ESV muddies the interpretive waters by adding the possessive pronoun "Their" to read "Their wives." "Their" is not in the original text. Were it in the text, it would strongly suggest "wives." Its absence supports the translation "women."

Chapter Eleven: Voices into the Culture

1. Aimee Byrd is the author of *Housewife Theologian*; *Theological Fitness*; *No Little Women*; *Recovering from Biblical Manhood and Womanhood*; *The Sexual Reformation*; and *Why Can't We Be Friends?* You can access her work at www.aimeebyrd.com.

2. Raleigh oversees the Let My People Go Ministry (www.lmpg.org) and is the author of *Vulnerable: Rethinking Human Trafficking*.

3. Carolyn McCulley (www.carolynmcculley.com) is the author of *Radical Womanhood: Feminine Faith in a Feminist World*; *The Measure of Success: Uncovering the Biblical Perspective on Women, Work, and the Home*; and *Did I Kiss Marriage Goodbye? Trusting God with a Hope Deferred*.

4. You can access Wendy's work at www.theologyforwomen.org. She is also the author of *Companions in Suffering: Comfort for Times of Loss and Loneliness*; *Is the Bible Good for Women?*; *By His Wounds You Are Healed: How the Message of Ephesians Transforms a Woman's Identity*; *Practical Theology for Women: How Knowing God Make a Difference in Our Daily Lives*; *The Journey: A Walk Through Scripture*; and *The Gospel-Centered Woman: Understanding Biblical Womanhood through the Lens of the Gospel*.

5. Brian Croft is the founder of Practical Shepherding (https://practicalshepherding. com).

6. You can access Dr. Prior's work at www.Karenswallowprior.com. She is the author of *Booked: Literature in the Soul of Me*; *Fierce Convictions: The Extraordinary Life of Hannah More—Poet, Reformer, Abolitionist*; and *On Reading Well: Finding the Good Life through Great Books*. In partnership with B&H Publishing, she is also releasing a series on the classics which now include *A Guide to Reading and Reflecting* on *Frakenstein*; *Jane Eyre*; and *Sense and Sensibility*.

7. Quina Aragon is the author of *Love Made: A Story of God's Overflowing, Creative Heart* and *Love Gave: A Story of God's Greatest Gift*. She is also a spoken word poet. You can access her work at quinaaragon.com.

8. Todd Bordow's dissertation "A Rethinking of the Traditional Divorce Exception Understanding of Matthew 5:31–32 and Its Implications for Pastoral Counseling" is available at http://kingdomkompilations.com/wp-content/uploads/2018/09/Dissertation-What-Did-Jesus-Really-Say-About-Divorce-2.pdf.

9. Learn more about Christine Caine at https://christinecaine.com/index .php?site=true.

10. You can find out more about Rachel at www.racheljwelcher.com. She is the author of *Two Funerals, Then Easter* and *Talking Back to the Purity Culture: Rediscovering Faithful Christian Sexuality* and is an editor at *Fathom Magazine*.

11. You can access Justin and Lindsey's work at www.justinholcomb.com. Justin is the author of numerous books on theology and the creeds. In addition, together Justin and Lindsey have authored *God Made All of Me: A Book to Help Children Protect Their Bodies*; *God Made Me in His Image: Helping Children Appreciate Their Bodies*; *Rid of My Disgrace: Hope and Healing for Victims of Sexual Assault*; *Is It My Fault? Hope and Healing for Those Suffering Domestic Violence*; and *Children and Trauma: Equipping Parents and Caregivers*.

Scripture Index

Old Testament

Genesis